D0983227

Pearl: Image of the Ineffable

The publication of this work was substantially assisted by the generosity of Alex G. Spanos.

PEARL: IMAGE OF THE INEFFABLE
A Study in Medieval Poetic Symbolism

Theodore Bogdanos

The Pennsylvania State University Press
University Park and London

Library of Congress Cataloging in Publication Data

Bogdanos, Theodore.
Pearl, image of the ineffable.

Includes bibliography and index.
1. Pearl (Middle English poem)
2. Faith in literature.
3. Symbolism in literature.
4. Christian art and symbolism—Medieval, 500–1500.
I. Title. PR2111.B63 1983   821'.1   82-42783
ISBN 0-271-00339-1

Contents

For Herta Helene
and for Toula, Hans, and Elisabeth

Acknowledgments

My foremost debt is to Professor Phillip W. Damon of the University of California, Berkeley, who directed this study in its early stages. For me, he has always stood as a beacon of excellence, academic and personal. To Professor Raymond Oliver I owe the encouragement of the work's germinal idea. While it was developing into a book, he upheld my occasionally sagging spirits through kinship of conviction and led me to many critical insights. I also thank Professor Janette Richardson for often dragging me out of the comfortable world of abstractions to confront the actual texts at hand.

I have been honored and helped by the advice of several scholars who were kind enough to read the manuscript and comment on it: Professors Charles Muscatine, Bertrand H. Bronson, Norman Rabkin, and Wayne Shumaker of the University of California, Berkeley; John M. Fyler of Tufts University; Winthrop Wetherbee of the University of Chicago; and C. David Benson of the University of Colorado at Boulder. I am indebted to my dear friend Professor John R. Trimble of the University of Texas at Austin for some delicate surgery on my prose, painful but salutary. I owe special thanks to my friend and colleague Professor Charles Ludlum of San Jose State University for countless instances of expert counsel on English idiom, medieval and modern. I am deeply grateful to Professor Robert W. Frank, Jr., editor of *Chaucer Review,* for his wise criticism and guidance. I also thank Mr. John M. Pickering, editorial director of the Pennsylvania State University Press, for his patience and courtesy in handling the publication of the work. Finally, I should never forget that it was Professor Paul Piehler of McGill University who first kindled my love for medieval literature when I was a student at Berkeley.

My deepest debt is to my wife and children, who surrounded me with much love and patience during the writing of this book. It is to them that I dedicate it.

1

Introduction

In this book, I propose a reading of the fourteenth-century English poem *Pearl* that I have come to through a particular interpretation of its symbolic development.[1] At the same time, I wish to shed some light on medieval poetic symbolism as a whole, dealing especially with the artistic problem of representing the apocalyptic and the ineffable. More specifically, I want to show how the medieval symbol, often thought of as a static, self-enclosed metaphoric unit, can be transformed in the hands of a master poet into vital drama and therefore vital art. *Pearl* stands as a supreme example of such an achievement.

Curiously enough, despite their professed philosophical flexibility, modern critical works seem at times more uncompromising than medieval ones in maintaining at all costs certain thematic preconceptions at the expense of a more open-ended and "dynamic" view of medieval poetic symbolism. (I do not use "dynamic" here as a euphemism; I merely mean "active," "flexible.") Perhaps such rigor should be applauded as historical fidelity. But it becomes a serious misunderstanding when a religious poem like *Pearl* is accounted for as an artistic event by a few crystalline theological concepts and nothing more. It is my purpose to remind the reader that an interpretation of the poem's symbolism that recognizes all levels of perception and response, however multiplex and contradictory and even irresolvable, is truer to the fundamental mystery of the Christian faith than any conceptualization.

I regard *Pearl* as a dramatization of man's encounter with divine reality as this particular poet has envisioned this encounter and has rendered it into a poetic experience with an order and significance of its own as artistic statement. I am speaking, in fact, of the drama of faith—"the tension of belief," as Walter Ong so aptly calls it—which is at the core of medieval (and, I would add, timeless) spirituality. In the poem's milieu, the late Middle Ages, when man's mood begins to darken into pessimism and deepening melancholy about the transience of earthly life, this tension becomes more pressing, even fraught with panic. Man's ultimate goal, Paradise, appears now more fragile and inaccessible.[2] Art and literature present man diminished, pathetic, even comic—and therefore less worthy of such an attainment.[3] In *Pearl*, the antagonists of this drama of faith are man and God, so bound by love yet so irreconcilable by nature. The poet aims at a definition of their relationship, existential rather than theoretical, and displays a certain attitude toward this relationship, which weaves in and out of the poem's emotional crises like a pervasive contrapuntal theme. The poem shows man at a moment of profound loss and spiritual confusion. In the dream, where desire battles actuality,[4] the hero gravitates toward an ideal realm, seeking to fathom the mystery of ultimate reality, to reconcile his loss with the universal scheme of things, and to find consolation. His personal desire is gradually transformed and expanded to its anagogic form as the nostalgia for Paradise.[5] He attempts to unite himself with the divine, at least through understanding, so that he can transcend the contradictions of this life. The divine beckons him to itself and ravishes him with its perfection, only to reject him, withdrawing at his searching touch into its awesome mystery. Yet it leaves a profound claim upon his life with its promise of final "cnawing" and immortality.

The poem has a narrative dramatic order, which has been well delineated by A. R. Heiserman. It involves essentially the development of character and action between the Maiden and the dreamer. It unfolds as a pattern of emotional oscillations, of "controlled discoveries and disappointments" for the poem's hero, in a narrative full of suspense, leading to the climactic event of his rejection from the New Jerusalem. Then follows the happy resolution: the dreamer finally understands all and reconciles himself to divine reality and its decrees.[6]

I agree fully with Heiserman's view of the poem's dramatic order, except for his interpretation of the ending, as I shall explain. What I want to explore in this study, however, is another dramatic order that unfolds not in the narrative action but on the imagistic surface of the work. It is here that the two antagonists, divine and human nature, vie with each other in the most concrete and perceptible terms. In fact, the poet draws our attention to the poem's symbolism as the dramatic arena: He confines physical action to a few mourning and ritualistic gestures, except for the dreamer's plunging across the stream. At the same time, he lavishes much craft and visual wealth on shaping his imagery, even though he borrows a great deal of it from tradition. The imagery thus becomes the means through which we may experience the poem's confrontation and conflict in a concrete form. Drama is caught in symbol, and symbol is released into drama.

I want to trace the pattern of imagistic development that the poet contrives in order to convey to us in a palpable manner his particular vision of divine reality and of man's quest after it with its accompanying hopes and fears. This pattern can be seen as a gradual process of distancing, of increasing alienation, between the imagery and our experience. It thrives on the mounting metaphoric tension, the increasing violence of relationship that builds up between human similitude and divine reality, between the symbol and the object of its representation. The poet begins presenting man's encounter with the mystery of ultimate reality on familiar ground. The dreamer—as well as the reader—faces the question of life and death, the two poles of our experience, so opposite to each other yet mysteriously inextricable and even mutually sustaining. We come across this paradox in the garden of his lamentation, puzzled by the notion of life being born of death as in the seed. But our puzzlement becomes more profound when nature ceases to act as comforter, when its familiar cycle of regeneration is broken by the strange transformation of the rose to a pearl. The variety of associations, traditional and contextual, in these images as symbols of transience and eternity are too self-contradictory to make this transformation easily acceptable to the human sensibility. An irresolvable dialectic, initiated and guided by the poet, begins in the reader's mind, between his intellectual cognition of certain traditionally established symbolic values and his experience, which tries to decide what best represents eternity: the renewal of the transitory or the deathlike stasis of the permanent.

In his grief and confusion, the dreamer moves to an ideal visionary world, which, we must assume, has a dual dimension, interior and exterior: It is a construction of the desiring psyche, but it also has an objective reality of its own as a cosmos that man will confront in the anagoge of his existence. The dreamer hopes to transcend in this realm the contradictions of finite existence—only to find them in his vision of the ideal in a crescendo of symbolic paradoxes. The poem becomes an extended antithesis of viewpoints and essences, which the dreamer and we as readers try to reconcile. The essential antithesis is caught very concretely in this paradox: The ideal world, which is meant to transcend time and space, is represented here by its very contradiction, an image, an artifact of time and space. Ironically so, the poet's own creative absorption in that artifact betrays the transcendent aim, weighing down the supernatural with pigment and brilliant opulence. Furthermore, each image brings with it a variety of traditional and contextual associations, sacred and profane, creating an imagistic compound of complementary values and sensibilities. The poet counts on this contradictory multiplicity to express his meaning and to shape his art. The tense, irresolvable interplay which he sets in motion between divine tenor and human vehicle conveys a sense of divine mystery more convincing than any conceptual formulation. Mystery here becomes infinitude of meaning, not its paralysis. This is not only an important theological insight but also a crucial artistic advantage, because the ineffable never ceases to challenge the human imagination to new invention of forms and relationships between realities, however distant. In its silence, the ineffable becomes a potent and energizing force.

The climax of this pattern of symbolic distancing is the vision of ultimate reality in its apocalyptic form. The pearl, the poem's central symbol, with its own complementary values, is the seed of this mounting dramatic and symbolic *discordia concors*. Taking the pearl as the symbol for the kingdom of God—within the tradition he borrows—the poet cleverly spreads the pearl's qualities and engulfs with them the anagogic realm. As the dreamer and we with him seek to enter this realm with our perception and thus to possess it, it freezes into an icon, a perfect artifice of ideality, ingathering and enclosing in an impenetrable, enigmatic image the mystery that we are after. In its grotesqueness, this image reveals an aspect of divine reality that is awesome and terrible. It fills man with both ecstasy and revulsion. Various scholars have remarked on the violent complementarity of the numinous and the apocalyptic, its mixture of joy and terror, and its threat to the human identity and to familiar order.[7] It is my aim to show how the Pearl Poet turns this complementarity to artistic advantage, giving it utmost immediacy by making it part of a specific human dramatic situation. It is a situation racked, indeed, with the "tension of belief." And just as Augustine and Aquinas capture this "tension of belief" in a verbal conceit, using the incarnate Word as sacred prototype, so can Dante—and the Pearl Poet in a lesser way—create a corresponding imagistic conceit, whose sacred model is the incarnate God "in the flesh." The apocalyptic vision in *Pearl*, then, is an imagistic conceit of eternity. It is significant that the dreamer and we are cut off from the vision of the ideal at the point of total symbolic irrelevance. Finally, I want to show how the poem's denouement is also played out in both narrative and symbolic terms.

To read the poem's symbolic imagery in the manner that I have suggested presupposes a certain approach, whose basic premises can be found in medieval symbolist thought. This approach requires, first of all, that we respond to the poem on all levels of our perception— physical, emotional, intellectual—simultaneously. Although critical analysis separates these levels, we must constantly try to synthesize them again into their whole, without letting go of the work's less rational aspects. In spite of its strong thematic preoccupation, medieval poetry demands the same multiplex response as all poetry. A medieval poem, too, cannot be reduced to its paraphrase or its theological theme. Hence, medieval poetic symbolism also must be experienced on these multiple levels.

The Pearl Poet grounds the relationship between symbol and idea in familiar experience. Even at the height of apocalyptic incongruity between symbol and idea, it is familiar experience that acts as the point of reference for our responses, as the criterion of our judgments. The poet uses this dependence of the reader's mind to carry out his symbolic strategy. His progressive intensification of the visual values of the poem demands that we respond to his images, like the dreamer, "in yȝe and ere"—that is, sensually and emotionally as well as intellectually. The physical aspect of the symbolic image is crucial to its spiritual meaning. It should not be—in fact, it cannot be—transcended by any intellectual leap to purely conceptual values. Immaterial meaning is made to depend on the material qualities of the symbolic image and even to behave like them. This suggests a rather commonplace view of the relationship between spirit and matter in medieval theoretical thought, often overlooked in medieval poetic practice by both medieval and modern critics. Fettered by their Neoplatonic distrust of the physical and their thematic preconceptions about a specific work, they sift and choose only those corporeal and affective values in the image that are consistent with these preconceptions. I shall insist on recognizing a variety of such values in each symbolic image, however opposite and complementary. This complementarity is significant: From a theological standpoint, it is at the center of Christian mystery. Poetically, its ceaseless dialectic between conceptual definition and experiential resistance produces vibrant art.

The multivalence of the medieval poetic symbol, especially in its representation of the supernatural, is not the invention of any modern critical predilection for "tension" and "paradox." Nor is it part of a modern attempt to rescue medieval literature from its dullness. It finds its philosophical and, less definitely, artistic justification in the medieval notion of analogy. I do not mean to rehearse here in any detail the philosophical premises of this notion. We know that it deals in ontological terms with the capacity or inadequacy of human similitudes to represent divine reality. (By "ontological" I am referring to the essential nature of the object in itself.) My main interest is to highlight the artistic possibilities of analogy as metaphoric process, affirming the centrality of the physical aspect and seeing it in dynamic counterpoise to the spiritual aim of any poetic similitude.

Let us first consider Pseudo-Dionysius the Areopagite, who, together with Saint Augustine, helped shape medieval symbolist thought. As a Neoplatonist, he has been traditionally viewed as one who "denies" the analogical image. Its physical nature relegates it to a world of illusion where matter is, at best, a degraded and false imitation of a higher reality. Too much stress, however, has been placed on Pseudo-Dionysius's ultimate quest for mystic ignorance (*mystike agnosia*) through the *via negativa*. We overlook his own admission that, nonetheless, man by his nature follows rather the *via affirmativa*, aware of the paradox that the descriptions he makes of God are both true and untrue. In fact, he considers the analogical image as an instrument of man's spiritual elevation (*anagoge*). When he mentions the celestial realm, Pseudo-Dionysius gives free rein to his poetic imagination as he describes "the many-voiced trumpets" and "the streaming lights" of the angelic world, the flaming, beautifully graduated colors and configurations. Here is a Neoplatonist celebrating the very image he renounces, speaking of pure spiritual essences with the language of the refined sensualist. The more rarefied his images, the more exquisitely they touch our senses. Pseudo-Dionysius explains—and emulates—the biblical poet's symbolic strategy in using "dissimilar similitudes" (*anomoious homoiotetas*) to keep us aware of the distance between divine reality and its human representation. The dissimilar similitude will serve as a key metaphoric concept in our present study. Pseudo-Dionysius discusses this concept, of course, in theological terms, dealing mainly with man's true knowledge of God. Yet in the choice of his terms, which refer mostly to shape and color and to difference within similarity, he displays an aesthetic appreciation of analogy as well. This aesthetic appreciation becomes more evident when he points to the paradoxical function of the symbol: it reveals truth while veiling it.[8] This is metaphor of the highest order, in my view. It stimulates the human imagination to move back and forth on a tense and engaging metaphoric continuum, attempting to absorb a double truth, maintaining a taut awareness of the similarity and the difference that coexist dynamically between the means and the object of symbolic representation. The Areopagite's denial of the veil seems rather an admission of its inescapable impact on our perception, of how much it imposes its physical reality upon the intended spiritual meaning. In effect, Pseudo-Dionysius seems to say that there is no similitude that is totally "negative" or self-transcending. For while it says what God is not, it is saying what it, the similitude, is. His very style, like that of Augustine's *Confessions* and of most medieval mystical writings, shows the tension between aspiration and achievement: he describes his ascent to a purely intellectual experience of God with the contradictory earthbound language of human desire, "the violent intemperance . . . of the intense and unswerving and unrestrainable . . . love [*eros*] for divine beauty."[9]

As is well known, Augustine, despite his Platonic leanings, sees the physical world sanctified and redeemed in God's act of the creation. In fact, he seeks to understand God in his creatures, whether in the created cosmos or in the Scriptures as *signa*. In order to know God and to comprehend his Word better, we need to study the things around us more closely. To Augustine, the physical aspect of each analogical similitude is indispensable to its higher meaning. He therefore institutes the senses as channels of spiritual knowledge, when, for instance, he insists on the prerequisite necessity of our having experienced sensuously the oil's smooth surface in order to comprehend the olive twig that Noah's dove brought back to the ark as a symbol of God's mercy.[10] Augustine earnestly embraces Saint Paul's conviction that the *invisibilia* of God can be understood through the *visibilia* of this world—a conviction that guides all medieval analogical thought.[11] (I shall have more to say about Augustine's views on analogy.)

Though he repeats the warnings of his intellectual mentor—Augustine—not to dwell too long on the charms of the physical world, Hugh of Saint Victor celebrates, nonetheless, its physical beauty as a symbol of God. According to Hans Glunz and Edgar de Bruyne, Hugh is the first medieval thinker to develop a systematic aesthetics of analogy and, especially, of the surface of God's own analogical symbol, creation.[12] Speaking of the first, he observes at one point, for example, that analogies and similitudes engage us not only because they are pleasantly obscure but because they have beauty and because they *surprise* the mind into new revelations. Speaking of creation, Hugh insists that the "spiritual" reader scrutinize it closely in order to come to a better understanding of its maker. The sensible universe, he tells us, is a book written by the finger of God.[13] Hugh delights in the paradox that the humblest creature hides some vast, profound truth. He elevates all five senses—not only sight and hearing—to indispensable instruments of spiritual truth through their perception of this world's beauty: the innumerable colors, the shapes, and the smells of God's creatures. He does not hesitate to render spiritual regeneration more accessible to our sensibility by describing it in terms of delectable sensual gratification.[14] Hugh finds in every physical attribute of the analogical similitude a corresponding spiritual significance, in such a way that the spiritual significance seems to behave like and to derive from the physical attribute. It is this close interdependence between matter and spirit that acts as the sacramental and aesthetic principle of the Pearl Poet's and Dante's imagery.

Although his discussion of analogy and similitude is more epistemological than aesthetic, Saint Thomas Aquinas's conclusions on the subject help focus, at least historically, our approach to medieval poetic symbolism. Thomas, too, insists repeatedly on the indispensability of sensory perception to intellectual knowledge. To form and sustain any spiritual truth, the human intellect, despite its abstractive tendencies, needs to refer to sensate objects, to correspondent "phantasms."[15] Thomas reaffirms the value of sensible creation as a symbolic vehicle to knowing God.[16] Walter Ong has discussed with penetration Thomas's acknowledgment of the necessity of similitudes both in theology and in poetry, implying strongly that their concrete surface helps translate their meaning through the senses.[17] "Analogies of God, for Thomas, are *aenigmata,*" Marcia Colish reminds us. Thomas felt—without ever being able to resolve it—the continuous tension between the similarity and difference that reside simultaneously in each analogate, each metaphor.[18]

In his *Itinerarium mentis in Deum,* Saint Bonaventura speaks of the sensible world as a "ladder" for the mind's ascent to God. In order "to know God . . . to bless Him and to love Him," we must study his creatures well. It is for our instruction that he imprinted his traces (*vestigia*) on them. Saint Bonaventura dwells lovingly on their "light, sound, odor, savor," which constitute their beauty (*speciositas*), emphasizing the function of all five senses as "doors" not only to sensuous perception but also to spiritual apprehension. "The invisible things of God"—he echoes Paul and Augustine—"are clearly seen from the creation of the world, being understood by the things that are made." Furthermore, the symbolic significance of each creature is part of its nature, built into it by God rather than invented by man.[19] Franciscan spirituality and its aesthetics, as well as its emotionalism and its appeal to earthbound, familiar experience, increase the impact of the symbolic surface in any poetic context. Without committing the excesses of the late Middle Ages, *Pearl* shares this temper; it has its own *gloria passionis.*[20]

The simultaneous multiplicity—and even contrariety—of meanings in the analogical similitude is a notion spun into the very fabric of medieval symbolist thought. It was based on traditional exegesis. Augustine points to the opposition of meanings—a good and a bad sense—in several similitudes. The lion, for instance, represents Christ as well as the Devil. The serpent serves as an example to the wise; but it also reminds us of the serpent in the Garden of Eden.[21] A look at medieval *distinctiones* reveals the same symbolic complementarity. To Alanus de Insulis, fire signifies the illuminating light of the Holy Spirit but also the consuming heat of concupiscence.[22] The breasts of the spouse in the Song of Songs represent Mary's loving arms that held Christ as well as the seductive rhetoric of amorous dalliance.[23] According to Augustine, such multivalence was built by God into every symbol, scriptural or creational, as part of his art.[24] It is the source of both spiritual insight and aesthetic pleasure. Theologically, in its yoking of distant realities, it proclaims an underlying unity in the complex scheme of things, instituted by God himself—a comforting and reassuring thought to man. Aesthetically, this frequently contradictory multiplicity of meaning adds to analogy a highly engaging and pleasing obscurity. As Augustine puts it, "things [divine truth] are perceived more readily through similitudes and . . . what is sought with difficulty is discovered with more pleasure."[25] Boccaccio responds to the pleasure of obscurity in figurative expression in similar terms: "It is obvious that anything that is gained with fatigue seems sweeter than what is acquired without effort."[26] More specifically, this simultaneous contrariety of meaning vitalizes analogy as metaphoric process by the tense irreconcilability of its terms—a tension that energizes great poetry and excites the imagination. As Père Chenu reminds us, the medieval masters delighted in this polyvalence, even at the cost of conceptual clarity.[27]

Any survey, then, of medieval analogical theory reveals, in the medieval thinker, a continuous awareness of the aesthetic possibilities of the analogical relationship: the multivalence of the symbol, the importance of its physical aspect, and the interplay between different but simultaneous levels of response. The medieval poet, as we can see in the *Pearl*, recognized and exploited artistically the dynamic qualities of the analogical process in his own symbolism. In fact, he made human drama out of them.

Medieval analogy based its validity on the sacramental connection between the material and the spiritual, the human and the divine, which God effected through his Incarnation. In it, the two opposing natures are brought together in a dynamic relationship, fused yet distinct.

The Incarnation does not stand as the sacred prototype of the yoking of these opposite natures in an ontological and theological sense only. In the medieval period, God's primal sacrament becomes an aesthetic prototype as well. "In the Middle Ages," Gerhart B. Ladner reminds us, "the central tenet of Christian theology was also the greatest justification of Christian art."[28] Human nature was worthy enough of God's assumption. Man, then, was God's closest analogue.[29] In this function, the visible, physical aspect of man became increasingly significant in the later Middle Ages, the milieu of *Pearl*. "Before the Incarnation of the Word, only the internal form (that is to say, the soul) of man was similar to God, but beginning with the Incarnation of the Word even the external form (the body) of man became the form of God." So writes Helinand of Foridmont, reflecting "a reawakening in the twelfth century of the incarnational aspect of the image of man, which in the early mediaeval west had been largely eclipsed by the spiritual and eschatological aspect." Saint Bernard of Clairvaux, who would tear down all images because they interpose themselves between man's vision and God (we recall his letters to Abbot Suger), admonishes us, nevertheless, that our "love for Christ . . . must begin with love for Christ's body, for His *caro,* His very flesh."[30] The increasing naturalization of the human figure in Gothic art in the depictions of Christ shows that the medieval artist, like the medieval theologian, was asserting more and more the reality of Christ's humanity and the importance of physical form as a means of incarnating divine truth.

I do not intend to dwell on the theology of the Incarnation. I shall focus more on its aesthetic implications in medieval poetry. At least two such implications need to be restated here, because they are central to my approach: If the Incarnation insists on the reality of the physical as means of representing the spiritual, and if the spiritual is to be understood in terms of the physical, then the very qualities and distinguishing characteristics of the physical shape the spiritual meaning in our minds and they become part of it. In every incarnational representation we are asked to respond to these qualities in their own concrete reality—as Augustine does with his fingertips, touching the smooth surface of the oil for a full understanding of God's mercy.[31] As we saw, the analogical thinkers of the period imply strongly the necessity of such a response. Second, if the reality of the physical and the spiritual, the human and the divine terms, is to be equally emphasized in any metaphor of the ineffable, the tension between these two terms, as they try to establish themselves in the perceiving mind, increases considerably. When the medieval poet manipulates and patterns this tension, the result can be a powerful spiritual and artistic experience.

Charles S. Singleton has argued that Dante wanted his *Divine Comedy* to be interpreted like the Scriptures by constructing it on the same allegorical principle. Since Dante's poem is an imitation of God's way of writing and an analogue to God's poem, the universe, the reader must regard its truths as an extension of those in the Bible. In this connection, the poem participates sacramentally in the reality of its sacred model. Invoking Thomas Aquinas's emphasis on the historical reality of the literal event or thing as an indispensable basis to any subsequent spiritual meaning, Singleton insists on the historical veracity of Dante's journey as necessary to its incarnational efficacy.[32] Singleton's view has, in the meantime, been modified by Richard H. Green, Phillip Damon, and Robert Hollander.[33] These critics contend quite sensibly that

Dante, through his artistic strategy, indicates clearly the fictional nature of the poem's event. This fictiveness, however, in no way annuls or diminishes the validity of the poem as spiritual experience and its capacity to incarnate sacred truth through its literal content. The medieval poet, therefore, as imitator of God the arch-poet, could always claim for his fiction and his handiwork a sacramental connection with sacred truth.

In this sense, then, Dante's art is incarnational like God's. The literal and the physical aspect of his poetic representation has a presence and historical reality of its own. It is the basis on which the poem's spiritual meaning has been built. Dante, like Christ, uses the humble images of this earth to "incarnate" divine truths, quite aware of their sensuous and affective impact and the paradox of their incongruity. So the human figure at the center of Dante's ultimate vision asserts the indispensability of the human framework as point of reference, not only in theological understanding but also in the representation of its opposite, the superhuman. This final configuration is Dante's most powerful statement of the Incarnation as his poetic principle. Earlier in the poem, Dante had asserted the poet's unique right to readapt God's incarnational art when he embodied the ineffable mystery of Christ's dual nature in a creation of the poetic imagination and of fantasy—the griffin. What the sacrament is to God, then, the poetic symbol is to the poet, his imitator.

It is my conviction that the author of *Pearl* places the same demands on his reader as Dante. He too wants his poem read as an analogue to God's Word. To emphasize his demand, he risks the reader's boredom and refuses to create an anagogic world of his own invention—unlike many of his colleagues in their dream visions and otherworld journeys.[34] Instead, he borrows or, rather, daringly appropriates the anagogic telos of the Bible and makes it the dramatic denouement of his own private experience. He claims to have seen what John the Apostle saw. He claims to have actually encountered the sacred prototype of anagoge itself, the New Jerusalem. Can a poet imitate God's way of writing more closely than this? Still, his claim is placed on the truth of the poem as an experience of its own and not on its historical probability. On this basis, then, the Pearl Poet forms his images to function incarnationally; their corporeal form shapes their spiritual meaning. Physical perception becomes spiritual illumination.

In bringing together such vastly different natures, the incarnational symbol holds the maximum metaphoric tension, because it is more than metaphor. It insists on a sacramental identity between its terms, which all levels of human perception contradict. Because the tenor is unknown and fundamentally inexpressible, the vehicle tends to engulf it with its own reality and define it totally in its own terms. Yet the human mind resists this engulfment, escaping at the same time into new vehicles and new analogical relationships between distant realities. This ceaseless failure turns simultaneously into creative activity, in which the poet as artist creates an infinitude of forms and patterns and, therefore, meaning. It is in such an instant that the medieval poet saw himself imitating and sharing in the creative fecundity of the arch-artist, God. The Pearl Poet and Dante were no exception to this realization.

The Pearl Poet's incarnational art is not seen only in his symbolic imagery. Just as his images bring together opposing natures and sensibilities, his verbal structures, too, combine in one corporeal (verbal) form a multiplicity of meanings. We see this in his incessant word play, his link words, and his verbal echoing of the same idea in new contexts. I do not intend to dwell extensively on this verbal aspect of *Pearl*, since enough has been said by other critics.[35] All I want to establish is that the Pearl Poet handles his words as analogues of the Word, just as he handles his poetic symbols as analogues of the sacrament of the Incarnation. Verbal form functions with a symbolic efficacy of its own. As equally palpable experience, the poem's verbal surface is part of its *visibilia,* intended to lead to its invisible spiritual meaning.

Finally, the poet delights in re-incarnating within infinite verbal and imagistic patterns that principle which holds the medieval world together: variety in unity and unity in variety.[36] His poem is structured on this pervasive cosmological and aesthetic principle. The poem itself, therefore, is an incarnational symbol of God's universe.

These are, then, the critical premises on which I shall base my reading of the poem's symbolic imagery and, inevitably, of the poem as a whole.

2

In the "Erber Grene"

The opening section (I) of *Pearl*, which describes the hero's lamentation in the garden, establishes the direction of the poem's symbolic and dramatic development. The author reveals his intention as well as his method of relating symbol to drama. He defines the hero's crisis and initiates the expectation of its resolution. The poem's central themes begin to emerge; its general tone and emotional temper are set. This outlay of forces takes place in a progressive fashion but with startling economy and concentration. A careful glance at the first stanza shows this well:

> Perle, plesaunte to prynces paye
> To clanly clos in golde so clere,
> Oute of oryent, I hardyly saye,
> Ne proued I neuer her precios pere.
> So rounde, so reken in vche araye,
> So smal, so smoþe her sydeȝ were,
> Quere-so-euer I jugged gemmeȝ gaye,
> I sette hyr sengeley in synglere.
> Allas! I leste hyr in on erbere;
> Þurȝ gresse to grounde hit fro me yot.
> I dewyne, fordolked of luf-daungere
> Of þat pryuy perle wythouten spot.
>
> (1–12)

The first word we encounter is "Perle." Isolated by a caesura and charged with dramatic force as an apostrophe, it transfixes us with its total arbitrariness as "the beginning"—the first essence to be contended with. Through such an emphatic confrontation, we are made to recognize immediately the importance of this image. The first stanza thus posits the pearl as the poem's central symbol and, at the same time, relates it to a personal human drama: it is the object of the hero's loss and bereavement. We are forced, therefore, to formulate an approach by which we can discover its identity and its dramatic significance. Since the pearl brings into the poem a rich background of traditional values, it is essential for us to be aware of the constant counterpoise between symbolic tradition and poetic context and of the meanings resulting from their interaction. We may thus develop some principle of inter- pretation that we can apply to the poem's other symbols and to medi- eval poetic symbolism in general.

Recent critics of *Pearl* have revolted against using extrinsic sources— medieval lapidaries, social history, scriptural commentaries, and so on— to define the meaning of the pearl image in the poem.[1] I agree with them that the ultimate shaping force of the symbol's meaning is the poem's context. But to appreciate fully the transformative impact of this new context, the reader—whether an educated man of the fourteenth century[2] or a modern critic—should be acquainted with the symbol's traditional values. This cumulative tradition, after all, stands as a power- ful context in its own right. The poet wants us to have such an aware- ness, so that we may perceive more keenly his particular treatment of the image and the intention behind it. The more established and resistant the value to be altered, the more tense and aesthetically engaging the interplay between it and the pressing new milieu. In fact, the poet sets up the anticipation that the symbol's traditional values will remain un- changed in their past cohesion—only to dash such an anticipation into new coherence. This pattern of "traditional" expectation and contextual frustration in the poem's imagistic development operates in *Pearl* as the concrete embodiment of the human drama unfolding in it. The poet's method of selection and symbolic transformation becomes, in essence, the work's thematic and formal principle. I would like, therefore, to survey the pearl's symbolic background—touching on some of its salient values—before following its reconstruction within the poem.

One is overwhelmed by the wealth of associations that the pearl came to possess as symbol in the Middle Ages, from many levels of experi- ence. W. H. Schofield and P. J. Heather have shown that lapidaries were very popular in that period and were studied assiduously.[3] That the Pearl Poet was acquainted with these works appears indisputable.[4] In them, we can see what the pearl and other precious stones meant to the medieval imagination. Gems possessed magical powers: they could protect the wearer from harm,[5] they could be used to influence men's and nature's behavior,[6] they could even test a woman's chastity[7]—not a very sublime connection with pure maidenhood, a key spiritual value in

Pearl. Most of these properties had a salutary effect on the body and the mind. Thomas Usk, a contemporary of the Pearl Poet, paraphrasing Jacobus de Voragine's life of Saint Margaret in the *Legenda Aurea*,[8] summarizes them in his *Testament of Love:*

> But special cause I have in my herte to make this proces of a Margarit-perle, that is so precious a gemme whyt, clere and litel . . . in whiche by experience ben founde three fayre vertues. Oon is, it yeveth comfort to the feling spirites in bodily persones of reson. Another is good; it is profitable helthe ayenst passions of sorie mens hertes. And the thirde, it is nedeful and noble in staunching of bloode, there els to moche wolde out renne. [III, i, 34–51][9]

Usk goes on to translate the pearl's physical qualities into the spiritual virtues of his courtly-divine mistress: her purity, her humility, and her healing effect on him.

Added to these enchanting and healing powers was the exquisite exoticism of the oriental pearl, which was considered peerless in texture and form.[10] Oriental pearls were highly praised and attached to fabulous adventures in medieval works like the *Cursor mundi* and *The Travels of Marco Polo.* These associations must have aroused in the medieval sensibility the complementary feelings of suspicion and attraction toward the pagan beauty of the East and its unbridled sumptuousness. We discern this mixed attitude in the author's ideological resistance to yet descriptive relish in the glittering, brilliantly colored vistas of heathen armies in the *Chanson de Roland,* for example. The Pearl Poet appreciated and adapted to his use the pearl's exotic, oriental background.[11] We observe this in his own visual abandon as he describes the precious holy vessels in Belshazzar's palace (*Purity,* lines 1469–72). Any sanctity still lingering in these objects is soon dispelled by their sensuous luxuriance. The mystery of the sacred turns almost into magical fascination.

Because of the poem's religious theme, patristic interpretations of the pearl image in medieval scriptural commentary are highly pertinent here.[12] They constitute the symbol's spiritual tradition and make up a good part of its philosophical and conceptual aspect. This background affects significantly the pearl's evolution within the poem's drama of belief. These patristic interpretations are based mainly on two biblical parables: the pearl (the Word of God) that must not be cast to the swine (the spiritually unprepared) (Matt. 7:6); and the pearl of great price (the kingdom of God) that the good merchant (the wise man) must buy, sacrificing all other possessions (Matt. 13:45–46). To Augustine the pearl stands for the knowledge of the Word in its purity and self-consistency of meaning, while for Jerome it represents "the knowledge of the Saviour, the sacrament of the Passion and the mystery of the resurrection."[13] To these fathers and to Chrysostom the pearl symbolizes the mysteries of the Christian faith, which should be kept away from the uninitiated and the nonbelievers and thus remain unsullied.[14] Bede speaks of the pearl as the celestial life.[15] Albertus Magnus sees reflected in the pearl Mary's purity, her humility yet utter singularity.[16] Aldhelm, among others, associates the pearl with virginity, describing holy maidens as "Christi margaritae, paradisi gemmae."[17] Medieval verse employs the foregoing exegetical significations quite frequently. The Pearl Poet, for one, uses the pearl as symbol of spiritual purity repeatedly, as in *Purity* (lines 546, 1113–32) and in *Sir Gawain and the Green Knight* (lines 2364–65).[18]

It is essential to note, at this point, that almost invariably the medieval exegete will scrutinize intently the physical and, more subtly, the affective attributes of the image, using them as points of departure and as concretizing vehicles for correspondent spiritual values. The pearl's whiteness, for instance, images virginity; its flawless texture incarnates spiritual purity; its smallness, humility; its spherical shape, self-sufficient perfection and, hence, immortality: "Margarete is sayd of a precyous gemme or ouche that is named margaryte, whyche gemme is whythe, lytyll, & vertuous. So the blessyd margarete was whithe by virgynite, lytyll by humylyte, & vertous by operacyon of myracles."[19] "Heaven is a pure body . . . in the form of a sphere," Albertus Magnus adds, speaking of both its physical and its spiritual perfection.[20] Spiritual value, therefore, is derived from and expressed through the material attribute. The tension between idea and concretion—between spirit and matter—in their irreconcilable difference yet profound interdependence is constantly present in these interpretations. Hence, the pearl as symbol of perfection already carries within itself from tradition the principle of analogical contradiction, which the poet translates into moving human drama in *Pearl*.

We have noted that traditional exegesis often invests biblical images with contrary meanings. What complicates—and greatly enriches—the pearl as symbol of perfection in medieval literature is its simultaneous association with the less perfect things of this world, as Rabanus Maurus shows:

> *Margarita* est coeleste desiderium, ut in Evangelio: "inventa una pretiosa margarita" [Matt. 13:46], id est, concepto in mente desiderio coelesti. Per *margaritas* spiritualia sacramenta, ut in Evangelio: "Ne mittatis margaritas vestras ante porcos" [Matt. 7:6], id est, interna mysteria non committatis immundis.

Per *margaritas* homines justi, ut in Apocalypsi: "Duodecim mar-
garitae, duodecim portae" [Rev. 21:21], quod homines sancti
per fidem apostolorum aditum habent ad regnum coeleste. Per
margaritas deliciae terrenae, ut in Apocalypsi: "Mulier erat or-
nata margaritis" [Rev. 17:4], quod fallacia hujus saeculi terre-
nis deliciis nitet.[21]

To him, the pearl symbolizes the desire for heaven, the Holy Sacra-
ments, the divine mysteries that must be protected from the uniniti-
ated, and then faith itself through which man passes into eternity as
through the precious gates of the New Jerusalem. But the pearl also
represents the depravity of worldly riches, seen here as the adorn-
ments of the fearsome eschatological figure of the *mulier,* the Whore
of Babylon. It also stands for the pleasures of this earth ("terrenis
deliciis"). One chapter later (Rev. 18:11–17), we come upon the de-
struction of the city of Babylon, where its princes and merchants weep
among the ruins for their lost treasures and precious stones. The
Bible itself presents the pearl as a symbol of perfection as well as of
mutability and even moral corruption. How does the reader, then—
medieval or modern—react to the heavenly city, built as it is with the
reckless opulence of the earthly city? How far can thematic context or
the poet's clearly announced thematic intention prevent the fusion of
these two cities into one complex poetic experience, eliciting an
equally complex response?

Together with its spiritual aspect, we must keep in mind the pearl's
secular values as equally immediate to the medieval sensibility. The
nobility used precious stones inordinately in their pomp and self-dis-
play—their fashionable attire, their crowns, and their rings—much to
the admiration and obsessive envy of the rest of medieval society.[22] In
literature, personifications of worldly wealth, such as Richesse in the
Roman de la Rose and Lady Mede in *Piers Plowman,* appear heavily
bedecked with pearls and other jewels. In his castigation of human
covetousness and self-exhibition, Walter Hilton, a contemporary of the
Pearl Poet, admonishes his age to set "no greater value on a precious
stone than on a lump of chalk."[23] It is these associations that have led
Sister Mary V. Hillman and John Conley to view the pearl at the begin-
ning of the poem strictly as the material wealth that the misguided hero
has lost and now laments—until, of course, he learns to seek instead the
riches of heaven.[24] These critics assume that the pearl symbol eventu-
ally transcends in the poem all mundane and corporeal values, ceasing
to affect any other level of perception in the reader except the purely
intellectual and spiritual—a mistaken assumption.

Associated thus with the life of the medieval aristocracy and, inevitably, with its literature, the pearl image acquired strong courtly overtones. These added to its secular character. Medieval romance is rife with ladies being compared to precious stones.[25] To these belong Machaut's Marguerite, Chaucer's Alceste, and Usk's courtly-divine mistress. We also encounter precious palaces of love, such as the temples of Venus in Chaucer's *House of Fame* and in *The Destruction of Troy*. An interesting example is the castle in the fairyland of *Sir Orfeo*, compared by the author to the New Jerusalem itself (lines 330–52).[26] A similar mixture of romance fantasy and sanctity is seen, as I have pointed out, in the Pearl Poet's own description of the holy vessels in Belshazzar's hall (*Purity*, lines 1467–74). We shall note repeatedly in *Pearl*—as part of its complex sensibility—motifs and impulses that derive, without doubt, from the romance.

Perhaps the most tantalizing and puzzling connection exists between precious stones and mortality in the Middle Ages. We are struck by the sumptuous adornment of tombs and shrines—such as the richly ornamented crosses and altars erected by Edward I to the memory of his wife Eleanor—and the gilded effigies of the time.[27] In literature, we come across the heavily decorated tombs of Antony in Chaucer's *Legend of Good Women*, in Gower's *Tale of Iphis*, and the preciously vested corpse in the grave of *St. Erkenwald*. The lapidaries give no clue as to the impulse behind this curious connection. One can speculate on the moral lesson intended in such a gripping juxtaposition. Nonetheless, one cannot escape the macabre fascination, assuredly felt by the medieval audience, in observing how precious opulence translates itself into oppressive overripeness and decay—and the reverse. This translation is worth noting, since we shall encounter it in *Pearl*.

It must be evident by now that there is nothing more deadly to poetic analysis than a catalogue of sources and analogues. As a list of dissected, discrete items, it contradicts by nature the vital continuity of the work analyzed. Furthermore, it always remains peripheral to the work and its meaning because it refers to criteria outside it.[28] When incorporated, however, into a more intrinsic approach, such background criticism does enhance our appreciation of the work at hand.

In the foregoing survey, I have tried to demonstrate the rich complementarity of meaning that the pearl brings into the poem from tradition. It combines various and often opposing sensibilities—from the sacred to the profane—which we cannot extricate from each other at will to fit certain thematic preconceptions. Furthermore, we see that the pearl's spiritual values are grounded trenchantly in its material qualities and are therefore considerably defined by them in our perception. This interdependence results in continuous analogical tension between these spiritual values and their concretizing vehicles, since they derive from contrary orders of being. The dynamic interplay between levels of meaning and disparate sensibilities leads us to expect the pearl symbol to continue shifting and expanding within the poem's own context, resisting reduction to a single concept or theme. This inherited complexity allows the author to make the pearl the concrete vehicle for the poem's equally complex drama of faith, where man seeks to reconcile the divine with the human, the spiritual with the material. Finally, the pearl's traditional multivalence, and therefore irresolution of meaning, forces us to turn even more to the poem's context as ultimate shaping force.

It does not take long upon entering *Pearl* to discover that its author handles his imagery on the incarnational poetic principle that I have reiterated: Physical form shapes spiritual meaning, or—put another way—spiritual meaning behaves like the material attribute. Sensuous perception becomes simultaneously metaphysical penetration; the physical and the intellectual fuse in one instantaneous act of understanding. The Pearl Poet insists on the importance of the pearl's corporeal qualities by dwelling on them with meticulous intensity. Consequently, any change in them signifies a redirection in the symbol's spiritual meaning—a key premise in my critical method.

The poem's opening eight lines are essentially a formula out of a medieval verse lapidary. Several of the traditional meanings that I have mentioned are established in these lines as part of the hero's lost object. The pearl is given great worldly worth, recalling the aristocratic and mercantile society that esteemed it. It carries with it the exoticism and romance of the Orient. Its flawless shape and texture make it peerless and singular. The poet presents these qualities, however, with a particular coloration, which has considerable anticipatory value. The pearl's enclosure in gold (2) stresses its precious singularity and immaculateness. It protects and enhances the gem; but it also transfixes it in a curiously isolating perfection—immobile, impenetrable, resisting scrutiny or possession. In a sense, then, the golden enclosure defines symbolically the pearl's relationship to the hero and to us, beckoning to us with its beauty yet keeping us at an irrevocable distance from it.

The protective and subtly erotic tenderness of "So smal, so smoþe her sydeȝ were"—to be echoed and further clarified later (190)—the use of the feminine pronoun "hyr," and the tone of the hero's lament complicate the pearl's identity. It is more than a material gem that the hero mourns. "Araye" means the stone's setting, but it also suggests a person's attire. "Smoþe sydeȝ" obviously refers to the pearl's surface; yet simultaneously it brings to mind a woman's soft flanks.[29] If indeed we did not have some sense of the pearl's human identity, we would have soon dismissed the hero's lament as ludicrously exaggerated, if not grotesquely maudlin. The poet, therefore, establishes her human dimension almost immediately by having the hero speak as a bereaved lover, "fordolked of luf-daungere" (11). The hero's grief becomes more appealing and worth identifying with, especially for a courtly audience. Nevertheless, the poet does not weaken any of the pearl's gemlike qualities but insists upon them. In sum, the poet begins to concentrate on the pearl an increasing number of loves and relationships significant to the life of the hero, leading eventually to the final and most important relationship sought by him on an anagogic level.

We are confronted, consequently, with the question concerning the true nature of the object of the hero's quest. Its shifting character has predisposed us toward a further expansion of its identity. So far, we have perceived it as something supremely desirable yet difficult to attain—a complementary quality that initiates the poem's dramatic pattern of desire and frustration. To the hero, the pearl will indeed become the "grounde" of both his "blysse" and his "bale" (373). His courtly complaint suggests, furthermore, the futile wooing of some distant and unresponsive entity—an aspect of significant premonitory value.

It is part of the poet's dramatic strategy to keep the pearl's identity ambiguous for some time in the work and to further complicate its character by investing it with a multiplicity of sensibilities and relationships: courtly, spiritual, worldly, personal. Because it embodies so many disparate realities, the pearl obviously—as object of quest—becomes a potent dramatic force in the hero's effort to reconcile the contradictions of his existence. "The author's plan," Schofield observes, "is to let the symbolism of the poem disclose itself slowly."[30] This delay in symbolic identification, as part of a personal drama, generates suspense and the desire for final clarification and resolution. Moreover, as long as the object of loss stays obscure, consolation, too, remains unfocused and distant, becoming more desperate by its very uncertainty. Finally, in the symbol's counterpoise of the two elements—the precious stone and the human figure—the poet offers us an imagistic prefiguration of the poem's central antithesis and its two protagonists: human nature and the order of being that the pearl will finally come to represent. Having, then, selected and reconstructed some of the pearl's traditional meanings in the first stanza, the poet indicates that the poem's symbolic imagery as a whole will develop out of the interaction between established value and contextual pressure—a process thematically significant and aesthetically vitalizing.

The hero's initial lamentation is charged with powerful, even self-luxu-
riating emotion, which establishes the poem's general temper. Emotion
is intrinsic to the poem's dramatic order, and yet it has been side-
stepped as too elusive and subjective for discussion in favor of clear
ideas. Emotion, nonetheless, not only humanizes the poem's event but
also brings to it, as aesthetic experience, variety of tempo and tonality.
Heiserman is right in stating that "the poem works through a dialectic
of emotion, of controlled discoveries and disappointments,"[31] although
he forces his point too far by making this emotional dialectic the work's
organizing principle.

The initial two stanzas are a good sample of the poet's intricate
handling of emotion. The first eight lines are arranged by asyndeton
into a group of paratactic clauses, which sound like spasmodic exclama-
tions, culminating in the cry, "Allas! I leste hyr . . . " (9). The poet
captures the hero's inner turmoil in palpable form through the power-
ful image of the heaving chest and by the explosive, bellowing allitera-
tion: "My *b*reste in *b*ale *b*ot *b*olne and *b*ele" (18). The poet's constant
interest in realizing inner states concretely through image and verbal
form—rather than remaining on an abstract moral or psychological
level with them—is additional evidence of his "incarnational" mentality.
Moreover, the hero's emotional violence is made to suggest a corre-
sponding degree of impotence. Such prostration on his part makes the
object of his quest appear even less attainable, thus increasing the
poem's dramatic suspense and promising greater complication.

This feeling of precariousness is intensified considerably by the tim-
ing of the hero's desperate exclamation, "Allas! I leste hyr in on
erbere" (9), because it raises the gnawing question about his final
consolation. We try to distinguish here—as throughout the poem—the
different voices of the "I." Who mourns here—the confused, hopeless
hero undergoing the experience *then,* or the narrator, supposedly en-
lightened and comforted after the event, relating it to us *now* with a
wiser perspective? A series of statements by the narrator in the pre-
sent tense gives us the impression that much of his initial bereavement
has continued beyond the poem's actual occurrence to the time of its
telling: "I *dewyne*, fordolked . . . " (11). "Ofte haf I wayted, wyschande
þat wele" (14)—when? Since the consolatory vision? Even now? Fi-
nally, the narrator breaks out in bitterness against a universal experi-
ence still taking place all around him: "O moul, þou marreʒ a myry
iuele" (23). These disconsolate utterances at the beginning of the
poem function as a dramatic device of foreboding. They linger in our
memory, as the situation unfolds, generating suspense and apprehen-
sion in us, especially during the hero's moments of self-abandon and

ecstatic optimism in the ideal realm. Why does he still lament? What kind of consolation has he derived, if any?

The poet introduces early in the poem a significant source of consolation which we must consider at this point. The narrator recalls that, during his mourning,

> 3et þo3t me neuer so swete a sange
> As stylle stounde let to me stele.
>
>   (19–20)

Patricia Kean opposes the view, held by E. V. Gordon, that this song is the poem itself in germination. She suggests that the hero is listening, instead, to the voice of God—of "resoun" and the "kynde of Kryst"— that is comforting him.[32] The poet does not actually define the song. Whether its source be divine or human, this comforting voice is a song, nevertheless—that is, a construction of conscious artistry. In medieval thought, every human artistic creation imitates God's artifact, the world. By indirection at least, the Pearl Poet suggests his poem's role in the process of consolation. He offers it as a poetic incarnation of the beauty and coherence of God's poem, the universe, so that the hero— and we by participation—may contemplate it and absorb it as an ordering principle for our spiritual integration. The poet introduces here, then, the idea of art as source of consolation.

With him, however, this is not an abstract notion only. He points directly at the very surface of his work where this idea operates in concrete, experienceable form. The consolatory rhetoric can be heard in the soothing whisper of the alliterative s's (19–20). It is woven into the fabric of his artifact. The intricate yet set stanza form, too, asserts palpably the poet's intention to control vital human experience within the order of his art, saving it in some manner from chaos. I believe, therefore, that Kean's and Gordon's views are both true and can be reconciled into one thesis. That the "kynde of Kryst"—the nature of Christ—should console man in the form of "a sange" claims for human poetry the capacity to carry on the reconciling and ordering work of the incarnate Word. By this juxtaposition, the author reasserts once again the Incarnation as his poetic principle.

The poet returns many times to the garden of his loss, before that unique entrance "in Auguste":

> Syþen in þat spote hit fro me sprange,
> Ofte haf I wayted, wyschande þat wele,

> Þat wont watȝ whyle deuoyde my wrange
> And heuen my happe and al my hele.
>
>   (13–16)

He chides life bitterly for its injustice to him. He tries to place his loss in the universal scheme of things, to comprehend it, to justify it. In the garden, he encounters the irresolvable contradiction of earthly existence: the symbiosis of life and death—two irreconcilable yet profoundly interdependent principles. The poet incarnates this paradox through the physical form of the "erber." Its gripping interplay of beauty and decay functions as imagistic dramatization of this existential enigma and its resulting anguish. Drama becomes image; the image contains the dramatic action.

The hero is overcome by the spectacle around him of beauty undergoing desiccation. He is racked by the thought that his "priuy perle wythouten spot" is "so clad in clot" (21–22). The "spot" to which he comes for comfort is "þer such rycheȝ to rot is runne . . . /Per hit [the pearl] doun drof in moldeȝ dunne" (25–30). The poet succeeds in making the "erber grene" a universal garden of mutability, the earth we dwell in. But he also makes it a landscape of the soul, an imagistic reflection of the hero's inner state.[33] The garden's natural beauty, the "blomeȝ blayke and blwe and rede," and the "Flor and fryte" (26–29) are presented with an opulence that gluts the senses, evoking an oppressive overripeness on the brink of festering. The landscape objectifies the languorous, damp melancholy that suffocates the hero—and perhaps now the narrator, in a renewed paroxysm of despair.

The narrator suggests, however, that he was aware in the garden of the natural and spiritual principle that death begets life. He states it, in fact, with a certain syllogistic intentness, using logical connectives, as if trying to convince himself of its rationality:

> *For* vch gresse mot grow of grayneȝ dede;
> No whete *were elleȝ* to woneȝ wonne.
>
>   (31–32)

The seed reconciles in itself the universal garden and its opposites. A lowly creature embodies in its natural cycle the lofty promise of the Resurrection. This is the language of Christ himself (John 12:24–25), employing the physical world as eloquent spokesman for spiritual truth. Corruptible nature is presented, paradoxically, as the image of man's regeneration and immortality. The poet recalls also another biblical similitude: that "the kingdom of heaven is like to a grain of mustard seed . . . the least of all seeds" (Matt. 13:31–32). On an ineffable, sacramental level, the humble seed and the kingdom of heaven become one—a fusion instituted here by the incarnate Word. The seed, therefore, embodies analogically the Incarnation itself as principle of reconciliation between opposing realities. Through its own union of matter and spirit, it holds out the promise of its sacred prototype: man's final reconciliation and union with God.[34] But the narrator fails to comprehend fully this function in the seed or to be consoled by it—either before or after the instructive vision.

In this failure, we encounter for the first time what is in essence the poem's central event: man's drama of faith with its tensions, as he tries to grasp transcendent reality with the limited yet indispensable similitudes of his own earthly conception. Through its natural familiarity, the seed makes the mystery of the Resurrection seem accessible to our understanding and even our perceptual experience; for man relates to the idea of perfection to the extent that it appears to be the fulfillment of what he has experienced imperfectly. Simultaneously, however, we become aware of the impossibility of ever verifying the adequacy of the seed as representation of immortality. The tenor being beyond human experience, the vehicle is essentially irrelevant. The two exist in different modes of being, which are irreconcilable as corruptible nature and incorruptible divinity. The seed as similitude, therefore, cannot explain to the hero of *Pearl* the mysterious kinship of life and death. It only restates the paradox by one more failure of representation. Through such a realization, the poet helps us understand and identify with the hero's inability to absorb the seed's consolatory message of the Resurrection. Dramatically, we grow apprehensive as to his further success in fathoming ultimate reality and its paradoxes through human metaphor.

By means of the seed similitude, the poet has accomplished several things. As part of his symbolic strategy, he has guided the reader to look for spiritual meaning in physical form. By employing Christ's own metaphor, he has asserted emphatically the incarnational function and authority of his own imagery. Finally, he has made us experience the stress in such a process of spiritual perception in existential terms: through the hero's personal drama.

Nature fails as comforter, also because its cycle includes both decay and regeneration—that is, elements of change. Therefore, as metaphor of eternal fixity and immortality, it contradicts itself. The hero in his despair, on the other hand, wants to find permanence—even if it means suspending cosmic and natural law.

The hero's quest for permanence has been viewed variously. When he asks that "Flor and fryte may not be fede / Per hit [the pearl] doun drof in moldeȝ dunne" (29–30), he wants the flowers that grow out of the dissolution of the pearl to remain "unfaded." He pleads that

So semly a sede moȝt fayly not,
Þat spryngande spyceȝ vp ne sponne.
(34–35)

"So seemly a seed must not fail, that springing spices do not spring up from it." This is the prevailing interpretation of the hero's wish among critics today, articulated best by Patricia Kean.[35] This view preserves, no doubt, the distasteful, macabre associations of natural beauty feeding on the rotting body of the pearl–human being. These associations certainly accentuate the hero's sensuous preoccupation with death and decay, forcing us to savor it. On the other hand, it is not clear why the same individual who a few lines earlier had lamented the pearl's loss through decay welcomes now its becoming food for growing plants and its being transmuted into another substance—flowers—however immortal.

One critic, at least, has disagreed with the thesis of "immortal flowers" springing from the decaying pearl. Edward Vasta points out that there is no linguistic basis for translating "fede" as "faded." He takes "fede" to mean "fed," as the past participle of OE *fedan* and ME *feden* "to feed." According to Vasta, the hero prays that flowers "may not be fed" from the pearl and that it remain unchanged. He pleads, therefore, that "so seemly a seed must not falter, so that springing spices do not [ever] spring up from it." The pearl's beauty must not become subject to corruption.[36]

I think that these interpretations can be reconciled, because they relate essentially to the same impulse. The hero wishes the pearl to maintain a vibrant, "organic" life, but at the same time he wants to capture that life in some permanent, unalterable form. Since this suspension of natural law is not possible within the mode of his existence, the hero turns inevitably to ideality. The poem's drama unfolds upon the manner in which this quest for permanence is fulfilled in the realm of the ideal—as the poet envisions such a fulfillment.

In these initial lines of *Pearl*, we are listening not only to one man's lament against death but also to the dread and dismay of a whole age. Johan Huizinga and T. S. R. Boase have described vividly the obsessive preoccupation of the late Middle Ages with the experience of death.[37] It expresses itself often with odd relish in detailed description of the process of physical putrefaction, of the dust and the worms of the grave, and of half-decayed corpses. The age seems to demand a concrete image of death, not in order to face mortality with pious, mature realism but to give vent to its frantic sensual horror of it, perhaps as a form of cathartic foretaste. And Huizinga comments with great perceptivity: "A thought which so strongly attaches to the earthly side of death can hardly be called pious. It would rather seem a kind of spasmodic reaction against an excessive sensuality." To him, such a reckless exhibition of the horrors of death reflects, "indeed, a very materialistic sentiment, namely, that all beauty and all happiness are worthless *because* they are bound to end soon. Renunciation founded on disgust does not spring from Christian wisdom."[38] What concerns us here more is that such a vision of death demanded an equally palpable and convincing image of immortality. Already by the thirteenth century, in *La lumière as lais,* heaven was depicted as a place of spiritual but also physical delights, where the five senses are in a state of perpetual ravishment.[39] Subsequent visions of heaven took on an increasingly concrete and sensually appealing form[40] in parallel with the increasingly concrete and sensually appalling vision of death.

That *Pearl* is preoccupied with the experience of death and, specifically, with human decay is evident throughout:

> Er moste þou ceuer to oþer counsayle:
> *Py corse in clot mot calder keue.*
>
> (319–20)

> *Alþaȝ oure corses in clotteȝ clynge,*
> And ȝe remen for rauþe wythouten reste,
> We þurȝoutly hauen cnawyng.
>
> (857–59)

> Þat is þe borȝ þat we to pres
> Fro *þat oure flesch be layd to rote.*
>
> (957–58)

These references are to actual, not figurative, death. They dwell on the very process of physical dying and decomposition. *Pearl* does not share in the necromaniac hysteria of its milieu. Yet it displays a keen sensuous awareness of mortality, which seems to invite an equally material conception of immortality. The first is poignantly felt in the image of "smoþe," virginal beauty "so clad in clot" (6, 22) in the garden; the second materializes in the manner in which the poet constructs the ideal world. Significantly, that construction of permanence begins in the very womb of mutability—in the "erber grene," which the hero enters now, "In Auguste in a hyȝ seysoun" (38–39).

The author begins the narrative of his entrance by asserting his dual role as protagonist—the "I" of the poem—and as conscious artist ordering his experience as poetic statement:

> To þat spot þat I in speche expoun
> I entred in þat erber grene.
>
> (37–38)

While he invests his work with considerable authenticity and immediacy by becoming its hero—that is, by making the experience his own—the poet establishes an aesthetic distance between himself and the event, between the event and us.

Not only the "erber grene" but also the time and season of the hero's entrance reflect the contradictory nature of human experience, intensifying further the paradox that resides in the garden: the coexistence of life and death. One need not preclude the associations that various critics have tried to establish between the time of entrance and the season's major holidays.[41] The medieval reader, of course, must have responded to these connections more readily than we. If one were to consider the otherworldly transformation that takes place in the pearl and in the landscape, then the Transfiguration (August 6) suggests itself as sacred prototype. If one wishes, on the other hand, to emphasize the resemblance between the Pearl Maiden—the transhumanized dead daughter—and the Virgin Mary, "þe Quen of cortaysye," certainly the Assumption (August 15) only strengthens the comparison.

A more immediate and inescapable response needs to be noted here, however. The harvest is a festive, happy occasion in man's life. It brings to mind God's plenitude and the satisfaction that follows human toil. Yet, as prelude to an enlightening vision, the time of entrance in the garden is not the conventional May morning of regeneration and springtime. The harvest sustains man, yet it deprives the face of the earth of its fruit, its signs of life and fertility. The "croke3 kene" gather the life-sustaining corn; but they also function as a metonymic evocation of death. This association will take on a sharper edge when the Maiden will call her death God's harvest, when she was reaped "as newe fryt to God ful due" (894). The poet touches our nerve endings with the tearing, sawing cr's of the line: "Quen corne is coruen wyth croke3 kene" (40). He succeeds through image and verbal form in incarnating through this humble natural event the contradictoriness of human existence and the keen anguish it causes the hero, compelling him to seek to transcend it.

The description of the "huyle," too, dramatizes symbolically the paradox of life coexisting with death, of beauty intermingling with decay. The poet avoids obvious effects; he does not describe the "huyle" as glaringly macabre. He works, rather, by subtle indirection. He decorates the grave with flowers and spices of delectable color and fragrance. They bring from medieval symbolic tradition the promise of healing and comfort,[42] which the hero apparently begins now to experience:

> On huyle þer perle hit trendeled doun
> Schadowed þis worteȝ ful schyre and schene,
> Gilofre, gyngure and gromylyoun,
> And pyonys powdered ay bytwene.
> Ʒif hit watȝ semly on to sene,
> A fayr reflayr ȝet fro hit flot.
>
> (41–46)

The beauty of the flowers, however, evokes a dual response. It blunts grief and assuages the ugliness of death—only to exacerbate it the next moment, intensifying that ugliness by standing in poignant contrast to it. One cannot, furthermore, blot out the unsavory thought that such beauty has fed on the decaying pearl or rotting corpse beneath. The flowers and spices seem to carry in their heavily rich texture and pigment the fertilizing liquids of the dissolving body. As a result, the pearl, the object of desire, becomes simultaneously the object of revulsion. This duality sets a significant pattern of ambivalence in the reader's perception affecting the dreamer's object of quest—a complementary interplay to continue to the end of the poem. The "huyle" becomes a sumptuously ornamented grave mound; the heavy fragrance of its spices and the damp overripeness around it exude a powerful odor of mortality. Opulence turns into decay.

We note, moreover, that these plants have been brought here out of their natural context and season,[43] in an artificial arrangement of the poet's own making. The phrase "powdered ay bytwene," according to C. A. Luttrell, suggests a heraldic ornamental design.[44] The flowers, which already shine with a plastic intensity, have been patterned and riveted into a beautiful mosaic. (Throughout this study, I am using the term "plastic" only in reference to the plastic arts.) The enumeration of the plants, as architectonic and syntactical sequence, reveals a ritual structure imposed by the artist on the inscrutable, shifting reality that surrounds him in order to secure in it stability and coherence. Such patterning—to be seen again in the poem—is part of a style that man erects here as defense against the dissolution of order in a world of flux. It constitutes, in a sense, the poem's rhetoric of consolation as wrought upon its verbal and imagistic surface. Its impulse toward schematization and permanence will lead us to significant insights in the realm of the ideal—the visionary landscape and the New Jerusalem.

The hero's loss of his beloved pearl and its incomprehensibility in the scheme of things cause in him a profound spiritual crisis. The poet presents the hero's *psychomachia* as a violent splitting of the self into two antithetical voices: "resoun" and the "kynde of Kryst" versus his "wretched wylle" that "in wo ay wraȝte" (55–56). We shall have to wait for "resoun" to take on a more articulate form later through the Maiden's discourse. In the meantime, the hero has encountered the "kynde of Kryst" incarnated in nature, the seed of wheat. But its comforting voice is enfeebled by the "fyrce skylleȝ" of his grief, his incomprehension, and his obstinate self-will to bend God's universal order and its natural laws to his private wish. His inner conflict leads to exhaustion:

> I felle vpon þat floury flaȝt,
> Suche odour to my herneȝ schot;
> I slode vpon a slepyng-slaȝte
> On þat precios perle wythouten spot.
>
> (57–60)

Relying on symbolic tradition, several critics have assumed that the fragrant spices have begun to heal the hero at this point.[45] We must note, however, that it is not through their spiritual virtues—as defined within this tradition—that the flowers soothe his sorrow. They do not restore in him a clearer judgment, nor do they sharpen his spiritual insight. Their effect is, rather, soporific. Combined with the opulent beauty of the garden, the spices overwhelm his senses into anesthesia: the "slepyng-slaȝte."

This "slaying sleep" has been often viewed as a preliminary step to mystic illumination. Such suspension of the senses is the contemplative's "closing of the eyes of the flesh to the image of this world,"[46] leading to a more intellectual vision of divine reality. The means of transporting the hero's "spyryt" to an ideal world evokes, however, an ambivalent response in the reader by its oppressive sensuality. The sleep is brought about by a suffocating *voluptas,* where spiritual awareness seems totally absent as link to the next illuminative stage. In it, ravishment passes into deathlike passivity and languor. Such a curious transference sets up a disturbing dialectic between ecstasy and death, suggesting an indefinable, threatening, yet exciting relationship between them. The late medieval sensibility responded to and even relished this odd sentiment in its artistic depictions of Death as wooer. Late medieval mystics, like Juliana of Norwich, expressed it in vivid detail when describing their *raptus:* "Then the rest of my body began to die. . . . I knew for certain that I was passing away. . . . I desired to suffer with him [God]. . . . We shall never cease wanting and longing until we possess him in fulness and joy." She knew, indeed, the tantalizing mixture of sensations and emotions accompanying such an event, where death and ecstasy fuse into one experience: "This revelation," she tells us, "was . . . horrifying and dreadful, sweet and lovely."[47] Is the "slepyng-slaȝte" a foretaste of total fulfillment or total self-annihilation—or both by some mysterious kinship?

The "slepyng-slaȝte" fits in form the archetypal event of the hero's initiation into another mode of existence. Such an initiation often destroys the old self, leading to its resurrection and renewal. The hero passes from earthly actuality, on the road to the ideal, to absolute reality,[48] an ascent which, in *Pearl,* culminates in the New Jerusalem. Obviously, such an archetypal connection excites in the reader the corollary hope of the hero's final consolation and spiritual restoration. We cannot avoid responding also to the similarity of the hero's profound sleep to Adam's and Eve's creation and to Christ's death and resurrection. Dante used the first of these biblical associations in the pilgrim's dream in the Garden of Eden to stress the creation of a new self in him. Christ fell into the sleep of death to rise from it in his full divinity. Both associations connecting the "slepyng-slaȝte" with these sacred prototypes—and perhaps also with Dante's experience—add enormously to the expectation that the Pearl dreamer's "sleep-death" will be similarly regenerative and fulfilling.

The "slepyng-slaȝte," however, even as initiation to ideal reality, carries on within it the paradoxical and irresolvable counterpoint of life and death found in the "erber." In its irresistible devastation of the hero's consciousness, it arouses fear. The desire for the ideal, and yet the concomitant threat of losing one's self in the attempt, makes the "slepyng-slaȝte," like the garden, an experience of both attraction and revulsion. Is the "slepyng-slaȝte," then, as transitional event from human actuality to transcendent ideality, a foretaste of the hero's final encounter? To what extent does its duality—its ecstasy and dread—foreshadow his anagogic experience? We are left wondering.

Throughout my analysis, I have imposed certain interpretations on the poem's symbolic imagery: its effect and the responses it elicits from the reader. One may contest these interpretations by a series of legitimate questions: Who is the Pearl Poet's intended ideal audience? If a medieval audience only, how can we define it today? Was this audience meant to respond to the poem's imagery in the manner that I have proposed here? If, on the other hand, the poem has been written for all time, how can we guard its intention and let it mean to us as well?

Defining an ideal medieval audience has become a *locus desperatus* because of a number of historical uncertainties already extensively debated. It is best to assume by the poet's range of subject matter and sensibility that he was writing for an audience sophisticated enough to be aware of the problem of faith and its place within the human condition and, therefore, capable of fully responding to any poetic dramatization involving this problem—as in *Pearl*.[49] The audience was also cultivated enough to recognize the aesthetic framework within which the poet as a medieval artist worked and to judge by it.

To appreciate the poet's intentions better, we must, no doubt, acquaint ourselves with the ideological and aesthetic values of his milieu. Let us not pretend, however, that such an acquaintance, coupled with the greatest historical earnestness on our part, can prevent entirely the projection of our own critical predispositions into medieval poetry. When I speak then of "the reader," I am actually referring to a near-impossible abstraction, in which, admittedly, I cannot avoid exercising my own prerogatives. The variety of approaches to *Pearl* in our time attests to the problem of "proper interpretation"—if the ceaseless rediscovery of a work of art is to be considered improper and a problem.[50]

A more intrinsic objection to my imagistic and dramatic evaluations would raise the issue of the various levels of awareness in the work: Does the poem's "I" respond to and report on the symbolic imagery according to my view of it? How can I claim a different effect than that which the hero openly experiences? We must ask whether the author intends the poem's "I" to dictate and control our responses as readers throughout or wants us to separate ourselves from the hero at some point and move to a different, if not superior, perspective. Finally—what in this work is an excruciating question—how does the author as the all-encompassing intelligence in the poem relate to the ever-present "I"[51] in identity and in level of awareness? Fortunately, there is no neat distinction between hero, poet, and reader as centers of consciousness in *Pearl*. If there were, the result would be predictable and insipid. It is the fluidity and potential identity among them that energize the poem with multiple interweaving patterns of response. Yet the author initiates and guides throughout the poem a definite interplay among levels of awareness—the poet's, the hero's, and the reader's—in order to carry out his thematic and artistic aims.

To clarify this interplay, let us consider, for the moment, the historical connection between the poet and the poem's "I." Much of the criticism in the early part of the century concerned itself with determining the autobiographical link between author and event in *Pearl*. The debate became more complicated when W. H. Schofield denied categorically the historical actuality of the event (the Pearl Poet lamenting the death of his infant daughter) and redefined it as pure allegory based on fiction.[52] Since there is no biography of the poet extant and his name remains unknown, critics have not been able to decide on the connection between the poem's situation and the author's real life, despite his reference to the dead girl as "nerre þen aunte or nece" (233). E. V. Gordon has questioned the possibility of a purely fictitious "I" in fourteenth-century visionary literature while admitting that real events or persons have served as point of departure for extended fictional and allegorical works at the time.[53] Recent critics in general have sought to combine views, allowing for the poem's allegorical aim while acknowledging its literal dimension as indispensable to its human validity, its immediacy, and its power of genuine feeling.[54] The author could have easily attributed to himself a fictitious experience—so have Dante and Chaucer, for that matter. The fictionality of this event, however, does not diminish the work's power as poetic experience or annul its capacity—as analogue to God's arch-poem, the universe—to participate in sacred truth.

The "I" in *Pearl* remains historically ambiguous. He calls himself, for instance, a "jeweller"; yet the appellation slips from our fingers, taking on multiple meanings—mundane and spiritual—just like his pearl. He speaks like an expert gemologist, but, as soon as his pearl reveals a human dimension, he becomes more than that. One sense, at least, of "jeweller" becomes evident. There is an air of connoisseurship and refined taste in his lapidary comments that materializes on the poem's own surface: the finely wrought style of the verse, the brilliant sumptuousness of his imagery, the intricate construction of his stanzas. Even in profound grief, he is an irrepressible craftsman who likes to display his art, capable of shaping the random material of human experience into beautifully smithed pattern. Is the poem going to be, then, a precious artifact—a verbal rediscovery of the lost pearl, so to speak?

Having commented, though briefly, on the historical identity of the poem's "I," let me focus on its relationship to the author and to the reader from the standpoint of awareness, staying for the time being within the first section of the poem. To some critics, these distinctions are artificial and ultimately invalid. Charles Moorman emphasizes the centrality of the narrator over the Pearl Maiden. He is the spectator and the sufferer in the work; the poem is about *his* experience. The Maiden "cannot be said to function, except peripherally, in the narrative movement of the poem." The hero-narrator, therefore, is "the central intelligence of the poem," controlling the reader's responses throughout with his own. After all, he is supposed to represent us in the work as Everyman.[55] Following Moorman, A. R. Heiserman claims that the poet succeeds in making the reader's responses identical with those of the hero-dreamer, annihilating any critical distance betwen them.[56]

I disagree with this indiscriminate identification between hero-narrator, poet, and reader. We have a sense of a double perspective in the "I": the hero who is undergoing the experience for the first time, whose understanding naturally lags behind the occurrence in naive wonderment; and the narrator who remembers and relates the event, having learned from it. We tend to assume that the narrator is also the poet casting the related experience into aesthetic form. As I have indicated, however, the poet distances us from the narrator as well, when the latter's disconsolate cries during the relating raise in us doubts as to his final consolation. The poet wants to make us indeed aware of the problem of consolation in the poem. In that conscious strategy, he begins disengaging himself and us from the hero *and* the "matured" narrator to a different perspective, which becomes more definite at the end of the work. Still, the poet never allows a facile delineation of perspectives; he preserves the engaging ambiguity of the "I" as hero, narrator, and self-conscious poet and their relationship:

> To þat spot þat I in speche expoun
> I entred in þat erber grene.
>
> (37–38)

Concerning the interpretation of the imagery, I have shown that the hero—as well as the still-grieving narrator—cannot fully grasp the seed's incarnational and consolatory function, nor has he profited by it. What is more, he displays no clear awareness of his human limitations for such an understanding. In that sense, the reader is placed by the poet at a superior level of evaluation—which ultimately turns upon him as well. For the dreamer's crisis of belief is Everyman's. The poet seems to command here an absolute position, subjecting the judging reader to his own judgment, with some philosophical irony.

Furthermore, the context builds certain associations into the imagery that the hero cannot fully perceive. His inadequate understanding of the symbolic spectacle before him prevents him from reacting to its premonitory function. This discrepancy in the perception of symbolic realities between him and us and his inability to anticipate through them impending frustration create in the reader anxiety and dramatic suspense, which are further intensified by the dreamer's euphoric optimism. His wish for permanence, for example, in defiance of cosmic order—valid in its human despair as it might be—promises in its pathetic impossibility a reversal. This, in his grief, he cannot foresee. Thus, in his lack of awareness, the hero becomes the object of dramatic irony, from which we are not entirely exempt in our similar human impulses.

In sum, the Pearl Poet uses the hero-narrator "as a *dramatis persona* whose awareness is measured against norms provided by the whole poetic context," remaining below the poet's "absolute awareness." This definitive comment by Phillip Damon pertains to Dante's "io" in the canzone of *La Vita Nuova* and in the *Commedia*,[57] but it is equally applicable to the poet and the "I" in *Pearl.* It is unrealistic, then, for us to confine our responses to those of the hero-narrator rather than attempt to discover directly through them the poet's own views and intentions. These intentions become clearer once we grasp his symbolic and dramatic strategy as a self-consistent pattern unfolding progressively throughout the poem.

Perhaps the most significant distinction between identities and perspectives in the poem's "I" is the following: The hero-narrator pleads at some point the ineffable. But the poet continues speaking, inspired by that silence into effulgent eloquence with which he creates an anagogic vision of his own, until it is consummated by its sacred prototype, John's apocalyptic vision. In that creation, the Pearl Poet delights in the inventive power of his artistic imagination, while at the same time he captures in concrete form and with sinewy intellectual control the enigma of that ultimate reality. To this we shall come presently.

3

The "Fayre Londe"

Enough has been written on the visionary tradition—from Odysseus's descent to the underworld in *Odyssey* XI to *Pearl*—that another thorough survey would be superfluous here. Since ancient times, dreams were considered as revelatory, especially in initiating the dreamer into supernatural reality. There he would derive guidance for his earthly existence. This revelatory function was greatly enhanced in Christian literature, beginning with John's Revelation and followed by other apocalyptic works, such as *The Shepherd of Hermas* (c. 160) and the *Visio Paoli* (third century).[1] By the fourteenth century—the time of *Pearl*'s authorship—the dream vision had become a popular literary type.

Several medieval thinkers concerned themselves with the psychological operation of the dream vision and debated intently its revelatory value. Founding his observations on an intricate system of the soul's makeup, Synesius (370–c. 430), an early significant commentator on the subject, dealt extensively with the dream in his *De insomniis*, as means leading either to higher vision or to distorted illusion, depending on the soul's inherent order and equilibrium.[2]

Using Artemidorus's *Oneirocritica* (first century) as his basis, Macrobius (late fourth century) developed a descriptive scheme that influenced considerably the evolution of dream criticism in the Middle Ages. To him, there are five species of dreams: In the *oraculum*, "a parent, or a pious or revered man, or a priest, or even a god clearly reveals [to the dreamer] what will or will not transpire, and what action to take or to avoid." The *somnium*, on the other hand, is a type of dream "that conceals with strange shapes and veils with ambiguity the true meaning of the information being offered, and requires an interpretation for its understanding." The remaining three types are the *visio*, a prophetic vision that comes true in waking life; the *phantasma* or *visum*, in which an apparition "comes upon one in the moment between wakefulness and slumber"; and the *insomnium*, or nightmare, which "may be caused by mental or physical distress, or anxiety about the future."[3]

By definition, then, the dream in *Pearl* would fit both the *oraculum* and the *somnium,* since it is both revelatory and enigmatic, embracing, actually, two radically contradictory impulses. The poet makes it immensely engaging when one impulse serves the other: the enigma becomes, in essence, the revelation; the revelation remains an enigma. We shall observe this exchange alternately in the symbolic spectacle and its "rational" explanation by the Maiden. One could well argue also for certain qualities of the *insomnium* pervading *Pearl* in its troubled and violent, though often ecstatic, temper.

Through his study of scriptural visions—being particularly attracted to Paul's question whether he was "in the body . . . or out of the body" during his vision of Paradise (2 Cor. 12:2)—Augustine arrived at his own categories. He appears to be concerned, however, more with the manner of occurrence than with the subject matter of the dream vision. He distinguishes among three types of visionary experience: the *visio corporale* [*sic*], received directly through the body's natural senses; the *visio spiritale* [*sic*], in which "spiritual forces impress themselves upon the imagination like sensory images"; and the *visio intellectuale* [*sic*], in which spiritual truths are communicated without the interposition of word or image—that is, on a purely intuitive and ineffable level of perception, the external senses entirely suspended.[4]

If we attempt to fit *Pearl* to any visionary type defined by Augustine, we meet with certain complications; happily, these remind us of the distance between theory and practice and save us from smug, simplistic classifications. The dreamer tells us—with greater assurance than Paul—that, during his vision, he was "out of the body," leaving it lying on the mound in the garden, his spirit having sprung up to God:

> Fro spot my spyryt þer sprang in space;
> My body on balke þer bod in sweuen.
> My goste is gon in Godeʒ grace.
>
> (61–63)

There is no apologetic "io non son Enëa, io non Paulo sono" (*Inferno* II, 32) here. In other words, the dreamer claims to have undergone a *visio intellectuale.* This is the highest form of visionary experience aspired to by the medieval contemplative: Richard Saint Victor's *somnium mentis,* Saint Bernard's and Walter Hilton's bodily sleep and inner wakefulness.[5] The Pearl dreamer's inner wakefulness, however, is experienced and communicated to us as a brilliant kaleidoscope of images, though he keeps pleading the ineffable. These images do not waver or dissolve in dreamy mistiness. Their sensuous sharpness and clarity of form contrast curiously with their elusive, shifting spiritual significance. Ambivalence is rendered with great precision of outline—an important perceptual paradox in the poem. Despite the suspension of the body's natural senses, the hero's inner senses operate in the dream with extraordinary keenness, acting as crucial channels of spiritual perception as well. Contrary to the dreamer's claims, then, we must view the *Pearl* dream—referring back to Augustine—predominantly as a *visio spiritale*.

Attempting to classify *Pearl* according to medieval dream psychology—a continuing preoccupation with the poem's critics—is, nevertheless, peripheral to its meaning and soon turns into a sterile Aristotelian exercise. As conscious artistic statement, obviously, the poem is not an exact reproduction of an original visionary experience—if, indeed, there were any. On the contrary, it shows the poet exercising at every turn rational, "undreamlike" control over its form and significance. To digress a little, we do not judge aesthetically the stream-of-consciousness novel for its fidelity to the actual occurrence of free, disordered associations. Rather, we admire its capacity to gather chaotic experience into intense, intricate order—which, paradoxically, renders chaos more meaningful and powerful. As Austin Warren well expresses it, "psychological truth is an artistic value only if it enhances coherence and complexity—if, in short, it is art."[6] We must, therefore, judge the *Pearl* vision not from the standpoint of psychological verisimilitude—even in a medieval sense—but according to the author's success in exploiting this verisimilitude and theoretical background to further validate his art.

Let us turn, then, to more intrinsic considerations guiding the author's use of the dream genre. The poet cannot allow the dreamer a *visio intellectuale* as a matter of thematic consistency and artistic practicality. Achieving such a supreme form of mystical experience would have been inconsistent with the resolution of the poem. And, second, the author needs the expressive elements of the lesser vision—image and word—in order to give concrete shape to his poem. The alternative would have been "awed, absolute silence."[7]

Further, the poet exploits the dream's traditional oracular and revelatory value in order to invest his work with unquestioned authority. In the end, he tells us emphatically that he had a "veray avysyoun" (1184). This authority, combined with the traditionally enigmatic character of the dream, liberates the author from the demands of common actuality that are made at the constant expense of illusion and, consequently, of considerable artistic autonomy. Rationally conceived spatial and temporal relationships can be annihilated under the felicitous guise of the irrational in the dream state. Visionary relationships are moral and metaphysical rather than realistic,[8] transfixing our attention by their unnatural shape on crucial thematic statements or startling us pleasurably with novel, unexpected formal patterns.

In a broader sense, the lack of logical and naturalistic restraint has permitted the visionary poet to bring together under one glimpse very distant realities. This violent yoking surprises the mind into new, hitherto unrealized connections between these disparate essences. As a result, the allegorical dream vision allows for a highly energetic analogical process, which is metaphysically significant and metaphorically engaging. As genre, it tends naturally toward becoming a symbolic drama precisely because of its inherent impulse to juxtapose highly resistant identities in a vision of potential reconciliation.

Tradition has expanded this inclusive and fusive capacity of the allegorical dream vision by secularizing it. The *Roman de la Rose,* a glorious result of this expansion, had a profound influence on the development of the literary dream in the Middle Ages. I shall not go over well-trodden ground and survey this development, except to underscore the bringing together into one literary form of two vastly opposed sensibilities—the sacred and the profane. Their mutual resistance as contrary principles yet inevitable intermingling on an imaginative level resulted in a powerful and irresolvable metaphoric interplay that could only vitalize and enrich the genre as poetic experience.

Pearl is indebted to both the religious and the erotic visionary tradition of its time. Several critics have established its association with the *Roman de la Rose* by comparing the "erber" and the visionary landscape with the love garden in the *Roman.*[9] Patricia Kean, however, has resisted this association, because it weakens the author's "seriousness of theme." She points, instead, to the biblical earthly Paradise and the *hortus conclusus* of the Song of Songs as the true models. Such a resistance proves arbitrary and unhistorical, since the *Roman* garden is itself an adaptation of the biblical gardens, however parodic. Kean herself acknowledges the frequent blending of sacred and profane prototypes in medieval literary landscapes. She even undertakes to demonstrate in some detail the similarities—if not indebtedness—of the *Pearl* landscape to secular works like the Alexander romances, Chaucer's dream poems, the French prose romance *Huon de Bordeaux,* and Mandeville's travels.[10]

That the Pearl Poet was acquainted with the *Roman* is by now an indisputable fact. He mentions its author "Clopyngel in the compas of his clene Rose" in *Purity* (line 1057) and alludes to the work itself in *Pearl* in the dreamer's question to the Maiden as to her true nature (750–52). He employs in *Pearl* several motifs found also in the profane poem: the entrance to the paradisal garden, the dreamer's quest for the beloved who is described as a symbol (rose-pearl), the multicolored, brilliant landscape with its singing birds and flowing brook, and the languorous language of frustrated wooing ("luf-daungere").

The Pearl Poet has deliberately and with great delicacy mingled the devotional with the erotic aspect of human experience, but not merely for the delectation of his courtly audience. He wants, rather, to reaffirm the analogical and sacramental bond between human and divine love—a dominant theme in medieval literature. At the same time, he puts at his disposal the immense metaphoric vitality of this relationship, whose exploration becomes, in effect, the poem. Consequently, in *Pearl,* the dream form itself functions as an incarnational vehicle: It brings into dynamic reconciliation essentially irreconcilable natures. It blends disparate levels of experience and their contrary sensibilities. It employs different modes of perception, translating spiritual truths into sensory images—although as dream it has no sensory substance of its own. Perhaps its most intriguing paradox is that dream acts as the vehicle of reality and its symbol. The extensive debates on the revelatory value of the dream vision in the Middle Ages were more than a dispassionate intellectual game; they reflect, rather, the time's intent awareness of this paradox.

As another key artistic advantage we must finally consider the dramatic pattern that the allegorical dream vision acquired early in its development, from *The Shepherd of Hermas* (c. A.D.160) on: The dreamer-hero finds himself in a profound spiritual crisis. One or several authoritative figures appear to the dreamer in one or several visions and help him place his crisis in a new perspective of truth. Such truth is communicated to the visionary hero through symbolic imagery and through rational, conceptually articulate dialogue in which the authoritative figure engages the dreamer. Their encounter takes place in a visionary landscape that has an objective reality of its own (as a supernatural realm, for example) while at the same time functioning as an imagistic concretization of the dreamer's own psychic reality, as an objective correlative of his inner state at each stage of his spiritual progress. The exchange between the dreamer and the authoritative figure and the movement from his initial resistance to his final conversion become sources of dramatic tension. We witness the clash between two opposing natures and viewpoints of reality, which finally comes to a climax at the resolution of the dreamer's crisis.

Pearl follows this dramatic order, unfolding into a pattern of "controlled discoveries and disappointments," of violent emotional oscillations and of suspense, all leading to the climactic event of the dreamer's coming face to face with the apocalyptic Lamb in the New Jerusalem. Heiserman, whose description I have repeated here, completes this dramatic sequence with the conventional happy ending of the dreamer's enlightenment and consolation.[11] No doubt, *Pearl* follows the traditional order and sets up the corollary expectations—only to subvert the denouement in a thematically significant and aesthetically energizing manner, as we shall see.

It has been widely recognized that, in human experience and in art, the dream is the area of maximum conflict between desire and actuality. Northrop Frye tells us (in somewhat esoteric terms) that, on the archetypal level, the *dianoia* of any poem in general is the representation of this conflict.[12] Looking at the dream on both an archetypal and an "anagogic" level, Frye claims that "its limits are not the real but the conceivable . . . the limit of the conceivable in the world of frustrated desire emancipated from all anxieties and frustrations . . . the conceivable or imaginative limit of desire, which is infinite, eternal, and hence apocalyptic."[13]

In *Pearl,* the dreamer's desire shapes the world of his vision into the order of coherence he seeks after a profound loss and confusion in the waking world. What limits the dream here, however, is not the conceivable, whose only possible confine is "the world of fulfilled desire emancipated from all anxieties and frustrations." For the conceivable shackles, rather than emancipates, desire with frustration. Desire, after all, cannot become emancipated from frustration; it is born of it. Hence, it is not only desire that shapes the dream but also the frustration and anxiety that derive from the dreamer's painful realization of the very limits of his power of conception. Desire and frustration fall into a dramatic pattern that becomes, in effect, the organizing principle of the dream vision. Although Frye acknowledges the constant presence of this dialectic in poetry, he manages to annul it somehow in the anagogic dream, perhaps as a result of his strict categorizing. He separates the anagogic into two symbolic realms, the "apocalyptic" and the "demonic," associating the first with the fulfillment and the second with the frustration of human desire.[14] Yet the literary anagogic world[15]—as we shall also see in *Pearl*—combines almost always both realms and both impulses. It is seldom one or the other.

Since in the dream it is human wish that shapes reality, the visionary world of the *Pearl* germinates from the dreamer's object of quest: the pearl. His desire expands it into the ideal universe of his vision. The poet confirms this expansion by diffusing throughout the landscape the pearl's physical qualities—and, inevitably, its symbolic associations.

One cannot imagine a more felicitous "coincidence" for the Pearl Poet than to have at his disposal countless precious landscapes from metrical romance and other world visions with which to construct his own world of wish fulfillment. This background has been studied extensively: from a general standpoint by Howard R. Patch and in relation to *Pearl* by Patricia Kean.[16] The variety of contexts in which these landscapes appear—sacred and profane—excites a corresponding variety of expectations in the reader who encounters the visionary landscape in *Pearl* for the first time. Because of their multitude, I shall follow only a few of these conventional expectations as they are transformed and redirected in the new context.

The poet initiates the visionary event as a knight's departure for the exotic fairylands of romance and other world journeys, in quest of *auenture:*

> My goste is gon in Godeʒ grace
> In auenture þer meruayleʒ meuen.
> I ne wyste in þis worlde quere þat hit wace.
>
> (63–65)

Such a description functions as a narrative device arousing in the reader wonder and anticipation. Furthermore, the poet grounds the dreamer's spiritual quest after the mystery of ultimate reality in the image of the chivalric quest, in order to invest it with familiar human form. The poet thus reminds us that all human quests somehow incarnate and participate in the reality of that final quest toward self-fulfillment: union with God. Yet the comparison will not tolerate a thoroughly serious attitude from the reader. The sunny, adventuresome beginning, borrowed from the world of the romance, asks that we counterbalance our earnest seriousness with a feeling of "gomen" and "meruayl." The poet wishes to teach but also to entertain. By bringing to mind the event's fictiveness, he does not mean to negate its essential truth but means to help us maintain our distance from it for a better spiritual and aesthetic judgment. He keeps up the attitude of "gomen" throughout with various amusing strokes, especially in the dreamer's thought and action. In this manner, he intimates a "comic" perspective of his own, which is philosophically important and also rescues the work from unmitigated, monotonous gravity. Finally, he asserts his unique prerogative as poet to readapt God's incarnational art by giving shape to ineffable reality in a creation of fantasy and the poetic imagination.

It is a strange and exotic landscape that we enter with the dreamer, a land "remote from normal experience," as Dorothy Everett once put it, rather mildly.[17] Every object in it, however, is sharply outlined despite the visionary ambience. There is no dreamlike film covering all or a melting of one image into another as in Dante's *Paradiso*. The effect is one of sensuous keenness. The corporeal values of the landscape are asserted powerfully, as if the poet signals to us that his meaning resides in them. This clarity and unalterability of outline, "so cler of kynde" (74), makes for visual intensity—and, simultaneously, for a curious effect of static permanence.

Kean has traced well the landscape's visual organization—how the poet directs the reader's eye "from mass to detail: from cliffs and forests to rocks and trees, and to details of the trees; from a distant view of the river and its banks to a close-up."[18] This progressive visual movement continues, guided by the dreamer as he journeys up the riverbank:

> I welke ay forth in wely wyse;
> No bonk so byg þat did me dereȝ.
> Þe fyrre in þe fryth, þe feier con ryse
> Þe playn, þe plontteȝ, þe spyse, þe pereȝ;
> And raweȝ and randeȝ and rych reuereȝ,
> As fyldor fyn her bonkes brent.
> I wan to a water by schore þat schereȝ.
>
>   (101–7)

The unfolding sequence acts as a "pointer," a gradual visual and kinetic buildup to the solitary figure that he will come upon soon on the other side of the stream.

The setting is a forest with gleaming cliffs and "rych rokkeȝ" (68):

> Þe lyȝt of hem myȝt no mon leuen,
> Þe glemande glory þat of hem glent.
>
>   (69–70)

The crystallike, precious quality of this rocky background makes the landscape seem, indeed, an expansion of the poem's central symbol, the pearl. There is an indelible sense of power and autonomy in the cliffs framing the scene. Viewing stones as archetypal images, Mircea Eliade mentions the hierophantic effect on early religious consciousness of their "hardness, ruggedness, the permanence of matter." They stand in contrast to "the precariousness of [man's] humanity," suggesting "an absolute mode of being."[19] In the visionary landscape of *Pearl,* they seem to rise as an initial counterpoise, solid and immovable, before the intruding dreamer.

The dreamer reinforces the sense of strangeness and impenetrability that so far dominate the visionary landscape when he confesses for the first time his inability to comprehend and express its splendor: "Þe lyȝt of hem myȝt no mon leuen" (69). The ineffable enters here as a dramatic force in the poem's dialectic of desire and frustration, functioning mainly on the level of symbolic perception. I shall delay discussing its role for the moment.

The second section (II) of the poem, which describes the visionary landscape, is a mutiny of the senses, of image and sound. In a manner that eludes explicit analysis, the style here becomes the event. The verbal surface is the more immediate landscape to be traversed and experienced by the reader rather than the landscape that is being described. The forests are strangely luminescent (66–72), with trees whose trunks are "blwe as ble of Ynde" (76) and whose leaves shine like "bornyst syluer" (77). By employing metallic images, the poet sharpens the sensory effect, eliciting, however, a significantly ambivalent effect. We hear the leaves' foillike, whispering yet curiously harsh, sound as they sway and shimmer in the unearthly brilliance of the landscape: "Wyth *sch*ymeryng *sch*ene ful *sch*rylle þay *sch*ynde" (80). If the image stimulates so keenly sight and hearing, it is inevitable that other senses—touch in this instance—are also mobilized. The metallic leaves evoke the mixed sensation of fine, polished texture, yet also of hard, cold surface. That the poet means to translate sound into touch—to make us, in other words, experience his imagery throughout synesthetically—becomes more explicit in his description of the gravel. The sound is wed to the touch because it emanates from it. The dreamer tells us that he feels (with his heels, obviously) the gravel grinding from under him as he treads on it. And that touch produces the crunching noise that we hear re-created in the verse: "Þe *g*rauayl þat on *g*rounde con *g*rynde," made of "precious perleȝ of oryente" (81–82).

The medieval literary audience no doubt must have enjoyed this glutting of the senses—as in the heathen scenes of the *Chanson de Roland,* in the luscious garden of Deduit in the *Roman de la Rose,* or in the detailed description of Gawain's rich attire and armor in *Sir Gawain and the Green Knight.* One discerns in the foregoing description in *Pearl* a self-defeating excess, nonetheless. We shall face this question repeatedly in the poem; the explanation lies partly in the artistic mentality of its milieu but more significantly in the poet's conscious thematic and aesthetic intention.

This sensual excess is relieved momentarily by a fine variation of delectable images (86–106). We encounter many-colored birds, "boþe smale and grete," flying "in fryth in fere [together]," and singing "wyth a swete asent." And there are "þe plontteȝ, þe spyse, þe pereȝ," "So frech flauoreȝ of fryteȝ were." These are welcome, familiar images. But a certain intensification in their appearance prevents us from responding to them with natural enjoyment—the "flaumbande [glowing] hweʒ" of the birds, the rich, exotic indigo of the tree trunks, and the rivers coursing through the landscape "as fylldor fyn" (fine gold thread).

Most elements in the visionary landscape come from the familiar waking world, whose recollection will act constantly as the criterion of our reaction and judgment in the ideal world of the dream. These terrestrial objects, however, have undergone "a kind of alchemical transmutation,"[20] changing their natural texture to rich pigment and to hard, precious brilliance. By allowing these images, still, their natural shape and leaving some of them yet unaltered—"þe plontteʒ, þe spyse, þe pereʒ" and "frech flauoreʒ of fryteʒ" (104, 87)—the poet strengthens the impact of the transformation: He maintains the contrast between natural and altered elements sharply before us. Furthermore, he creates the marvelous impression that the transformation is still active because incomplete, spreading itself with wondrous imperceptibility over the terrain. Nature has passed into artifice—a transition that prefigures the poem's fundamental symbolic development.

The most poignant imagistic counterpoise between the two worlds—the mutable world that the hero tries to transcend and the ideal world that he seeks—is found, appropriately, at the very threshold that separates them: the stream to which the dreamer comes. The poet captivates us with the stream's music: the swirling sounds in "*Sw*angeande *sw*ete þe water con *sw*epe" (111) and the gurgling and cackling of the brook, "Wyth a rownande rourde raykande aryʒt" (112). He evokes a feeling of nostalgia for the good earth, which the dreamer must have felt, moving in spirit at the far reaches of the universe,[21] looking like Dante upon our "threshing floor." We feel a keen coziness in the snug sleep of the "stroþe-men" in the cold winter night, the vast starry skies over them (115–16). These elements combine to create a natural scene of exquisite rustic concreteness.

But the "*b*onkeʒ *b*ene" of the river are "of *b*eryl *b*ryʒt" (110); the thick alliterative sound makes us even hear their solidity. The pebbles at the bottom are like precious stones fixed in a brilliant mosaic:

> For vche a pobbel in pole þer pyʒt
> Watʒ emerad, saffer, oþer gemme gente,
> Pat all þe loʒe [pool] lemend of lyʒt.
>
> (117–19)

The image stiffens; the idyllic stream seems to freeze into an icon. Yet it remains transparent as "glas" (114). The dreamer appears to see in it for a moment the outskirts of the precious Apocalyptic City awaiting him at the terminus of his journey. The stream, therefore, is a concentrated example of the transformation taking place in the visionary realm. While it recalls the familiar world of man, it also anticipates as image the anagogic world still to be encountered.

As I have stated earlier, the poem's ideal realm germinates from the dreamer's object of desire, the pearl, taking on its physical and, inescapably, its symbolic values. We must maintain, nonetheless, a simultaneous sense of its dual nature and dimension: It is a construction of the dreamer's psyche. Therefore we must view the visionary landscape and its transformations as an imagistic objectification of the dreamer's intuitive perception of the ideal and his relationship to it. This is an intrinsic function of the landscape, for which we have been prepared earlier in the poem, when we began to view the "erber" as a complex image reflecting the hero's inner state. At the same time, the visionary landscape is a conscious construction of the poet, a composite symbol of the ideal as an objective, irrevocable reality existing independently of man. The poet reveals in this symbolic construction his own particular conception of that reality and man's relationship to it—by the medium he chooses and the shape he gives it.

The dreamer's wish for permanence, expressed so intensely in the garden of mutability, the "erber grene," begins to materialize in the dream. The earthly landscape which was subject to change and decay has hardened now into a more durable domain. Contrary to our expectations that, as image of Christian ideality, the visionary landscape should transcend the mundane values of the earthly garden, we find it being caught in them by the very act of its self-assertion. In other words, the more persistently it states its freedom from this world's materiality, the more trenchantly bound it becomes in it by the material intensity of that statement: the brilliant colors, the metallic denseness, and the overripe opulence that has been transformed from flowers and spices to precious gems. In the attempt to escape the contradictions of his earthly existence, the dreamer encounters now—in the eyes of the reader—a more stunning paradox: the inescapable continuity between the ideal and the actual in the utter dependence of the former to articulate itself in terms of the latter.

This dependence, however, in the Christian life, has been raised to its most successful and sanctified form in the Incarnation. The poet relates the dreamer's quest for final understanding and reconciliation to that achievement: he adapts the incarnational process so as to reveal those aspects in the sacred that make the life of belief a deep and intense drama. Let us follow this adaptation.

The Pearl Poet begins his representation of transcendent reality by using common, earthbound images such as the seed. This is the language of Christ himself, the incarnate Word. Let us recall that, as similitude, the seed represents the mystery of the Resurrection and participates in it sacramentally. We perceive this divine mystery as well as the actualizing of man's spiritual regeneration through the corporeal process of the seed's gestation and fruition. Spiritual meaning is made to behave like the physical form of the similitude. In this incarnational function, the seed reminds the dreamer and us of the achievement of its sacred archetype: the reconciliation of matter and spirit, of human and divine nature. We fail—as the dreamer does—to fully grasp the sacramental kinship between our world and higher reality. Yet we are left with the comfort that we still exist in an order of being that is intimate and intelligible to us but also participates in—and thus makes accessible to us, however mysteriously—that higher reality. In the seed similitude, the tenor is an unknown and ineffable entity; but the vehicle is a familiar one, and the reader's perception and understanding ground themselves in it inextricably. The mind has no choice. For, even at the height of analogical irrelevance between symbol and idea, it keeps referring to familiar experience as a framework of judgment. The poet knows this inescapable reliance in the reader's mind and exploits it to the utmost.

After securing the incarnational interdependence between divine tenor and human vehicle early in his imagery, the poet transforms the vehicle itself into an enchanting but unintelligible order of being, making it increasingly irrelevant as similitude. A process of gradual distancing begins between the imagery and our experience. It develops into a pattern of progressive alienation, of mounting incongruity, and therefore of growing metaphoric tension between symbol and object of representation. Its familiar order annihilated, the reader's mind is made to search even more urgently for some coherence between image and reality, for a new frame of reference. This mental search going on within the poem's metaphorical process is translated into the poem's human drama: the dreamer's own quest for meaning and relation after such profound loss. The estrangement between symbol and idea incarnates here poetically the estrangement between human and divine nature, between man and God. These two levels, the symbolic and the dramatic, are fused throughout the poem and brought together into one climactic order.

The poet further subverts familiar order and increases our sense of alienation from the visionary landscape as similitude of ideality by a strange, artificial fusion between different modes of existence: Organic nature turns into inorganic matter, objects with palpitating life freeze into brilliant but immobile artifacts, leaves are metallic, and rivers appear to be made of gold leaf. This unnatural crossing of natures jars the sensibility. Happening in a landscape symbolic of the ideal, it almost stands in parodic and grotesque contrast to the fusive and humanizing function of the Incarnation. Its visual absurdity threatens the dissolution of familiar, protective reality and consequently of the self—a fear adumbrated in the "slepyng-slaȝte."

Thus, the ominous element of the grotesque is found to coexist with ravishing beauty in the visionary realm.[22] It enters the poem here as a force that will display its full symbolic and dramatic significance at the final encounter. In the meantime, it begins to generate anxiety as to the nature of the ideal in which the dreamer seeks to submerge himself. This anxiety emanates from the ambivalent impact of the visionary landscape as symbol: We are fascinated by it as a brilliant product of the human imagination when free from common actuality and exercising its creative autonomy. Yet, what makes the fascination irresistible is the horror that mingles with it, as we confront the possibility of some terrible truth hiding in these unnatural symbolic relationships, threatening to shatter our world and our frame of reference. The poet attempts to capture through symbolic ambiguity the sense of joy as well as the sense of terror that accompany man's eschatological expectations. These complementary feelings are inextricably interwoven into the experience of belief; they constitute its tension. In the poem, they operate as powerful dramatic forces in opposition to each other.

The notion of the artistic imagination seeking liberation from common actuality and reveling in its own creative autonomy sounds undoubtedly Romantic. The wild fantasy of the margins in medieval illuminated manuscripts—the writhing reptiles, the grotesques, the orgiastic foliage—tells us otherwise. The nightmarish trumeau of the Benedictine Abbey of Souillac (c. 1130) with its fantastic entanglements of legendary creatures—men, animals, and monsters—which seem to be "worked up into the abstruseness of a delirium,"[23] reflects, together with its apocalyptic terror, the yearning of the medieval artistic mind to shape and celebrate its own anagogic vision. The fabulous yet often terrifying landscapes of otherworld visions and of the metrical romances offer additional evidence of the impulse toward artistic freedom from the strictures of the actual.

The Pearl Poet displays the same impulse in his visionary landscape, presenting it with the exuberance of an almost cosmogonic act, perhaps in conscious imitation of *Deus artifex*. But as poetic act this presentation is not a vehicle for private self-expression only. The author orders his creation with a sense of public thematic responsibility: he uses the success or failure of his art as a means of representation dramatizing man's effort to conceive and express the absolute. For, if human art could reproduce in each of its artifacts the pattern of God's universal order, then the creative process itself could best incarnate man's struggle—its joys and frustrations—for a higher vision of reality. Let us examine the Pearl Poet's symbolic adaptation of the creative process in the visionary landscape with this purpose in mind.

That he imposes a definite artistic order on his construction of the ideal becomes obvious by the materials he uses: the "bornyst syluer" of the leaves that could frame a sumptuous diptych, the rich indigo of the tree trunks to be found perhaps in a decorated initial of a psalter page, the rivers "as fyldor fyn," like gold-leaf threads tooled into an interlace relief design, the opulent tapestry ("webbeȝ") of the "rych rokkeȝ," the mosaiclike pebbles, and the stained-glass transparency of the stream (69–120).[24] Human art supplants nature as comforter and as incarnating vehicle of divine reality. There is a buoyant sense of visionary conquest and creative elation in the making of such an effulgent and intricately ordered symbol. But the poet reveals before us the ironic paradox that art fails as vision and as representation of reality, ideal or common, to the extent that it fulfills its own nature and order—to the extent that it succeeds as art. Let me be specific.

The careful visual organization and the listing of discrete objects— the forest, then the cliffs, then the trees, then the leaves, and so on— establish a ritual architectonic sequence. The effect, however, is curiously complementary. Such a ritual structure relieves our fear of chaos; it offers us the pleasure of control, coherence, and equilibrium. Yet it also suggests an overarching framework of values—in which the dreamer now moves—that restrict human desire and self-realization. The full significance of ritual order as it relates to the dreamer will become evident in the anagogic realm.

Moreover, the visual intensification of each object and its precise delineation create paradoxically out of order a sense of truncation and discontinuity.[25] However enchanting in its visual beauty, the visionary landscape is a spasmodic arrangement of isolated entities. Imagistically, this arrangement recalls the isolating perfection of the central symbol, "clanly clos in golde so clere" (2) and set "'sengeley in synglere"(8). Man's artistic vision, then, refracts and fragments in its intensity the ideal reality it tries to capture. Perhaps it was this bitter realization that moved Heinrich von Morungen (d. 1222) to sad reflection:

> Mirst geschên als eime kindelîne,
> daz sîn schonêz bilde in eime glase ersach
> unde greif dar nâch sîn selbes schîne
> sô vil biz daz ez den spiegel gar zerbrach.

dô wart al sîn wünne ein leitlich ungemach.
alsô dâhte ich iemer frô ze sîne,
dô'ch gesach die lieben frouwen mîne,
von der mir bî liebe leides vil geschach.

[It happened to me as to a small child, that saw its beautiful
image in a mirror and reached for its own reflection so much
[hard, often] that it broke the mirror completely. Then was its
joy turned to bitter sorrow. So did I think that I would be
forever happy, when I saw my beloved lady, by whom,
through love, I have suffered much pain.][26]

Although Heinrich speaks in terms of *Minnedienst*, he describes a uni-
versal experience very much in the center of medieval consciousness:
the fragility of the ideal image at the touch of man the lover, the
visionary, the artist.

To evaluate properly the Pearl Poet's use of art and its failures to
dramatize in *Pearl* man's limitations in conceiving and expressing the
ideal, we cannot confine ourselves entirely to his symbolic imagery,
despite the scope of our subject. We must remain constantly aware of a
concomitant and more inclusive aspect of his artistic order: his style.
Style is the reflection of a poet's attitude toward the reality he repre-
sents. It also reveals his intention in reshaping that reality into new
coherence. It is crucial, therefore, to ask: Why did the Pearl Poet
choose one style and not another in representing divine reality? Does
he vary that style? With what intention? If the poet has borrowed his
style from his milieu, then we can gain some insight into the *Weltan-
schauung* of his age, and especially its eschatological attitudes, which he
most likely shares. (I shall not ask the futile question: Which comes
first, the poet or the age?)

The Pearl Poet's "aureate" style in the description of the visionary
landscape has some precedent in Alanus de Insulis (c. 1128–1202), a
poet "aiming chiefly at sweetness and richness," as in *De Planctu Natu-
rae*, but frequently ending in "bizarre luxury," as in *Anticlaudianus*.[27]
Alanus must have inherited the habit of stylistic intoxication from an
earlier master, Sidonius Apollinaris (430–484), whose diction he
praises as full of gems and colors, like a peacock's splendid plumage:

> Illic Sidonii trabeatus sermo refulgens
> Sidere multiplici splendet gemmisque colorum.
> Lucet et in dictis depictus pavo resultat.[28]

D. W. Robertson has described the increasing brilliance and ornateness of artistic and literary style in the late Middle Ages.[29] It is a style associated with the growing emotional luxuriance of the age, which begins to blur the formal clarity and intellectual control of the High Gothic. It is a style especially associated with works of excessive and often macabre pathos: the sumptuously ornamented but grippingly realistic tombs and effigies, the overaccented representations of divine suffering in sculpture and painting, and the poetry of dissolution and death, equally oppressive in its grim realism and violent sentimentality. Johan Huizinga points to other important characteristics of the late medieval style: It is obsessively visual, "accentuating every detail, . . . developing every thought and every image to the end, . . . giving concrete form to every concept of the mind." It is turgid and overloaded with effect—in short, "a rhetorician's style." What adds to its heaviness is the increasing languor and melancholy of its tone, reflecting the *Zeitgeist* and the mood that began to predominate after the Black Death. Again, such infatuation with detail and ornament and with local effect could only break down the unity of a work of art and dissipate the rigor controlling its total form. Perhaps the characteristic most pertinent to our concerns here was the irrepressible tendency to crystallize, and thus rigidify, thought into image.[30] The effect of this tendency on the representation of spiritual reality in art and literature could be utterly self-defeating—and yet highly enriching. Of course, Huizinga is speaking of style in the late fourteenth and fifteenth centuries on the Continent. It is evident that the Pearl Poet, as an English artist of the time, does not share in the pathological realism, the hysterical emotionalism, or the unrelieved preoccupation with man's mortality found in his Netherlandish and Flemish contemporaries. He does, however, display the basic stylistic tendencies of that milieu, though in a restrained manner.

His description of the visionary landscape in its ornate sumptuousness carries on, in essence, the rhetoric of beauty of the "erber," attempting to anesthetize the sensibility toward the gruesome reality of death. His depiction of the ideal employs, indeed, "a rhetorician's style," which reflects in its brilliant invention a self-luxuriating flamboyance yet also a suasive urgency—a feeling of despair, almost—at the precariousness of its "argument." This argument is the attempt to capture eternity in a concrete, permanent form as a convincing counterforce to the concrete image of death seen in the garden. This attempt, as we have observed, preoccupied considerably the poet's milieu. In *Pearl* it results in a devastating contradiction: The more intense the poet's effort to invest spiritual reality with a palpable shape, the more it denudes it of its sublimity. The more he tries to define it and distinguish it as itself, the more he shackles and confines it in irrelevant terms. The poet, like the dreamer and like all men in the life of spiritual perception, cannot free himself from matter. In his construction of ideality, the transcendental is suffocated and weighed down by pigment and hard preciousness. As a result, the reader becomes too distracted by the dense rhetoric of the symbolic surface to penetrate to any underlying doctrine—unless the doctrine is in the surface and its failure.

Because of the intensely visual character of the Pearl Poet's style, my discussion of its general characteristics has unavoidably fallen back on its imagery. It is essential, however, to focus on other key elements— sound, rhythm, and verbal form—although admittedly with the primary purpose of relating them to the poet's symbolic-incarnational intention. As equally palpable experience, these elements, after all, are part of the work's *visibilia,* through which we are led to its invisible spiritual meaning.

A principle that pervades *Pearl* is the intriguing relationship between the poem's form and texture and its central symbol: how the one expands in verse or distills into image the essence of the other. As in the visionary landscape, the author diffuses the seminal qualities of the pearl symbol over the poem's verbal surface. This can be seen in its intricate stanzaic structure, its rhetorical ingenuity, the aureate richness of its diction, the luxuriance of its sound, the skillful rhythmical counterpoint of its lines, and finally its word play.

To begin with, the cosmopolitanism of the poem's versification reflects the Pearl Poet's characteristic impulse to bring together distant areas of experience—in this case, the poetic cultures of his time. The poet uses twelve-line tetrameter stanzas that combine alliteration with a complex rhyme scheme: *a b a b a b a b b c b c.* Though somewhat altered in its sound pattern from the Old English line, [31] the alliterative line in *Pearl* is the indisputable legacy of the English native tradition. It fuses with rhyme, an element taken from the Continental poetic tradition. Although one cannot really claim that this fusion is part of the poet's symbolic intention, it nevertheless produces the effect of dynamic reconciliation between different levels of sensibility, so characteristic of the incarnational symbolic process.

We are acquainted, also, with the linking of the stanzas by a key word that appears in the last line of the preceding stanza and then reappears in the first line of the stanza that follows. This rounding off of each stanza—the gathering of ends into a self-contained unit—suggests the spherical self-sufficiency and isolating perfection of the pearl.[32] At the same time, the hooking-over from one stanza to the next creates a web of connections—much like a rich interlace pattern—which, as verbal technique, incarnates the accumulative intricacy of meaning in the poem's central symbol. Since the stanza linking is associated with verbal wit and word play, its full symbolic value will become more apparent in my discussion of these two elements later on.

Ian Bishop and Patricia Kean have identified with some thoroughness the rhetorical figures employed in *Pearl*.[33] Kean, however, loses contact with the poem by becoming immersed in the task of working up a systematic catalogue of its rhetorical formulas and *topoi*. Without subsuming these elements under one artistic aim, such a task—like the listing of analogues discussed earlier (chapter 2)—remains a tedious taxonomical exercise; it does not constitute true poetic analysis. In fact, I question some of Kean's characterizations. I cannot discern in the poem's initial lines, for instance, "the weightiness of a proverb" or the proverbial "clinching of an argument." Neither do I perceive an argument there, nor can I see the similarity in rhetorical structure and "epigrammatic form" that she claims to exist between the opening of *Pearl* and the openings of the *Roman de la Rose* and Chaucer's *Parlement of Foules*. Kean demonstrates well, on the other hand, how *amplificatio* is exploited as a technical vehicle for the presentation of the poem's evolving themes and ideas.[34] Still, the Pearl Poet does not use amplification only as *dilatatio*, "the purely linear extension, expansion, unrolling of a theme."[35] He makes it work simultaneously as αὔξησις, as elevation and vertical expansion of meaning. Thus, *amplificatio* as linguistic structure and technique incarnates verbally the ongoing expansion and elevation in significance of the poem's symbolism. It is beyond the scope of this study to enter an analysis of the poem in terms of its rhetorical *schema* as defined by the medieval *artes poeticae*. I wish to point out, nevertheless, that these figures are conscious manipulations of the poem's verbal surface, its *littera* and *sensus*. As such, they are no empty ornamental display; they shape the poem's *sententia* to the extent that outer form shapes internal meaning.

The diction describing the visionary landscape shares inevitably in the luminosity and luxuriance of its images:

> Towarde a foreste I bere þe face,
> Where rych rokkeȝ wer to dyscreuen.
> Þe lyȝt of hem myȝt no mon leuen,
> Þe glemande glory þat of hem glent;
> For wern neuer webbeȝ þat wyȝeȝ weuen
> Of half so dere adubbemente.
>
> Dubbed wern alle þo downeȝ sydeȝ
> Wyth crystal klyffeȝ so cler of kynde.
>
> (67–74)

If the visionary landscape is an expansion of the pearl's qualities, the diction helps create a corresponding verbal surface, the aureate words studding it like precious stones, adding to the lapidary effect of the verse.

Intricacy of design and sumptuousness of texture are not conceived in *Pearl* only plastically. The dreamer himself tells us that he experienced the otherworld "in yӡe and ere"—a direction to the reader by indirection to do likewise. All five senses become here channels of spiritual perception, as Hugh Saint Victor also would have pointed out to us.[36] The poem is a rich symphony of sound and rhythm in its assonance and alliteration:

> The dubbemente of þo derworth depe
> Wern bonkeӡ bene of beryl bryӡt.
> Swangeande swete þe water con swepe,
> Wyth a rownande rourde raykande aryӡt.
> (109–12)

Besides the sonal luxuriance *an sich*, we notice how sound also functions as rhythm. (I am using "sonal" as a pure adjective for sound, in order to avoid the modern technological associations of "sonic" and "acoustic.") The alliterative accentual pattern varies from four occurrences to three. Such variation of accent accumulates in the reader's memory, one line superimposing itself on the other in contrast. The result is a polyphonic counterpoint of rhythm, which is further enhanced by the counterpoint between the same alliterative sound and its various altering contexts, and by the way internal rhymes anticipate and resolve themselves in the external rhymes like musical motifs.

Very little has been written[37] and much needs to be said about the Pearl Poet's musical mentality and orientation. The foregoing passage is only a sample of the poem's pervasive musicality. A more thorough study than mine would show how much musical play creates tensions through discordant variety, to resolve them eventually into consonant unity—and back again. Thus, in *Pearl*, the pattern of sound and rhythm, too, reflects the dynamic evolution of the poem's central symbol. It also reasserts a key universal formative principle re-created by the poem as a whole: the interplay between unity and multiplicity. One cannot help recalling at such instances that medieval cosmology and aesthetics were to a great extent musically conceived; a literary work, as poetic incarnation of the cosmos, takes form within that conception.

Much of the word play—perhaps the most fascinating verbal structure in the poem—occurs at a distinctive place of attention: the linkage of the stanzas. Both E. V. Gordon and Dorothy Everett recognized, although without elaboration, the thematic value of these refrain words. O. D. Macrae-Gibson has devoted an entire study to the function of the link words in constructing the poem's thematic structure, exploring in some detail their play with meaning.[38]

I wish to recall here Walter Ong's discussion of the conceit, the pun, and word play in Latin hymnody, as they were used by Augustine, Adam of Saint Victor, and Thomas Aquinas to incarnate verbally Christian mystery, operating as analogues of the incarnate Word. Such word play was more than clever ornament or "phonetic tinkering"; it was meant to represent palpably through its "linguistic tension" the experience of belief. This linguistic tension is generated by the stress between infinite spiritual meaning and the limited but utterly indispensable terms of human expression.[39] The word play, in other words, is the dissimilar similitude cast in verbal, rather than imagistic, form. Whereas in Augustine's and Thomas's poetry this tension is expressed essentially in metaphysical terms and is contemplated with some intellectual detachment in its universality, other poets render it into active drama—whether in Christ's or in man's life. Such translation inevitably calls for a strategy of selection and intensification—hence, of artistic ordering. Thus metaphysical tension becomes artistic tension as well. Theology becomes poetry and poetry theology in dramatic, existential terms.

The medieval English poets relished the use of punning and word play for a similar purpose, as the following well-known lyric shows with startling economy and ingenuity:

> Nou goth sonne vnder wod,
> me reweth, marie, þi faire Rode.
> Nou goþ sonne vnder tre,
> me reweþ, marie, þi sone and þe.[40]

Pun is the shaping principle here: *sonne* (sun)—Mary's Son; *wod* (forest)—the wood of the cross; *Rode* (complexion)—the cross; *tre* (tree)—the cross. The word play reasserts the sacramental kinship between the humble things of this earth and sublime sacred reality. Further yet, it mobilizes this incarnational relationship to play out symbolically the live drama of the Crucifixion. Finally, it claims for the poet the unique ability to imitate the incarnate Word by fusing in one verbal form opposing levels of being, natural and spiritual, human and divine.

The Pearl Poet employs his word play in a similar vein. Let us look at the refrain linking the stanzas of the opening section, uttered by the hero in praise of his pearl. Its verbal form remains the same, but its meaning shifts with each repetition in each new context. The phrase "þat precios perle wythouten spot" means at first, that precious pearl without physical blemish. As soon as the pearl takes on a human dimension, the phrase acquires spiritual overtones, implying purity or innocence. Yet, because of the ambivalent impact of the image of precious enclosure, "wythouten spot" carries with it the corollary implications of an entity existing without much contact or relationship with common reality but enshrined in its own isolating perfection. When eventually "spot" is used by the hero to designate the place of his mourning, the phrase begins to say that the pearl has no local habitation: it exists beyond familiar time and space. To be sure, this signification spiritualizes the pearl even more, but it also intensifies its precariousness as object of quest, directing the hero's search into a strange and elusive order of existence. The poet thus turns word play into an instrument of dramatic irony as well: he subjects the hero to the irony of his own utterance, his own unwitting verbal conceit and what it really forebodes.

The word play incarnates in verbal form the process of development of the poem's symbolic imagery and especially its central symbol. Appearing at this early stage in the work, it becomes a verbal prefiguration of that development: the pearl will remain essentially the same in physical form, but it will shift and expand in spiritual meaning. In both the word play and the symbol, we experience the immense tension between the changing invisible significance and the constant visible form which denies such a change. The reader is at war with himself on various levels of his perception: The visual shape and the sonal pattern speak to the nervous system with unremitting concreteness and physical pressure, forcing it to submit to the principle of sameness. But this physiological level of acceptance is agitated out of its complacency by the emotions and the intellect, which discern new affective colorings and cognitional qualifications in each successive context. This is one of the means by which the poet energizes the poem's drama of faith, compelling the reader to participate in it actively by indeed pitting within him one level of perception against the other—from the visceral to the intellectual.

In the manner that he uses versification, rhetorical figures, diction, sound, rhythm, and word play, we see, then, that the Pearl Poet makes verbal structure function incarnationally in congruence with his symbolic imagery. The two operate simultaneously, just as their sacred prototype and poetic principle existed simultaneously as God "in the flesh" and as God the incarnate Word. In this sense, *Pearl* re-creates poetically the unique process by which "verbum caro factum est." The word becomes image; style as verbal form becomes symbol.

The Pearl Poet's success in subordinating his aureate style to his symbolic aim challenges us to consider a more fundamental question: Does the style, functioning on its own terms, help make the poem a superior and well-integrated work of art? Is there a proper relationship between structure and texture, form and content? I have in mind an artistic lapse which is the more poignant because it results from the best of intentions. It is when style in its eagerness overstates its achievement, when it becomes artistry displaying itself, pausing to luxuriate in too many glorious but isolated moments, to the point that the work's overall design dissolves from our view. I am also pointing to a concomitant problem quite akin to what Yvor Winters has aptly called "the fallacy of expressive form." To the extent that form surrenders to or attempts to imitate its matter, it weakens the work's expressive force, it annihilates itself and, consequently, conscious artistic control. As a result, such style "leads to disorganization and unintelligence."[41] In case such criticism may appear blasphemously anachronistic, I would remind the reader of Thomas Aquinas's demand for *claritas*—brilliance of surface but also lucidity of form—as one of three prerequisite qualities for beauty and meaning.[42] Chaucer, no less, mocks with his eagle the destruction of clarity and restraint through "gret prolixite . . . / Of figures of poetrie, / Or colours of rethorike" (*House of Fame*, lines 856–59).[43] Is the Pearl Poet, then, in his attempt to make style subserve his symbolic intention, guilty of "the fallacy of imitative form," of undermining *claritas* as articulateness of form by too much *claritas* as brilliance of surface?

The poem's aureate style has drawn both praise and blame. Kenneth Sisam considers its effect as "highly wrought, almost overwrought," to the point that "the form distracts attention from the matter by its elaborateness."[44] Constance Hieatt counters Sisam's criticism with the rather general statement that it is precisely this elaborateness that makes up the poem's "special excellence." She mentions "the admirable symmetry of the poem, and its wonderful appropriateness of language and style to theme and form," all resulting in a "totality of effect" and simultaneously in a "fascinating complexity."[45] A more hallowed source, C. S. Lewis, lauds the poem's style without any reservation, comparing it to William Dunbar's *Golden Targe* for its splendid language, its dazzling imagery, "a peculiar brightness, as of enamel or illumination."[46] This is, however, a connoisseur's feel for fabric rather than meaningful form.

In his aureate style, the Pearl Poet commits certain excesses of local overintensification that often impede that exhilarating, instantaneous awareness of the individual element and the total framework. Expressiveness is frequently enfeebled by "prolixite" and overmanipulation of effect. Almost every enrichment of the verbal surface that I have mentioned—harmonized as it might be with the poet's symbolic intention—attracts undue attention to itself as unique, self-enclosed aesthetic moment. I do not think that such truncating artistic self-consciousness can be explained away as good medieval "inorganic form,"[47] for even in its additiveness such form is not inert but moves with a reduplicative continuity of its key motifs.

The Pearl Poet's intricacy sometimes turns into inertia by its own infinite convolutions. The stanza linking, for example, slows down movement and thus dissipates artistic vitality by the incessant returning motion. It is like an afterthought, a statement seeking constant reaffirmation in a past response. As predictable, invariable verbal structure and ritual form, the stanza linking has subtle symbolic significance, as I have already suggested; as poetry, however, it sometimes is just that—predictable and invariable. On occasion, the connection itself is forced, as in lines 612–13, where "inoghe" is linked to "now."

The sonal luxuriance of the verse, while delectable, can be too arresting in its self-conscious artistry. I am returning to a passage I have already praised extensively:

> The dubbemente of þo derworth depe
> Wern bonkeȝ bene of beryl bryȝt.
> Swangeande swete þe water con swepe,
> Wyth a rownande rourde raykande aryȝt.
> In þe founce þer stonden stoneȝ stepe,
> As glente þurȝ glas þat glowed and glyȝt,
> As stremande sterneȝ, quen stroþe-men slepe
> Staren in welkyn in wynter nyȝt.
>
> (109–16)

Such insistence upon the reader's response, if unrelieved—as it often is in *Pearl*—can become strained and then ineffective through mere custom and repetition. In its subservience to a set format, it continues to operate even with the infelicitous result of cacophonous, cloddish monotony:

> Quen *J*ueȝ hym *i*ugged in *J*erusalem.
>
> (804)

> Wyth *g*ret delyt þay *g*lod in fere
> On *g*olden *g*ateȝ þat *g*lent as *g*lasse.
>
> (1105–6)

Similarly, word play, committed as it is to an invariable pattern, goes on anyway, sometimes with tortuous ingenuity. Although Macrae-Gibson has tried to work out a thematic antithesis between the limitations of this earth and the infinitude of heaven,[48] the employment of "date" as linkword in section IX is not so clear thematically. As refrain, it does not reveal any particular thematic pattern or progression of thought, because some of its meanings are unusual and far-fetched even for its own time.[49] Here they are used in a forced and scattered fashion: goal of heavenly achievement (492), limit to God's goodness (493), right time of year to cultivate the vine (504), season of year (505), end of day (516), beginning of day (517), end of day (528), hour or point of day (529), end of day (540), hour or point of day (541). Are such juxtapositions part of a symbolically meaningful *discordia concors* or rather an unsuccessful, if not careless, attempt at verbal wit?

Obviously, then, in the poem's aureate style, form frequently surrenders to its symbolic matter in trying to imitate it. The style's extravagant sumptuousness, its unrelieved intricacy, and the parasitic ostentation of some of its effects suffocate our perception of the work's total design. The style often produces the same ossifying and fragmenting effect as the imagery by the heavy delineation and individual enrichment of each verbal structure. From a symbolic standpoint, such a style is irreplaceable here; but from the standpoint of clear, well-integrated form, it falters. By dwelling on some limitations of the Pearl Poet's aureate style, I have not meant to detract from its overall achievement. In fact, the achievement seems the greater since the poet, intuitively at least, has turned these limitations to advantage by making them the specific and concrete means of conveying his particular view of the reality he is representing in the poem.

After all, the Pearl Poet is equally a master of bare, colloquial realism—the stylistic "other self" of the late Middle Ages. We shall be examining his use of that style in later passages, although not as extensively.[50] His virtuosity shows itself early in the poem in several lines that are interjected into a heavily aureate context as contrasting elements. He can evoke a feeling of tender, lambent intimacy with his plain diction: "So smal, so smoþe her sydeȝ were" (6). He relies on simplicity and directness for dramatic effect: "O moul, þou marreȝ a myry iuele" (23). Later on he will re-create a familiar, bustling reality with stark but sinewy concreteness:

> Wryþen and worchen and don gret pyne,
> Keruen and caggen and man hit clos.
>
> (511–12)

This style, of course, fits in with the world of the seed and the vine as symbolic foil to the pearl and *its* style.

The autonomy and essential irrelevance of the visionary landscape as composite symbol of divine reality raises several pressing questions in the reader's mind: Why has the poet chosen this imagistic medium and not another? What aspect of the sacred is he trying to accentuate? How are these powerfully stated corporeal values to be transmuted into spiritual meaning? In analogical terms, what does this veil reveal by hiding? We crave—and we imagine the dreamer does, too—an authoritative voice to translate the symbolic spectacle into rational, intellectually comprehensible terms.

The poet, who has of course nurtured and energized this desire in the reader as part of his strategy, proceeds to satisfy it not in abstract but in existential, identifiable terms. He grounds these questions in a particular human drama and, more urgently, in the hero's passionate expectation to transcend life's painful paradoxes upon entering the realm of the ideal. The poet intensifies our curiosity through the dreamer's own reaction to the landscape, full of wonder and taut anticipation:

> My goste is gon in Godeʒ grace
> In auenture þer meruayleʒ meuen.
> I ne wyste in þis worlde quere þat hit wace.
>
> (63–65)

The splendor of this domain makes his "goste al greffe forʒete" (86). He is refreshed by the "frech flauoreʒ of fryteʒ" (87) and the fragrance of the plants and spices (104). He is soothed into happy tranquillity by the "swete asent" of the birds' song (89–95) after the exhausting dissonance and strife between "resoun" and his "wreched wylle" (51–60). He bursts out into exclamations of incredulous rapture, "Lorde, dere watʒ hit adubbement!" (108), until finally he succumbs, intoxicated by the strange beauty around him: "I bowed in blys, bredful my brayneʒ" (126). Surely, Paradise must be near, he thinks, "þer ouer gayn þo bonkeʒ brade" (137–38).

Both Charles Moorman and A. R. Heiserman would insist that the poet has succeeded in making our reactions identical with those of the dreamer—the poem's central intelligence—and that, at this point, we would share his joy and refreshment without any qualification.[51] The poet, however, has already established some critical distance between the reader and the poem's "I," as I have shown, in the "erber." We remember his incapacity to accept the laws that govern the universal garden of mutability and to derive comfort from its incarnational eloquence. We recall his pathetic wish to suspend such inexorable laws in his quest for permanence. Moreover, his disconsolate words, uttered "after the event," still linger in our memory, functioning as elements of dark foreboding, foreshadowing some impending reversal. If the familiar earthly context alienated him so, we ask, how will the dreamer relate to this strange world and to what point of reference in it? The estrangement between symbol and represented reality, which the poet has initiated in the visionary landscape, intimates greater conflict betwen juxtaposed natures. The poem's metaphoric process takes on a vital dramatic function: the increasing violence—which is, in essence, mutual rejection—between terms incarnates an increasing sense of distance and alienation between the human hero and the ideality he seeks, in this case God.

This sense of distance—and with it our suspense—is heightened by the growing resistance that the ideal realm is putting up against the dreamer's comprehension and expression. He mentions this repeatedly and with increasing helplessness:

> Þe ly3t of hem my3t no mon leuen.
> (69)

> Þe derþe þerof for to deuyse
> Nis no wy3 worþé þat tonge bere3.
> (99–100)

> I hope no tong mo3t endure
> No sauerly saghe say of þat sy3t.
> (225–26)

The ineffable, as part of the poem's metaphoric experience, becomes an intensifying dramatic factor with its silence. It begets frustration, thus vitalizing the poem's interplay of wish and fulfillment. Symbolically, it is a silence more eloquent than any articulate statement about the nature of divine reality, delineating the dreamer's—and Everyman's—relationship to it. It is in such an elusive and mysterious reality, ironically, that we see the dreamer seeking understanding and consolation.

For these reasons—of which the dreamer is not aware—our responses cannot be the same as his, as Moorman and Heiserman wish to maintain. Consequently, we view the landscape's recuperative effect on him with skepticism that grows into tense apprehension at his mounting ecstasy and self-abandon. Such lack of awareness renders him doubly helpless before any impending disappointment; in effect, it can only lead to disappointment.

Our apprehension materializes in the dreamer's encounter with the stream. The poet translates here symbol into drama in a highly concentrated form. He sets up a concrete topography where he arrays opposite each other human wish and its ultimate fulfillment, Paradise, with a barrier in between them. The preoccupation of the author's milieu with the actual geographical location of Paradise must have given this topography greater immediacy than it has today.[52] Yet we feel no less the kinesthetic tension rising between the two poles of attraction over the barrier, as the dreamer paces up and down the riverbank looking for a crossing:

> Me lyste to se þe broke byȝonde
> . . . .
> Abowte me con I stote and stare;
> To fynde a forþe faste con I fonde.
> (146–50)

We cannot overlook the traditional symbolic valences of the stream as boundary in an otherworldly landscape. These values enter here in a preliminary fashion, to be reconstructed by the poem's own context, arriving at their full significance in the climax of the event. Mircea Eliade and Northrop Frye describe the stream or river as an archetypal symbol of complementary meanings.[53] Cosmologically, the waters are the *fons et origo* of creation and the means of its renewal. Sacramentally, they are the waters of spiritual cleansing and regeneration. But, at the same time, they symbolize death and the dissolution of form into chaos. The "old self" may emerge from this dissolution as a new being. Saint John Chrysostom expresses well the symbolic complementarity of baptism: "It represents death and entombment, life and resurrection. . . . When we plunge our head into water, as into a sepulchre, the old man is immersed, altogether buried: when we come out of the water the new man simultaneously appears."[54] The waters embody both meanings: the annihilating action of the Flood and the purifying effect of Christian baptism.[55] In the meantime, Howard R. Patch has shown through numerous examples how the river functions as barrier in the medieval romance and other world visions or journeys. It usually separates two different modes of existence. It is often a part of the landscape's enchanting appearance. Yet it frequently tests the venturing hero-dreamer with its dangers or prevents him, at the risk of his life, from passing from one realm to the other. In sum, it is made to invite the hero with its irresistible beauty, or the beauty of the "other" bank, only to stun him and transfix him with some hidden, unexpected peril.[56]

The stream in *Pearl* displays actively this traditional complexity of character. Its ambiguity is heightened, as we saw, by the curious counterpoise between natural beauty and the "plastic" transformation or alchemization setting in on it. The poet further intensifies this ambiguity by the duplicity of his language. To the dreamer, the inhibiting convolutions of the stream appear as only a pleasant diversion to his passage, "a deuyse / Bytwene myrþeȝ by mereȝ made" (139–40). Verbal play, however, increases the symbolic and dramatic efficacy of the image. E. V. Gordon interprets the phrase as "division made by pools, separating the delights." He proposes an additional meaning for "deuyse" as "device," associating it with the attractive but artificially constructed stream in the garden of Deduit in the *Roman de la Rose*.[57] David O. Fowler, on the other hand, points to another common meaning at the time: "strategem," "plot," "trick," or "deception."[58] The word's ambivalence stirs in the reader a wary attitude toward the stream. Appearance might mask with its beauty a perilous reality, just as the verbal form hides contrary meanings: enchantment yet treachery. Again, we are struck by the dreamer's unawareness of the stream's complementary nature as splendid but inexorable barrier. This, of course, adds to the dramatic *and* symbolic irony that is developing within the poem.

In the meantime, desire mounts in the unsuspecting dreamer; the refrain "more and more" (III) reflects with each repetition the emotional crescendo building up. Dramatically, the phrase "more and more" foreshadows his quibbling and his envious resentment toward the high status of the child that he has mourned so pathetically. It prepares us also for some expansion and redirection in the object of his quest. Furthermore, it forebodes conflict, for it sets no limits to itself. The phrase brings to mind a paradox central to the human condition, which the now wiser narrator articulates, looking back upon the event:

> As fortune fares þer as ho frayneȝ,
> Wheþer solace ho sende oþer elleȝ sore,
> Þe wyȝ to wham her wylle ho wayneȝ
> Hytteȝ to haue ay more and more.
>
> (129–32)

It is this insatiability for the absolute that has been man's curse, the cause of his fall; it is this insatiability alone that will earn him his redemption. The recollection of this paradox, especially by the narrator so early in the work, has powerful anticipatory implications for the outcome of the poem's event.

With ultimate felicity, Paradise, drawing him irresistibly to "þe fyrre londe" (148), the dreamer tries to wade the stream. But the depth of the water and its "woþeȝ" (perils) prevent him—an event reflecting and prefiguring the poem's dramatic development as a contrapuntal pattern of human pursuit and divine elusiveness. What Eliade, Patch, and Frye have described on the archetypal level as the obstacles to such a passage are present here as well; they all relate to the hero's natural incapacity to cross from his mode of existence to the zone of absolute reality. Yet the particular mention of depth merits our attention.

We notice that the poet has delineated sharply most of the images in the stream, whereas the depth with its perils remains vague. Around it linger the associations of the hero's descent into the abyss to confront and vanquish unknown enemies and of possible self-annihilation. Depth here does not seem to hide dragons or marine monsters but represents indefinability and fathomlessness, which, more immediately, suggest infinite mystery. The juxtaposition of ravishing beauty and rejecting dread makes this mystery awesome in its two-facednesss. I showed earlier that the bottom of the stream, while it re-creates an idyllic scene of this earth with its "stremande sterneȝ," also images in anticipation the Apocalyptic City with its precious battlements. How far does the present experience by the stream foreshadow in its ambivalence the final encounter?

The dreamer's repeated unsuccessful attempts to cross and his increasing longing bring the poem to a decisive confrontation. As skilled dramatist, however, the poet diverts the climax and relieves the tension—only to intensify it through complication and delay—by a surprising distraction, "a newe note": the appearance of the Maiden.

4

The Dialogue

THE ENCOUNTER

The appearance of the Maiden at this point initiates in the reader
certain expectations as to her function in the poem—expectations that
have been nurtured throughout the visionary allegorical tradition. Let
me define them.

In the preceding chapter, I outlined the dramatic order characteris-
tic of most medieval allegorical dream visions, which *Pearl* also follows.
I pointed to the dialogue between the authoritative guide and the
dreamer as a key element in this dramatic order. Its aim is twofold:
The dialogue attempts to translate into rational terms—and thus con-
trol further—the imagistic, inarticulate content of the dream. In addi-
tion, it leads to the resolution of the dreamer's conflict by persuading
him through argumentative discourse to place his spiritual crisis in a
new framework of values, a new perspective. This rational elucidation
and persuasion has been entrusted by allegorical authors—at least from
The Shepherd of Hermas (c. A.D. 160) down—to the authoritative figure
that encounters the dreamer in a visionary landscape, usually the
guide's domain. Hermas's Ecclesia, Boethius's Philosophia, Alanus de
Insulis's Natura, Dante's Beatrice, Langland's Holy Church are only a
handful—though an important one—among innumerable visionary
guides in medieval allegorical literature.

Appearing in works of conscious artistry, however, these figures are
subject to the author's thematic and artistic strategy. Relying on the
revelatory and supernatural character given to the dream vision by
tradition, the author reinforces the spiritual authority of his guide by
investing her, as Paul Piehler has shown, with certain archetypal and
oracular characteristics, adding to her a timeless and universal validity.[1]
By endowing the figure also with a historical identity—as Hermas does
with his Rhoda and Dante with his Beatrice—the author does not

weaken this authority. Instead, he humanizes it and further validates it, strengthening the bond between guide and dreamer with a living immediacy: actual historical passions continue to warm their new relationship, however spiritual. Dante's critics have explored the thematic and artistic function of the figure's historical dimension too well for me to elaborate on it any further.[2]

The author's strategy of amplifying the spiritual authority of his figure aims at establishing his work as unimpeachable spiritual and artistic experience. His message, too, uttered by such an imposing personality—especially within the supernaturally revelatory ambience of the dream—assumes an almost divine composure against the reader's possible skepticism. The author does not risk presumption by striking an oracular stance himself. Instead, he adopts the persona of the dreamer, with whom we tend to identify in our common humanity and by the fact that he anticipates and voices our objections. Thus we are gradually led to share not only his initial resistance but his eventual conversion as well. The author takes pains, in fact, to mock himself—in protective self-irony, of course—as the untutored, obtuse dreamer. Through such self-deprecation, safe because exaggerated, the author affects here a disarming modesty and even a quality of engaging pathos, both of which tend to enhance rather than diminish his stature.[3] The dreamer's obtuseness, mixed with an enterprising and often shamelessly insistent curiosity, invites further revelation, discursive or symbolic, from the spiritual guide. In sum, the author as typical allegorical dreamer takes on the role of naive pupil, as well as that of privileged transmitter of higher truth.

Within the generic tradition that I have been describing as frame of reference for *Pearl*, the authoritative guide has maintained a significantly ambiguous relationship to the dreamer. On the one hand, she acts as a personality external to him, descending from a supernatural realm, whose values she reflects symbolically and articulates discursively. At the same time, she functions as an innate part of the hero, emerging into affirmation and identity in the form of a distinct figure in his visionary experience, seeking to become reassimilated in a more reconciled and integrated self.

By isolating and objectifying this aspect of the self, the allegorical author attains to a purer definition of the forces contending within the dreamer. Yet he aims at something more than a delineation of the hero's inner self. The ambiguity of the figure's identity and her dual dimension as external and internal force are a vitalizing artistic means as well, because of the ontological and spatial paradox involved. The reader is asked to maintain a taut parallel awareness of both dimensions—a simultaneously cosmic *and* personal-interior view of the figure's true nature.

That he must do, in fact, with the entire visionary realm: To what extent does it embody the ideal as objective being, a cosmos unto itself, which *contains* man? To what extent is it a construction of the psyche, and thus *contained in* man? The author leaves the question unanswered, forcing the reader to seek out his own points of convergence between these essentially irreconcilable perspectives. The irresolution of this attempt stimulates the imagination into a creative activity through which the reader constructs his own patterns of synthesis between exterior and interior reality. Through such involvement the poet makes the reader his collaborator—a pleasure that lies at the core of the aesthetic experience. What adds, nevertheless, to the figure's internal dimension is the inevitability with which she reacts to the hero's inner state, materializing before him at a moment of desperate self-confrontation—as if invoked by it. Appearing at a similar moment, the Pearl Maiden recalls also the guide's conventional role of finally enlightening and consoling the hero, a key expectation in the poem's unfolding drama.

The Maiden is given a historical reality, kept vague for some time because of the alternating parental and courtly address to her by the dreamer, until it apparently settles down to a father-daughter relationship.[4] The bond appears to be deeply intimate, and it would indeed rob the poem of considerable emotional power and human authenticity if we were to dismiss its personal basis.[5] The characters in the drama themselves insist on it:

> Ho watȝ me nerre þen aunte or nece.
> (233)

> Þou lyfed not two ȝer in oure þede.
> (483)

> And, quen we departed, we wern at on.
> (378)

> Þow wost wel when þy perle con schede
> I watȝ ful ȝong and tender of age.
> (411–12)

We are not interested, however, in the Maiden's autobiographical veracity as much as in her impact and validity within the fictional—but no less real and meaningful—context of the poem's experience. No doubt, we must respond to her as a lost child and share in the dreamer's human bereavement. At the same time, we must also view her as an allegorical entity, a creature of the poet's symbolic imagination.

Morton W. Bloomfield has emphasized action as the attribute most crucial in determining the meaning of the allegorical personification. To him, it is the richest aspect from an aesthetic point of view, because "the personifier throws his creativeness into what he has his figures do."[6] In *Pearl*, however, the poet has translated most agency and action into image, confining physical movement to a few mourning and ritualistic gestures, with the exception of the dreamer's plunging across the stream. As I have tried to show, the poet intentionally draws our attention to the poem's imagistic surface as the dramatic arena, lavishing much craft and visual wealth in forming it. Consequently, we must view the Maiden's appearance—and eventually her discourse—as the more crucial to her identity. Further, we must analyze her physical attributes as those of a compound symbol rather than of a one-dimensional personification possessing only one meaning: that of its name. While he urges such a multiplex, "symbolic" reading, Robert W. Frank, Jr., warns that the allegorical writer's aim is not to baffle the reader but to clarify the personification's identity.[7] A glance at the Maiden, however, soon convinces us of a definite strategy of bafflement continuing from the initial pearl in the "erber" to the visionary realm to the Maiden.

Upon encountering her, the dreamer is overcome with astonishment: "more meruayle con my dom adaunt" (157). His statement is ironically prophetic—without his being aware of it, of course—foreshadowing not the persuasion but the daunting of his reason ("dom") by her doctrine as well as by her strange nature. Yet he insists that he knows her well and that he can recall her from the past distinctly: "I knew hyr wel, I hade sen hyr ere" (164). The description that ensues, however, proves how pathetically mistaken his assurance is. For the Maiden is not presented in familiar human terms. What transformation has she undergone that he fails to recognize? How does she still relate to him?

If the visionary landscape is the macrocosm touched and transformed by the hero's wish for permanence, the Maiden may be seen as the hero's wishful projection of himself into potential ideality, subject to a similar transformation. The germinating source is once again the pearl, expanded first into a visionary universe and now taking human shape in a vision of the self fused with its object of desire in a perfect state. In that sense, the poet-dreamer acts as a poetic Pygmalion sculpting an idealized self-image, carving into its grain his hopes and fears about ultimate reality and perfection.

Like its seminal source, the figure of the Maiden brings together multiple symbolic valences and levels of sensibility. These add to the rich confusion of her identity rather than resolve it—as hoped by the dreamer and the reader. Let us examine this multiplicity.

The poet deliberately initiates our scrutiny of the Maiden from the same topographical point as in our examination of the landscape: the crystal cliffs. Framing her in their effulgence and immovable power, they seem to reflect imagistically some essential quality in her. The juxtaposition effects a significant transference of attribute between Maiden and landscape:

> More meruayle con my dom adaunt:
> I seȝ byȝonde þat myry mere
> A crystal clyffe ful relusaunt;
> Mony ryal ray con fro hit rere.
> At þe fote þerof þer sete a faunt,
> A mayden of menske, ful debonere;
> Blysnande whyt watȝ hyr bleaunt.
>
> (157–63)

The impact is complex. "Meruayle" indicates excited wonder, "adaunt" an element of blunting fear as well, suggesting an ambivalent reaction in the dreamer.

The Maiden, like the pearl, displays certain courtly qualities in her appearance and demeanor.[8] I have already spoken of Thomas Usk's beloved Margarite (*Testament of Love*) as a contemporaneous courtly-spiritual rendition of the pearl symbol into human form. The Maiden's "fayre face" (169) and "yȝen graye" (254), her being "ful debonere" (163), "frech as flor-de-lys" (195), and "so smoþe, so smal, so seme slyȝt" (190)—all these courtly epithets have been used almost identically by Guillaume de Lorris on his Franchise and Beauté in the *Roman de la Rose* (lines 1197 ff., 1005 ff.).[9] The last phrase echoes the description of the pearl earlier in the poem (6). Thus it establishes in retrospect the pearl's human identity. But it also strengthens our impression that the Maiden is a human incarnation of the pearl symbol—even before the Maiden is identified or addressed as such. The mute and gradual presentation of their unique kinship through image rather than explicit statement involves in the reader a more intuitive and less definable level of recognition, positing this kinship as an irreducible symbolic event fraught with mystery, and hence potential significance.

The Maiden's courtliness is meant to accomplish several things: First, it must have pleased the poet's aristocratic or aristocratically aspiring audience. But more important, it preserves the ambiguity of her identity by keeping up the lover-beloved bond as one of several. The poet concentrates on the Maiden—as on the pearl—several loves, making her the embodiment of all human relationship lost to the hero. Moreover, her courtly aspect, appearing in a spiritual quest, reflects the author's intent desire—pervasive in his time—to reconcile human and divine love, fusing them metaphorically and seeking out their sacramental identity through the poetic symbol.

Nevertheless, the Maiden's courtly attributes also tie her to the world and rob her of her pure transcendentality. She is dressed as a fashionable lady of the time, inundated with pearls.[10] In her precious attire, the Maiden resembles Richesse in the *Roman de la Rose*. The opulence of her vestments thickens and draws down to matter her spiritual identity—much like van Eyck's heavily draped and bejeweled angels. The poet relishes every detail in his extended *effictio*, clothing her in the sumptuous brocade of his descriptive diction and thus adding inevitably to the figure's physical immediacy. His depiction of the Maiden gleaming "as glysnande golde þat man con schere" (165) matches in visual intensity and concentration Dante's "fresco smeraldo in l'ora che si fiacca" (emerald when it is newly split) (*Purgatorio* VII, 75) and Hopkins's grandeur of God "like shining from shook foil; / . . . like the ooze of oil / Crushed" (*God's Grandeur*). These images catch a moment of exquisite tension when the very pulp and texture of the object touches our senses in all its fresh vitality. They testify to the utterly refined but unimpeachable physicality of three supremely spiritual poets, whose common goal seems to have been the vindication of matter as metaphor of the spirit in a poetry of incarnation.

Several elements in the Maiden's appearance suggest unmistakably her spiritual character. These have been elaborated upon by various critics, who base their symbolic interpretations mostly on patristic exegesis and the medieval liturgical tradition.[11] My summary presentation of these values is meant to avoid undue repetition, not to deemphasize them. The Maiden resembles the Virgin in her white and gold. She wears the white robes of the newly baptized and of the apocalyptic brides accompanying the Lamb. She is bedecked with the precious stones of virtue; she is crowned with the heavenly "coroun," or aureole, of virginity. The Maiden stands, then, as a symbolic figure of purity and perfection. As with the pearl, these spiritual qualities are grounded imagistically in her physical attributes. She strengthens this connection by her self-description:

> He calde me to hys bonerté:
> "Cum hyder to me, my lemman swete,
> For mote ne spot is non in þe."
>
> (762–64)

"Maskelles," quod þat myry quene,
"Vnblemyst I am, wythouten blot."
(781–82)

If, however, the Incarnation as the work's poetic principle demands a full response to the similitude's physical aspect as vehicle of spiritual meaning, we cannot sift and choose only those corporeal and affective values that are consistent with our theological preconceptions. It is doubtful that the poet himself could have fully controlled our reactions simply through selective thematic announcements. On the contrary, the Pearl Poet deliberately stimulates a multiple response to the corporeal and affective qualities of his imagery, which he further complicates by pitting against these qualities articulate thematic concepts. The resulting complementarity is central to his intention. From a theological standpoint, it is closer to Christian mystery than any neat rational formulation. Poetically, its ceaseless though patterned dialectic between conceptual definition and perceptual resistance produces vibrant art.

This dialectic becomes highly active upon further scrutiny of the Maiden as announced symbol of perfection and eternal life. Several details in her appearance are borrowed from various literary portraits of ideal feminine beauty at the time: her golden hair (213); her gray eyes (254); her complexion, which is compared to the "flor-de-lys" (195). The predominant visual impression is one of lustrous whiteness: "Wyth whyte perle and non oþer gemme, / And bornyste quyte watʒ hyr uesture" (219–20). This impression remains to the end, when the dreamer last sees her amidst the apocalyptic throng: "Þen saʒ I þer my lyttel quene / . . . þat watz so quyt!" (1147–50). The poet accentuates this quality by eliminating from her complexion the rosy hue so usual to these idealized portraits.[12] While her spirituality may thus be heightened, the Maiden loses the warmth and color of the human visage, features imaging not only vital life but also the capacity for emotion. Her humanity is reduced and attenuated into a bloodless, crystalline purity.

The poet continues to use conventional courtly similes to describe her aspect: "Hyr vysayge whyt as playn yuore" (178), "Her ble more blaʒt þen whalleʒ bon" (212). But these epithets, which in another, more natural context would suggest refined feminine beauty, create here an ambivalent effect. The sheer whiteness of her complexion and its presentation in terms of hard, polished objects—ivory, whalebone—add to the Maiden a quality of ossification. She appears to have emerged from the sea change of death polished into plastic perfection, almost frozen into artificial permanence. As image of human ideality, she displays on her face, strangely enough, the interplay of life and death—a paradox that the dreamer had hoped to leave behind him in the earthly garden. Indeed, her appearance bewilders him and fills him with increasing dread:

> Hyr vysayge whyt as playn yuore:
> Þat stonge myn hert ful stray atount,
> And euer þe lenger, þe more and more.
>
> More þen me lyste my drede aros.
>
> (178–81)

Furthermore, her ivory face is curiously framed by her hair that shines like cut gold plate or gold leaf: "As schorne golde schyr her fax þenne schon" (213). Her face thus takes the form of the pearl "clanly clos in golde" (2), together with its affective and symbolic valences discussed earlier. The poet, who subtly succeeded in adding human character to the initial pearl, reverses now the process and transforms the human figure into a lapidary artifact. He completes this transformation by the repetition of the word "pyȝt" (adorned, placed, set, fixed) as the refrain of the section (IV): she is "a precios pyece in perleȝ pyȝt" (192); "her cortel . . . [is] / Wyth precios perleȝ al vmbepyȝte" (203–4); her complexion (possibly collar[13]) is "of precios perle in porfyl pyȝte" (216); the pearl on her breast "watȝ pyȝt" (228); finally, he is yearning "to sware þat swete in perleȝ pyȝte!" (240). The total effect is one of mosaiclike fixity—on every element in her appearance and, more significantly, on her place in the whole visionary ideal framework.

In essence, then, the Maiden is conceived as part of a process of expansion and concentration of the poem's central symbol: the pearl is diffused and expanded into an ideal universe, the visionary landscape, then shaped into an ideal human form, the Maiden, and finally distilled into the pearl that the Maiden carries "inmyddeȝ hyr breste" (222), as if it were the center of her being. The Pearl Poet effects an "entoptic" relationship[14] among the landscape, the Maiden, and the pearl on her breast—one enclosing or reflecting the other in different shapes, the essence remaining the same. Through this imagistic superimposition, the poet concentrates to the utmost the physical and spiritual impact of his central symbol, while he expands its dimension and depth into multiple forms.

The Maiden's human shape promises by association an incarnational function in her in that she might interpret divine values into familiar human terms. Yet it is evident that, as part of his strategy of symbolic alienation, the poet gradually removes her from the dreamer as possible incarnational intercessor through his plastic and grotesque presentation of her as an image of potential human perfection. Her grotesqueness is strangely intensified by the exotic beauty that mingles with it. The unnatural crossing of natures, seen first in the visionary landscape, is more gripping now, because it has altered the human visage itself. Half-transformed into precious effigy, the figure of the Maiden establishes an irrevocable sense of distance between man and the ideal form into which he wishes to be transmuted.

The poet-dreamer has rescued the Maiden—and by extension himself—through the shaping power of his art, from change and dissolution into beautiful permanence. Can the human sensibility accept her in this form as symbol of eternal, ever-vibrant life? Is it only because of the artist's failure of vision as man that she stands in contradiction to the higher reality she represents in her ossified, even repulsive splendor? Or is it possible that, as symbol, she actually participates in that reality, imaging an aspect in it that is dreadful and mysterious, withdrawing and enclosing its secret and its face, "clanly clos in golde," into an icon—a frozen image of hieratic ideality? Perhaps she reflects some devastating alteration of the self that we too must undergo within that ideal order, attaining to a different nature and form of beauty. If so, the Maiden functions then as a dissimilar similitude to potential human perfection, revealing the awesome paradox of that state by veiling it in a shape that is at once ravishing and terrifying, inviting and rejecting.

The dreamer does not grasp the nature of her change; his ignorance thus heightens the poem's dramatic irony and suspense. Yet he begins to intuit the distance separating him from her. His emotions oscillate violently between joy at her discovery and fearful astonishment, suggesting the mixture of ecstasy and dread felt by man as he confronts his own image within anagogic reality:

> Suche gladande glory con to me glace
> As lyttel byfore þerto watȝ wonte.
> To calle hyr lyste con me enchace,
> Bot baysment gef myn hert a brunt.
> I seȝ hyr in so strange a place,
> Such a burre myȝt make myn herte blunt.
> . . . .
> More þen my lyste my drede aros.
> I stod ful stylle and dorste not calle.
>
> (171–82)

The poet helps us relate to the dreamer's reaction by placing it within a familiar context rather than presenting it as an alien, unintelligible experience. He attains this by a descriptive stroke recalling the world of the court and the countryside, the romance and the beast fable:

> Wyth yȝen open and mouth ful clos
> I stod as hende as hawk in halle.
> (183–84)

This self-imposed simile diminishes the dreamer's human stature, casting him into the mute, unblinking stance of the bird. At the same time—following the typical medieval strategy of auctorial self-disparagement—the image makes the dreamer more appealing to us in his pathetic helplessness. Altogether, it reminds us of an all-encompassing ironic perspective that the author commands in the work as a mature artist, subjecting even himself to it.

The image of the predatory bird reflects, moreover, the dreamer's rapacious possessiveness toward the Maiden. The poet has caught the intentness of these emotions into suspended kinesthetic tension: the explosive immobility, the mouth shut tight, the wide-open, glaring eyes. He incarnates man's spiritual stance toward the ideal with pinpoint accuracy and concreteness. At the same time, he is able to suggest the precariousness of that ideal by capturing it in a moment of taut, excruciating concentration and expectancy. The image, finally, has an anticipatory function. Although as heraldic, noble bird the hawk manages to preserve something of the dreamer's human dignity, it initiates a series of animal images whose changing form will mark the gradual but relentless devastation of that dignity in the hands of the divine.

What further underscores the Maiden's metaphysical distance from the dreamer is the strongly defined ritualistic quality of her appearance and demeanor. The poet creates this quality through his *effictio* which handles each detail about her as in the landscape—delineating it sharply within its context and enriching it as a discrete, almost isolated emblematic entity, then fitting it to a strict architectonic sequence (163–80, 193–228). The poet appears to reinforce his Pygmalion-like relationship to the Maiden as construction of ideality by having her remain for a while still as a statue. Then, as if animated by his desiring gaze, she begins to move with selective motion:

> Þenne verez ho vp her fayre frount
> . . . .
> Þat gracios gay . . .
> Ryseȝ vp in hir araye ryalle
> . . . .
> Enclynande lowe in wommon lore,

> Ca3te of her coroun of grete tresore
> And haylsed me wyth a lote ly3te.
>   (177–238)

Her sparse but structured gestures obey a ritual order, reflecting, as symbolic action, the definite and irrevocable framework of values which she embodies and in which she moves in the visionary ideal realm. The dreamer's confrontation with this framework constitutes in essence the work's dramatic conflict.

The Maiden's greeting motion encourages the dreamer to speak, and immediately he tries to establish her identity:

> "O perle," quod I, "in perle3 py3t,
> Art þou my perle þat I haf playned,
> Regretted by myn one on ny3te?"
>   (241–43)

In ironic contrast with his initial assurance that he "knew hyr wel," the foregoing question betrays his mounting apprehension that she might be different from what he had hoped to find. But more subtly it discloses the dreamer's enterprising self-pity, a quality that humanizes and further validates his bereavement precisely because of its comic touch of self-interest and maudlin affectation. For, indeed, his question about her identity soon turns into a display of his injured feelings. His language of the courtly lover is all too conscious of its suffering and forlornness, reeking with languishing pathos. Earlier, there was "no gladder gome heþen into Grece" than he to find her again (231–32); now he almost reproaches her for living a happy life "in Paradys erde, of stryf vnstrayned" (248), while he mourns for her alone at night, "pensyf, payred, . . . forpayned" (242–46). His self-dramatization and the petulant indirection of his complaint take him to the brink of the ludicrous but also lend to his grief greater human authenticity.

Both as jewel "in gemme3 gente" and as human being "wyth y3en graye," she sets on her head "hyr coroun of perle orient" and responds to him (253–56). The poem develops now more explicitly into an extended confrontation between two opposing viewpoints and natures. A master of contrasts, the poet captures this antithesis in tonal counterpoint: the voice of the dreamer moves from optimistic exultation to whimpering self-pity, from pathetic lyricism to nagging envy. Against his violently modulating *duplum,* we hear the Maiden's crystalline, sober voice like a sustained *cantus firmus,* articulating evenly and inexorably the divine theme. Her hieratic gesture—like the wearing of the vestments of sacred authority—rules out any familiar proximity or intimate inclination toward the dreamer's private grief on her part. She corrects him "soberly" and with stern incisiveness:

> Sir, ȝe haf your tale mysetente,
> To say your perle is al awaye,
> Þat is in cofer so comly clente
> As in þis gardyn gracios gaye,
> Hereinne to lenge for euer and play,
> Þer mys nee mornyng com neuer nere.
>
> (257–62)

The image of the pearl "in cofer so comly clente" (259) revives the ambivalent effect (initially found in line 2) of exquisite fineness imprisoned in its own perfection. What complicates that ambivalence is the indelible duality of "cofer" as treasure chest and coffin. Perfect beauty is enveloped here by the trappings of mortality in an image that incarnates with stinging poignancy man's eschatological ecstasy and revulsion.

The Maiden informs the dreamer that what he lost

> . . . watȝ bot a rose
> Þat flowred and fayled as kynde hyt gef.
> Now þurȝ kynde of þe kyste þat hyt con close
> To a perle of prys hit is put in pref.
>
> (269–72)

She thus summarizes and brings to a focal point the transformation that has taken place up to now—in the "erber" and in the visionary landscape—from mutable nature to ideal permanent artifice, foreshadowing at the same time the manner of its anagogic fulfillment, in accordance with the poet's symbolic strategy. What overriding response is the poet trying to elicit in the reader by this crucial transformation from rose to pearl in his search for a symbol of eternity? Why did he make this choice?

Several critics of *Pearl* have viewed the poet's symbolic choice as uncomplicated:[15] The rose fades; thus it represents the transience of this life. The pearl, on the other hand, is precious, perfect in shape, and durable; it is then the obvious choice as symbol of divine effulgence and immutability and, therefore, of immortality. Patricia Kean, in her fine survey of past analogues and sources, is one of the few who have recalled the interchangeable use of the pearl and the rose within the Christian tradition as symbols for the same idea: the Virgin, sainthood, and above all immortality.[16] Unfortunately, Kean does not risk any personal response to the artistic possibilities of this complementary use, perhaps in fear of unhistorical subjectivism or undue evocativeness. Nor does she concern herself with the theological justification for such symbolic multivalence—a pursuit more akin to her critical interests.

Because of their historical interchangeability as symbols of divine reality, I consider the poet's choice of the pearl over the rose as well studied in intention. To fully understand this intention, we must keep in mind the values that either symbol brings into the poem from tradition as against the values that it is meant to take on within the poem's unique context. I have already enumerated some of the pearl's traditional significations (chapter 2). I wish to turn now to those associations that have established the rose as symbol of mutability yet also of perfection and immortality.[17]

In the medieval symbolic tradition, as I have shown, the pearl has represented transience when associated with earthly treasure and worldly pleasure, both being subject to misfortune and decay. The rose, on the other hand, has served as symbol for the brevity of earthly beauty and for man's mortality precisely because of its physical attributes and biological life: its blossoming into colorful vitality, then its full, ripe bloom, followed shortly by stooping and withering and then by festering decay.

Using Isaiah's "flos decidens" (28:4 and 40:6–7) as prototype, Boethius, Fulgentius, Gregory the Great, Alexander Neckham, and Robert Holcot, among other medieval thinkers, developed their own metaphors, comparing man's passing beauty and life to a flower, especially the delectable but fragile rose.[18] They anchor almost systematically each stage in man's life on the concrete attributes of the gradually altering flower. For example, in his comparison of life to the three flowers of fortune—the rose, the heliotrope, and the lily—Holcot utters the growing pang of his age at life's ephemerality, accompanied by an increasing preoccupation with the physical details of human mortality and putrefaction:

> For while the petals of the lily are blooming, they stay in place, and smell delightfully, and encourage the sight; but when they fall from the stalk, they stink horribly. Just so bodily graces seem best when they flourish in youth, but when we come to old age, when the eyes begin to darken, and the other senses decline to earth . . . then the petals of the blooming lily fall, and the miseries of our body are clearly revealed.[19]

After the Black Death, the voice becomes more frantic, as the poet's eye watches the flower of life fade "lite and lite" into insubstantiality:

> This erthly joye, this worldy blisse,
> Is but a fikel fantasye,
> For now it is and now it nis—
> . . . .
> Ne no burde so bright in bour
> Of thritty wynter, I ensure thee,
> That she ne shal faden as a flour—
> Lite and lite lesen her beautee.[20]

One is struck by the stark melancholy of these utterances. The late medieval poet seems to cling desperately to those fragile moments of life and beauty that the flower embodies, felt more intensely because so fugitive. This tragic realization dominates the spiritual drama of *Pearl*, caught in the image of the "rose / Þat flowred and fayled as kynde hyt gef" (269–70)—the youthful, fresh child now "so clad in clot" (22). The dreamer will forget himself in the ideal realm and call his Pearl with pathetic irrelevancy "þou so ryche a reken rose" (906) and "lufly flor" (962), echoing man's indelible nostalgia—even in heaven—for the delectable moments experienced on this earth. Dante cleverly accommodated this homesickness by making these moments metaphors of eternal bliss. The question we face is why the Pearl Poet turned away from these moments of vibrant though fleeting life, as embodied in the rose, to a different metaphoric and imagistic medium.

Nevertheless, in medieval literature, the rose, like the pearl, embraced contrary meanings. This traditional multivalence reminds us repeatedly not to commit our exegesis to one interpretation. For even if the immediate context asks explicitly for one meaning, the author cannot, as I have previously observed, delete by mere thematic statement the remainder of the symbol's life and efficacy. The incarnationally oriented poet—such as Dante and the Pearl Poet—being aware of the symbol's richness and of his own limitations in fully controlling its impact, channels such richness to serve a larger and more inclusive theme: the complementarity of reality and man's attempt in the life of faith to reconcile its opposites.

The references to the rose as symbol of physical and, more significantly, spiritual regeneration are as numerous as those of death and decay. Barbara Seward has surveyed the history of the rose as symbol of fertility and the fundamental processes of natural life in mythical and classical times. It was further connected with love, marriage, sex, and procreation, with springtime and festivity.[21] These values follow

the rose well into medieval literature, assimilated and transformed by
the new context, especially within the Christian and courtly ethic. Being
part of the natural cycle, the rose—like the "sede" and the "grayneӡ
dede" in *Pearl* (34, 31)—symbolizes rebirth after natural and spiritual
death. William Langland, for example, employs the growth of the rose
as a vehicle with which to give concrete, experienceable form to the
mysterious and ineffable process of man's inner regeneration:

> Riht as the rose • that red is and swote
> Out of a ragged roote • and of rouwe breres
> Springeth and spredeth • that spicers desyreth.
> Or as whete out of a weod • waxeth vppon eorthe,
> So Dobest out of Dowel • and Dobet doth springe
> A-mong men of this molde • that meke ben, or kuynde.
>   (A, x.119–24)[22]

Saint Bernard of Clairvaux in the twelfth century initiates a tradition
of comparing Mary to the rose: the white rose represents her purity,
the red rose her suffering for her son and her love for mankind as its
intercessor.[23] We find this analogical connection expressed with the
utmost delicacy and simple charm in several medieval lyrics: "Heo is of
colour and beate / As fresch as is the Rose in May" and "Lady, flor of
all thing, / rose sine spina," for instance. Coming to the Pearl Poet, we
note in *Purity* (lines 1078–84) that spiritual filth and rottenness are
replaced by the cleansing fragrance of the rose, the Holy Virgin, who is
the "plantatio rosae in Jericho" (Ecclesiasticus, xxiv.18). Later on, Wil-
liam Dunbar will use simultaneously the pearl and the rose to symbolize
Mary, the "place palestrall, / Of peirles pulcritud; / . . . Bricht ball cris-
tal, ros virginall."[24] One can see that, had the Pearl Maiden remained a
rose rather than been transmuted by "þe kyste" (271) into a pearl, she
would be no less a symbol of purity and spiritual perfection.

Through the rose's association with Mary, we arrive at a more signifi-
cant connection, theologically and poetically—that between the rose
and Christ himself—as in the following carol:

> Ther is no ro(se of) swych vertu
> As is the rose that bar Jhesu;
>   *Alleluya.*
>
> For in this rose conteynyd was
> Heuen and erthe in lytyl space,
>   *Res miranda.*

> Be that rose we may weel see
> That he is God in personys thre,
> *Pari forma.*[25]

The rose embodies here the mystery of the Incarnation, where "Heuen and erthe"—divine and human nature, spirit and matter—are brought into sacramental reconciliation. Worked into the symbol is the startling spatial paradox of infinite divinity "conteynyd . . . in lytyl space." The rose as humble material creature becomes the *speculum* through which we may perceive also the lofty mystery of the Trinity.

A poem of this kind is more than an intellectual game of emblematic deciphering. It re-creates the mysterious experience of the Incarnation by the irresolvable tension it elicits through a series of imagistic and verbal conceits. A lowly object and a humble style—as *caro* and *verbum*—despite their natural ineptitude, are made to express a vast and sublime notion. By either conscious design or intuition, the lyric poet heightens the tension in the paradox by his spare, understated expression. It is in a similar vein that Raymond Oliver responds to the incarnational subtlety and force of the famous "I syng of a myden," where the "imperceptible, refreshing" falling of the dew is "a flawlessly apt metaphor" for the ineffable descent of the germinating Holy Spirit upon Mary.[26]

Because of its capacity to embody divine mystery simultaneously in a complex intellectual form and in the form of the commonplace and everyday, the rose as symbol reconciles also the two different types of medieval spirituality and poetic mentality: the Thomistic and the Franciscan.[27] In that sense, it integrates all levels of perception and response in the act of faith. While it functions as intricate doctrinal conceit in a highly developed theological system, it also encompasses the less articulate, more affective, and therefore more popular aspect of medieval faith, which focuses more on the love than on the understanding that binds man with God.

Perhaps because of its association with earthly suffering and with mortality, the rose came to represent those who died for the love of God in martyrdom.[28] Inevitably, the red rose became the symbol of the Archmartyr, its red color representing his shed blood, in both a historical and a sacramental sense. Consequently, the Resurrection and its corollary promise of man's immortality were also symbolized by the rose: by its recurrent flowering within nature's cycle and by the splendor of its full bloom. These metaphoric connections with martyrdom and immortality have been developed with astonishing doctrinal and imaginative ingenuity by medieval writers, such as Saint Ambrose,

Walafred Strabo, Bernard of Clairvaux, and Albertus Magnus, to mention a few.[29] Especially in Franciscan spirituality, the rose, through its association with the Passion, became a vibrant symbol of God's ardent love for man, often borrowing the febrile, sensual language of human love to express itself.[30]

Indeed, what complicates—yet validates enormously—the rose as symbol of divine ardor is its age-old connection with erotic passion. It would be a futile and superfluous task to list here the countless *reverdies* and love lyrics of medieval Europe and England in which the rose stands for amorous desire and especially for the fragrant, delicate sexuality of woman. Such erotic symbolism culminates, as is well known, in the *Roman de la Rose,* a work of profound influence in its time, felt no less in *Pearl.* The tenor, woman, is hidden—yet delectably revealed— through an imagistic strategy of intricate suggestiveness, subtle and languorously refined in the hands of Guillaume de Lorris, robust and parodic in Jean de Meun's sequel.

In the fascinating exchange between the language—and consequently the experience—of divine love and human passion in medieval poetry, the rose becomes a rich vehicle in which these essentially antagonistic sentiments fuse. As long as the kinship between the two loves remains ineffable and paradoxical, it produces that stress which is at the core of medieval Christian spirituality and which results in vibrating poetry: Divine love takes on the fervor and concrete familiarity of human passion, while human passion, in its analogical function, is redeemed and elevated to its perfect form, which is in God. The power of the rose as similitude lies in the sense we have that somehow both loves, however different, are being simultaneously fulfilled in it. By achieving such a dynamic reconciliation, the rose as poetic symbol stands as a striking analogue to God's own sacrament of reconciliation, the Incarnation. As analogue, the poetic symbol participates in the reality of the sacrament. It is the sacrament conceived in an aesthetic order.

It was the realization of its metaphoric potency and inclusiveness, I believe, that must have stirred Dante toward the rose as eschatological symbol. In expanding this lowly creature into the very framework of his anagogic universe, Dante exploits to the fullest the tension that resides in the ontological and spatial paradox of that leap. The rose must have represented to him the maximum poetic approximation to the achievement of the Incarnation as metaphysical and poetic principle, and especially as the reconciliation between God and man. His symbolic choice was consistent, therefore, with the unitive fulfillment granted him at the end of his journey. So, too, I believe that the Pearl Poet's selection of the pearl as anagogic symbol, rather than the rose, reflects his particular sense of the proximity or distance between divine and human reality, between God and man, dramatized in the dreamer's own unitive attempt at the poem's climax. Whether the Pearl Poet was aware of Dante's work or not, we can better understand the intention behind his choice by comparing it with Dante's. Its effect will become more evident in our study of the New Jerusalem, where the pearl dominates as basic substance. In the meantime, we can make some preliminary observations.

The reader acquainted with the rose's symbolic background tends to experience a sense of loss upon the Maiden's announcement of its transformation into a pearl. With the rose, nature is dismissed here as comforter, as familiar similitude of regeneration. The pearl has been used as symbol of the precious uniqueness and the perfection of the divine. But as finished artifact and with its self-sufficient spherical shape it evokes an indelible sense of captive enshrinement within the isolation of its own perfection, barring off any lesser reality that surrounds it. Frozen into hard permanence, it lacks as image the life instinct and vital inner movement of the rose. It thus prevents us from participating concretely and with savor in the experience of spiritual self-realization through the symbol's own biological fulfillment. Though associated with the splendor and refinement of the courtly experience, the pearl—especially as depicted in the bloodless whiteness of the Maiden's visage—lacks the flushing emotion and the passionate ardor of the rose's fresh bloom and red color. To these qualities we cannot help responding more intimately as affective and sensual beings—a fact that the Pearl Poet is aware of. Finally, as symbol of martyrdom and divine compassion, the rose beckons suffering man to it; it does not keep him at a distance with the dispassionate composure of self-enclosed perfection. These preliminary evaluations would indeed seem precariously arbitrary if they were not supported by symbolic tradition and by the different ways in which Dante and the Pearl Poet construct the anagogic realm, placing questing man in it.

With the Maiden's dismissal of the rose from this realm and her establishment of the pearl as symbol of immortality, the Pearl Poet activates an irresolvable dialectic in the reader's mind, where intellectual cognition of a certain announced symbolic value vies with the contradictions of affective and sensuous experience: What stands best for eternity and for palpitating life—the cyclic regeneration of the transient or the unalterable fixity of the permanent? What, in fact, constitutes perfection—an infinite process of self-realization or the utter stillness of ultimate fulfillment? This dialectic lies at the core of man's eschatological anxiety.

THE DEBATE

The dreamer does not appear to understand the significance of the Maiden's transformation, nor does he follow the dialectic it initiates concerning the nature of anagogic reality and man's position in it. To be sure, he apologizes to her for having failed to recognize earlier her mode of existence. Yet he shows no greater insight now when with billowing emotion he congratulates himself for having found her, hoping to rejoin her (279–88). He tries to placate her with an overearnest courtliness ("My blysfol beste"), which soon becomes mangled by his possessive impetuosity: "I shall ma feste / And wony wyth hyt in schyr wodschaweȝ." His clumsy middle-class daintiness adds another comic yet humanizing touch to his character. His sweeping vow to love his Lord and "al his laweȝ" reminds us ironically of his previous unwillingness to abide by these laws when they did not accommodate him—as in the garden of mutability. Because too facile, his promise forebodes only further complication and conflict.

His buoyant optimism is punctured by a devastating rebuke. The Maiden relegates man's innate questioning as to the nature of things to a ludicrous collectivity, from which she separates herself: "Wy borde ȝe men? So madde ȝe be!" (290). This utterance articulates what was presaged imagistically by her precious enclosure: her remoteness from the human condition. Dramatically, it anticipates the state to which he will be reduced eventually, raving and pathetic. In contrast to his disordered happy outburst, the Maiden proceeds with merciless exactness to analyze the dreamer's "þre . . . vnavysed . . . wordeȝ" (291–92). Her answer has the detached tone and lucid structure of a *respondeo* in a scholastic *summa*. She counters his "objections" systematically by summarizing them and then expanding on each point in her response (291–324): First, she is not there just because he sees her, for man cannot base his belief only on what his senses validate. Second, he cannot hope to dwell with her "in þis bayly" without requesting what he essentially does not deserve: divine permission. And third, he cannot cross the stream barrier except "þurȝ drwry deth," because that right "watȝ forgarte [forfeited] at Paradys greue" by "oure ȝorefader."

With this response, the work has modulated from a symbolic to a discursive mode of presenting divine truth, though not as exclusively as it has been claimed in past criticism. The methodical articulateness of these doctrinal statements promises to elucidate divine truth and to effect some rational persuasion in the dreamer and us. It remains to be seen whether the Maiden's discourse is an explanation of divine law or a mere restatement of its axioms. I want to pursue this question by examining the rationality of some of her theological arguments and her means of demonstrating them through analogical similitudes.

A. C. Spearing, one of the poem's most astute critics, assumes that the change in mode at this point of the poem has taken place, because "the Dreamer has shown that he is unable to make any further progress through the development of symbolism." Hence, "the human drama of the encounter between Dreamer and Maiden continues to unfold . . . accompanied not by any symbolic development but by the development of argument and explicit doctrine." The pearl symbol—and I assume also the Maiden, since Spearing rightly objects to any symbolic distinction between them—undergoes no further development. After all, the pearl is mentioned only a few times and mainly in reference to what has gone on before. Spearing warns the reader not to search for any hidden allegorical meaning or any veiled mystery in the discourse. The Maiden herself provides exegesis whenever necessary in the form of the medieval sermon. The poet, furthermore, does not rely on the reader to interpret the discourse out of his own knowledge of current exegesis. The poet himself takes care to supply an explicit and careful interpretation.[31]

Let us, however, consider for a moment who the elucidator is. Despite the generic function of the rational guide that the Maiden brings into the poem, can the reader—after being exposed to her symbolic complexity—really expect her utterance to be more intelligible or less alien to the human sensibility? For, after all, her utterance is an extension of her symbolic substance as symbolic action in verbal form. I suggest, further, what may appear banally obvious but what is often forgotten: that the Pearl Maiden's discourse is subject to the same epistemological difficulties as all theology of revelation. In discussing these difficulties, I am guided by Thomas Aquinas's comments on metaphoric representation in both theology and poetry and its relation to rational statement.[32]

We have already observed the Pearl Poet's use of verbal wit and word play to assert the essential mystery of divine reality. He has used this verbal play in order to accompany and sustain the imagistic presentation of such a thesis in a crescendo of symbolic paradoxes. In the debate, he aims at strengthening that thesis by a series of discursive paradoxes as well, involving conceptual thought and its rational expression.

We discover that the Maiden's discourse has a tight syllogistic structure:

> "Thow demeȝ noȝt bot doel-dystresse,"
> Þenne sayde þat wyȝt. "Why dotȝ þou so?

> For dyne of doel of lureȝ lesse
> Ofte mony mon forgos þe mo.
> Þe oȝte better þyseluen blesse,
> And loue ay God, in wele and wo,
> For anger gayneȝ þe not a cresse.
> Who nedeȝ schal þole, be not so þro."
>
> (337–44)

The frequency of logical connectives—"why . . . for," "when . . . þen," "if . . . þen," "for þo þou . . . þou most," and so on—suggests rational cohesion and progression. But such structure is deceptive; it stands in ironic relationship to its content. For each of the Maiden's theological statements subverts its own validity by the metaphoric terms it uses to demonstrate itself. The cause of this subversion is the natural inadequacy of human terminology to explain a reality outside its own system. Each doctrinal dictum begins with concrete human terms as supporting "phantasms" and then moves to an abstract theological concept. But the mind can never return to the supporting concrete similitude to validate that concept through experience—the basis to all human understanding, according to Thomas. Similitude and abstract concept, in this case, derive from totally different modes of being. It is in this violent juxtaposition between divine concept and inept human metaphor that Walter Ong locates "the tension of belief."

We note, furthermore, that the tension becomes more powerful when the similitude tyrannizes over the tenuous, abstract idea, tending to define it totally through its own reality. The human mind of course resists this usurpation because it recognizes the fundamental irrelevance between analogical terms: the abstract notion and the concrete experience that is employed as its metaphor. Theology and poetry, being suprarational in nature, cannot survive on a purely abstract level and are at the mercy of metaphoric concretion. Man cannot transcend this stress of seeking cohesion between these terms—except through death. Then he can attain to a direct, intellectual, "angelic" comprehension of ultimate reality. This is what the Maiden offers to the dreamer: his "corse in clot mot calder keue" (320) for him to "þurȝoutly hauen cnawyng" (859), a prospect fraught at once with the terror and the promised ecstasy of that final quest. While still in historical time, the dreamer has no choice but to accept divine value "with the maximum of certitude and a minimum of understanding," as Walter Ong well puts it.[33]

Attracted to the problem mainly as an epistemological one—dealing, that is, with man's knowledge of God—Thomas did not pursue the artistic possibilities of the stress involved in the metaphoric exploration of ultimate reality. Neither does Ong in his brilliant commentary on Aquinas's views, limited also as he is by the compass of his chosen examples: brief doctrinal statements in verse. In longer works, like the *Divine Comedy* and *Pearl,* this stress lends itself to an extended dramatic order, which asserts its own value as aesthetic experience. In *Pearl,* let us remember, the comprehension of theological truth is not a game of dispassionate abstractions. It is presented, instead, as an immediate existential drama dealing with one man's deep personal loss, resulting in his rebellion against the universal scheme of things that permits such a loss. The hero tries to see his bereavement in terms of a higher unity by comprehending this scheme and its overarching imperatives. In that understanding lies his consolation. By ordering this spiritual effort into a complex pattern of human discovery and frustration, the poet not only evokes the character of his subject—divine mystery and the tension of belief—he also feeds the reader's aesthetic yearning for intricate, vital texture interacting dynamically with its delimiting outer structure. Such patterning does not function only as expressive form; it also gives the artist a sense of control, a form of conquest over ineffable reality and his experience of it. In that conquest, however partial, man feels an affinity with God the creator and orderer—a supreme realization which, too, offers him consolation.

To return to the text, in the Maiden's foregoing three-point correction, we are struck by the irony of at least one of these points. The Maiden warns the dreamer not to take appearance for reality (259–96) or to think of heaven in earthly terms. Yet she herself, through her language of accommodation, orients his perception of the transcendent along these terms in all their earthbound impact. She scolds him for the inadequacy of his vision, yet she thickens the veil before his eyes with her metaphoric images. Although she possesses a direct intellectual comprehension of divine reality, "cnawyng," in order to fulfill her role as spiritual guide, she must submit—as Christ did—to the necessity as well as to the inherent limitations of incarnational expression. This realization on the part of the reader is intended, I believe, to temper his patronizing attitude toward the dreamer as "hopelessly literal-minded"[34] and spiritually insensitive. Limited spiritual perception is not unique to him but is presented by the poet as part of the human condition—what Christ in his compassion understood and responded to by entering that condition.

The Maiden's rebuke and the prospect of self-dissolution that faces him, if he dares cross to her realm, catapult the dreamer from exultant hope to plangent despair, thus continuing the poem's emotional dialectic between joy and disappointment. No metaphysical argument can persuade away his anguish at the realization that discovering the ideal can be more painful for imperfect man than losing it:[35]

> Now haf I fonte þat I forlete,
> Schal I efte forgo hit er euer I fyne?
> Why schal I hit boþe mysse and mete?
> . . . .
> What serueȝ tresor, bot gareȝ men grete,
> When he hit schal efte wyth teneȝ tyne?
> (327–32)

Added to this is the equally painful and irreducible paradox, inherited from the fall of "oure ȝorefader," that the dreamer must first become what he must ultimately transcend: "clot," the earth (319–20).

The dreamer's "doel-dystresse" (337) appears to the Maiden not merely inappropriate and unworthy of compassion but curiously incomprehensible. For she asks—not merely in scolding but as if unaware of human motives—"Why dotȝ þou so?" (338). She responds to his misery only by erecting against it with stern detachment God's irrevocable decrees. The Maiden presents God's relationship to man in a significant fashion. God stands here as the inflexible "Dryȝtyn," who "of þe way a fote ne wyl he wryþe" (349–50). He is the awesome Romanesque judge, who does not seek to justify his ways to man; he demands total submission. She reduces man in his anguished questioning to a ludicrous, subhuman caricature of helplessness:

> For þoȝ þou daunce as any do,
> Braundysch and bray þy braþeȝ breme,
> When þou no fyrre may, to ne fro,
> Þou moste abyde þat he schal deme.
> (345–48)

The intent heraldic hawk—man about to clasp the rediscovered ideal—is changed now to a wild, braying animal cornered into subjection. We hear his struggle and bellowing in the explosive alliterative *b*'s (346). Dramatically, the image brings us closer to the poem's climax by foreshadowing it: the frenzied hero throwing himself against the barrier of the stream. The inexorability of the divine imperatives confronting the dreamer is relentlessly echoed by the repeated link word: "deme . . . deme" (VI). The Maiden demands that he "loue ay God, in wele and wo" (342), not out of any choice but because his anguish "gayneȝ . . . not a cresse" (343). By withdrawing that choice and by pointing to his total impotence, the Maiden annihilates the dreamer's human dignity, rendering him pathetic and even comic. Does this debasement of human sorrow and the near mockery of human infirmity reflect the poet's own view of man, or does it perhaps disguise some reproach toward God?

The Maiden's stern manner has been predominantly regarded as salutary to the dreamer and theologically correct. Dorothy Everett, for example, takes it for granted that it should be so:

> Since his [the dreamer's] serene confidence, and even his power to understand, was not achieved unaided, but was the result of divine revelation both direct and through the teaching of the Church, the person of the instructor is rightly represented as insusceptible of human emotion, remote and incomprehensible, while the person of the instructed remains human and prone to emotion, and for that reason able to arouse emotion.[36]

Yet we must note the poet's intentional accentuation of divine heartlessness: to this God—and to his visionary spokesman—man's tortured "mende3 [opinions] mounte3 not a myte, / Þa3 [man] . . . for sor3e be neuer blyþe" (351–52). There is an indelible air of relish in this statement meant, I think, to elicit a powerful response in the reader as human sufferer. The poet wishes to heighten the dramatic tension between man in his frailty and the absolute, inscrutable decrees he must measure up to. He therefore highlights that aspect of divine reality which is by nature "insusceptible of human emotion, remote and incomprehensible." The Maiden's manner is made to reflect this aspect as symbolic action but also in affective terms: stern, inexorable, alien, withdrawing. In this sense, emotion takes on a symbolic efficacy, while certain imagistic values brought about by her transhumanization—such as her plastic perfection—find now their full expression as feeling, not only as pure intellectual dialectic. Symbol becomes emotion, and emotion symbol.

What intensifies the mystery of the order of justice against which the Maiden measures the dreamer's complaint is, paradoxically, her use of familiar legal terms to explain it. These belong to the legal terminology of the feudal court—"þis bayly" (315), as the Maiden calls her heavenly dwelling. Man's fall from Paradise, for example, is described as a legal forfeiture ("forgarte" [321]). Terms such as "try3e" (311), to try a case; "sesed in" (417), to be the legal possessor of a thing; "herytage" (417), and so on, are used here with some technical rigor, in order to demonstrate to the dreamer the workings of divine law.[37] It is difficult to assess the effect of these analogies on the medieval reader. Being part of his everyday life, they must have held for him greater immediacy than for us; he could not dispel their concrete reality, even in his metaphoric thinking, as easily as we. One must allow, however, for a multiple response—then and now. The coherence and familiarity of these legal terms lend a sense of impartiality and fairness. On the other hand, applied as they are with exactness where mercy should reign and accompanied by the tolling refrain "deme . . . deme," they cast on divine justice an aura of unsparing, even fearsome impersonality.

To complicate matters, after orienting the dreamer's perception of divine justice along these analogical terms, the Maiden turns around and denies their relevance. Degree ceases to exist in the plentitude of God. His magnanimity overwhelms any exact estimate of merit—the measure that human justice applies. But the dreamer as man cannot possibly conceive the infinitude of God's mercy and abundance. Ironically, in her rigorous application of these analogues—even with the ultimate purpose of negating them—the Maiden establishes their reality all too strongly and thus shapes our conception of divine justice according to them almost irrevocably. No categorical abstract statement unverified by human experience can delete them from our consciousness, although intellectually we are aware of their ineptitude since they belong to a different order of being. Through our own perceptual stress, we are thus compelled by the poet to empathize with the dreamer's inability to transcend such terms in the course of the debate.

The dreamer's reaction to the Maiden's "legalistic" assessment of his spiritual crisis sustains with some tenacity the affective counterpoint of the work. However featureless he may be as a dramatic character and however public his feelings, he responds in an emotionally complex and well-modulated fashion, which helps us identify with him (361 ff.). He pleads forgiveness for his rash speech and explains his sorrow with touching restraint and courtesy. He recalls to her their past relationship and his present forlornness in simple, yet highly poignant language:

> And, quen we departed, we wern at on;
> God forbede we be now wroþe,
> We meten so selden by stok oþer ston.
>
> (378–80)

From plaintive pathos he plunges into profound self-debasement:

> Þa3 cortaysly 3e carp con
> I am bot mol and manere3 mysse.
>
> (381–82)

We cannot tell to what extent this is sincere self-appraisal, to what extent enterprising self-pity. Yet we cannot totally overlook the irony of her stinging speech having been "courteous"—perhaps a subtle reproach veiled in excessive compliment and bathos. The dreamer rebukes her piteously for her happy accommodation and her indifference toward his grief (385–88). Yet he is also dexterously resilient and cautious. He does not dwell on his complaint but sidesteps all previous rebuff and moves "wythouten debate" to more pressing business: locating her blissful dwelling, understanding her mode of existence, still with the hope of sharing in it (386–96). It can be seen, therefore, that the poet has created in the dreamer not a vapid allegorical type but a dramatic character of intricate specificity yet universal validity—qualities that characterize the poem's drama as a whole.

Upon his apology, the Maiden's tone softens, not because she responds now to the legitimacy of his sorrow, whose cause she has been, but because he promises utter obeisance. She proceeds, then, to explain heaven and her place in it (409 ff.).

In her description of divine reality, the Maiden continues to resort and with increasing tenacity to human analogues. She turns now to the images and values of the earthly court. She represents God as a chivalric king wooing his lady. Christ's virtues are those of a knight: "hys prese, hys prys, and hys parage [noble lineage]" (419). The Maiden presents herself as the wooed bride and crowned queen, dwelling in a castle, "þis bayly" (315).

Since the Maiden grounds the dreamer's perception so forcibly in the splendid images and the hierarchical coherence of the earthly court, it is inevitable that he should reach out to them as a means of grasping ineffable reality. To accuse him of viewing the Maiden's estate "in grossly material terms . . . as [being] something of a snob . . . [with] a keen sense of social status, a tendency to see reality in terms of social differences,"[38] would claim for the critic an "angelic imagination" which neither the Maiden nor the poet displays here. For the Pearl Poet luxuriates in the brilliance and grandeur of his royal similitudes, unheeding Pseudo-Dionysius's warning—echoed by the author of *The Cloud of Unknowing*—against the enticements of the material analogical image. He heeds, however, Pseudo-Dionysius's corollary conviction that the descriptions man makes of God are both true and untrue and that the analogical image, despite its inadequacy, is indispensable to man's spiritual vision and even spiritually uplifting.[39] The poet's achievement lies in his ability to impress upon us the irrelevance of his similitude while celebrating at the same time its own reality and beauty.

This "double truth" in the analogical similitude, which the human mind is constantly asked to absorb, is dramatized by the Maiden's attempt to deny the similitude's validity through the use of its own terms. When the dreamer, remembering Mary's supreme position, questions the Maiden's queenship—according to the analogical criteria that she herself has established—the Maiden draws a distinction between earthly and heavenly court. After structuring it according to human hierarchical principles, she now claims for the heavenly court a unique quality, "a property in hytself beyng" (446), of celestial egalitarianism. Yet the terms with which she describes this egalitarianism remain those of the human hierarchy: the divine denizens are made equal, yet they are still presented as kings and queens, existing in an order of rank where Mary reigns as "emperise" (441). The logical antagonism between hierarchy and equivalence is obvious. The Maiden's intent use of the terms of the former to sustain the latter—its opposite—only testifies to the paradoxical and inscrutable nature of the order of relation, of divine "cortaysye,"[40] that she tries to explain to the dreamer.

The poet's goal is twofold: He wants to impress upon us the essential inadequacy of all human formulation of the divine, symbolic or conceptual. At the same time, his *discordia concors* is not aimed at a totally negative realization, for it reminds us also of an overarching coherence, incomprehensible to man, where divine justice and the law of the court or the marketplace participate somehow in each other's reality, where these distant analogates are brought together in a state of mutual fulfillment and sacramental integration. Any total alienation between them would only truncate the unity of God's universal order.

The Maiden's legal and royal analogates—both as concrete images and as rational constructs—fail to clarify divine justice to the dreamer. In fact, he rebels against its arbitrariness, as she has presented it. Almost invariably, critics of the poem point to his spiritual insensitivity and his inability to transcend earthly values as the unreasonable causes of his rebellion. Both limitations are present in him, no doubt. But, despite the social terms he uses—"quene," "countes," "a lady of lasse aray" (486–92)—and his earthbound mentality, we cannot overlook his theologically valid complaint that the righteous man should be treated by God less favorably than those untested in the faith (469–85). He is astute enought to refer, through the Psalmist, to God's promise of rewarding man's moral struggle (591–96). Indeed, the eventual presence in the poem of Christ as man's fellow sufferer will elevate rather than diminish the worth of that struggle.

To be sure, the dreamer is not fighting here for the integrity of some universal principle as much as for his own accommodation. The irony is evident. Whereas before he had protested with passionate earnestness that he was "ful fayn" for the Maiden's worshipful "astate" (393–94), now the threat of his receiving less honor and bliss disgruntles him to no end and brings him to comic exasperation: "Bot a quene! Hit is to dere a date" (492). In response to his indignation, the Maiden repeats Christ's parable of the vineyard.

Several critics consider the parable's meaning in the poem explicit and rational.[41] It hides no undercurrent significance, no mystery to be further explored; the Maiden explains all. Christ used the vineyard in his parable and established its *significatio* for all time and in all contexts. This *significatio* has been further crystallized into conceptual clarity by exegesis. And, I would agree, once this intellectual stratum has been added to the similitude, we cannot ignore it any more than any other symbolic value. But we must see it in a tense dialectic with the other strata of the similitude—its sensuous and emotional impact and the pressure of the poem's context. Certainly, these affect any preestablished conceptual meaning and alter it.

The Maiden tries to explain to the dreamer divine justice, and especially divine rewards according to grace or merit, again resorting to the images and relationships of earthly existence in order to accommodate his human perception. As in her legal and royal similitudes, we see here once again symbolic irony working against her as divine spokesman in a significant way. She chides the dreamer for believing in appearances (295–96) and for thinking of heaven in earthly terms. Yet, as I have mentioned, she herself orients his perception along these terms, whose earthbound impact she increases by her intense statement of them—whether for an affirmative or a negative analogical purpose.

The vineyard comes from the world of the fading rose, which has already been rejected from the ideal realm because it is transient. With its harvest, the vineyard brings to mind the complementary associations of God's plenty but also of death met in the garden in a season, not of the traditional springtime context of regeneration, but "Quen corne is coruen wyth croke3 kene" (40). It was when his daughter was gathered up "as newe fryt to God ful due" (894). We cannot dispel from our experience—much as we try to intellectually—the autumnal emotional hue of the image, sombered by the shadows of the approaching night:

> Sone þe worlde bycom wel broun;
> Þe sunne wat3 doun and hit wex late.
> (537–38)

The poet goes so far as to depart from Matthew's narrative to make the vineyard a vital experience in its own terms. It is as if he insists passionately on the integrity of the *res* of his symbolic image—the thing in itself—as if he is saying that his spiritual truth will be as valid as his figure. This is a central principle in medieval symbolism, despite its Platonizing impulses.

The powerful images of movement, of human toil and noise, sustained by the imitative alliteration, cement our touch with the vineyard as an experience that asserts its own values indelibly:

> Wryþen and worchen and don gret pyne,
> Keruen and caggen and man hit clos.
>
> (511–12)

The colloquial, racy exchange between lord and laborers, not found in the biblical narrative, moves us from distant description to immediate reenactment:

> "More haf we serued, vus þynk so,
> Þat suffred han þe daye3 hete,
> Þenn þyse þat wro3t not houre3 two,
> And þou dot3 hem vus to counterfete."
> Þenne sayde þe lorde to on of þo:
> "Frende, no waning I wyl þe 3ete;
> Take þat is þyn owne, and go.
> And I hyred þe for a peny agrete,
> Quy bygynne3 þou now to þrete?
> Wat3 not a pené þy couenaunt þore?
> Fyrre þen couenaunde is no3t to plete.
> Wy schalte þou þenne ask more?"
>
> (553–64)

The poet mimics the tone of voice in the contending parties: the grumbling collectivity of the laborers ("vus þynk so") and the inhibiting confidence of the lord, challenging them with sharp, hard-nosed questions. The poet cannot resist the specific detail, even if he must invent it: "Þenne sayde þe lorde to on of þo" (557). To what extent is this concrete realism a serious limitation; to what extent does it facilitate the poet's thematic and artistic intentions?

Erich Auerbach speaks of the Bible's *sermo humilis,* "the lowly, or humble, style . . . in which . . . sublime mysteries can be brought within the reach of men." This style of expression parallels God's self-expression as man through the Incarnation. There exists a perpetual tension between the lofty event and the lowly style that articulates it, as there is tension between the essential antagonism of the two natures and the sacramental kinship into which they have been brought. "Simple, vul-

gar, and crassly realistic words are employed, the syntax is often collo-
quial and inelegant; but the sublimity of the subject matter," Auerbach
continues, "shines through the lowliness, and there is hidden meaning
at every turn."[42]

The tension between human vehicle and divine tenor is brought to
the breaking point by the Pearl Poet's concrete realism in his adapta-
tion of biblical narrative. This becomes evident earlier in his presenta-
tion of Paul's metaphor of the harmonious body, with Christ as its head
and men as its subservient members (1 Cor. 12:12–13). Paul's narrative
retains some suggestive generality which allows the sublime notion of
heavenly harmony "to shine through," at least enough to demand equal
attention as abstract concept. The Pearl Poet concentrates on the mate-
rial surface of the similitude too forcefully at times to allow the intellect
to penetrate its density and arrive at the intended spiritual meaning. In
this case, his keen eye is not content with Paul's "arme and legg"; it
must also find the "naule" (459). As with the disgruntled laborers, the
poet cannot resist a touch of comic realism in the squabbling members:

> Þy heued hatȝ nauþer greme ne gryste,
> On arme oþer fynger þaȝ þou ber byȝe.
>   (465–66)

He verges here on hilarious, rustic grotesquerie at the possibility that
the head would demand out of spite or, better, gall ("greme [or]
gryste") to wear a ring just like the finger. The parody on the contend-
ing members of the body distracts from the sublimity of divine "cortay-
sye," which it is meant to incarnate.

Similarly, in his more extended presentation of biblical narrative in
the parable of the vineyard, we almost lose sight of the didactic, tran-
scendental aim in vivid, anecdotal realism. The earthbound impact of
this concrete style shatters the aura of spiritual suggestiveness and mys-
tery. The poet holds us too fast in the earthly framework and within
time, in a front yard where they are all gathered after a day's work,
when "Þe sunne watȝ doun and hit wex late" (538). In a sense, then,
the vineyard as divine similitude betrays its spiritual aim to the extent
that it establishes its own reality—which is inevitable. Its cycle of effort
and reward is so strongly asserted in our sensibility as to resist any
intellectual attempt at negating that cycle in its familiar form. Added to
this experiential contradiction are certain arbitrary paradoxes that I
shall elaborate upon presently: the first are made last and the last first;
the rewards of heaven are the same while they are different.

As a similitude against itself, the vineyard becomes absurd here.
And, paradoxically, in that absurdity lies its meaning. For the poet

reveals something of the reality of heavenly justice in all its mystery through a "dissimilar similitude" that succeeds in its revelatory function only to the extent that it states, not negates, its own reality. We are made more profoundly aware of this mystery when we come to realize at some point that Christ's own Word—the sacred prototype, the *donnée* of the Christian faith—was never really an "explanation" but rather was a "revealing veil." Revealing veil: that is what saves the believing mind from paralysis but keeps bringing it back to explore this incarnational juxtaposition for that elusive similarity, or rather identity, between opposing terms, which only the sacrament promises.

This symbolic failure in the most articulate and rational part of the poem is a subtle but telling concretization of the dreamer's inner drama—his inevitable failure to grasp divine order and justice. We sense his frustration through our own. Our view of his incapacity to understand changes gradually; we hesitate more and more to judge him for his literalism; his drama of perception becomes ours as well. We cannot stay for long the ironic spectators of an obtuse, spiritually insensitive human exception, because we are made to identify with his loss and his confusion. He is Everyman. And so we repeat with him—if not with all the critics: "Me þynk þy tale vnresounable" (590).

To recapitulate, the Maiden's theological discourse, despite the rational tone and structure of its arguments, is subverted in its aim by its demonstrative earthly similitudes, as most revealed theology is likewise subverted. She does not explain divine mystery; she only restates it . In fact, she intensifies it by casting on it another veil of incongruous terms in one more symbolic representation.

Since the Maiden resorts to concrete metaphor in her discourse, we cannot accept Spearing's too exclusive statement that "throughout this large central part of the poem [i.e., the debate] the human drama of the encounter between Dreamer and Maiden continues to unfold . . . not by any symbolic development but by the development of argument and explicit doctrine," or—more specifically—that "for more than four hundred lines the pearl symbol undergoes no further development, and simpler, more explicit forms of exposition take its place."[43] The obvious involvement of similitudes and their failure, despite their familiarity and logical coherence, are part of the pattern of symbolic failure that builds up through the poem to its dramatic climax—the hero's encounter with the New Jerusalem. In this connection, then, the symbol continues to develop, incarnated in the human form of the Maiden but displaying its enigma during the debate on a more conceptual and articulate level—which is the more defeating to human perception precisely because it employs the most familiar forms of demonstration and exhausts all means of rational persuasion to no avail.

In the discourse, therefore, symbolic failure is sustained by a kind of syllogistic failure whose doctrinal and moral paradoxes are less palpable and definable but no less impregnable than those of the concrete similitude. These paradoxes are central to the Christian economy of salvation.

One of them is the fall of man and the process of his redemption. The question of divine mercy and justice, of salvation through grace and merit, relates to this vast and inscrutable theme. In the *Pearl* discourse, it focuses specifically on the nature of divine rewards and its relationship to two classes of souls: the untested and therefore morally unsullied, and the penitent who attain righteousness through struggle and frequent defeat. The vineyard parable is meant to clarify this relationship, but as dissimilar similitude it teaches us more what divine justice *is not* than what it is.

Looking at these theological issues on a more abstract, conceptual level, we meet with logical paradox. Divine rewards are identical in that they offer each soul total fulfillment in the presence of God. Yet, at the same time, they are different, since each individual soul experiences this fulfillment according to its unique capacity to realize God's presence.[44] In divine justice, then, the same is different, and the different is the same. This logical irreconcilability is further complicated by the ambivalence of two key terms in the discourse: "inlyche" (546, 603), which refers to the manner of spiritual payment, means 'alike,' 'thoroughly,' 'fully,' 'inwardly'; "rewarde" (604) means both the thing given and the capacity of deserving and receiving.[45] Now, if the spiritual given is the same, how does it reconcile itself with the limiting difference of its recipients in a world of no limits, no degree—no "more or less"?

I shall not delve into the theological intricacies of the corollary question of salvation through grace or merit and its relationship to the innocent and righteous.[46] Neither does the poet. He appears more interested in the existential than in the theoretical implications of this question. He wishes rather to dramatize the arbitrariness of God's justice and its frequently painful and perplexing impact on man's spiritual effort. The poet tempts orthodoxy, therefore, by having the Maiden present that effort as less deserving and more precarious than the passive, accidental perfection of the newly baptized infant (577–88). The innocent "wroȝt neuer wrang er þenne þay wente" (631). Their salvation is indisputable—a natural, effortless consequence of their unsullied state. The righteous, on the other hand, though they "*may* contryssyoun hente" (669), have erred; they "forfeted by sumkyn gate / Pe mede sumtyme of heueneȝ clere" (619–20). Hence, their salvation is subject to qualification: "may." Curiously enough, though she scolds the dreamer for demanding God's reward "by ryȝt" (XII), the Maiden

does not disdain claiming that right for the innocent and with empha-
sis. With each repetition, the refrain of the section (XII) takes on a tone
of superior self-satisfaction, which, I am sure, is meant to elicit a resent-
ful response in the reader as spiritual *agonistes:*

> Bot, hardyly, wythoute peryle,
> Þe innocent is ay saue by ryȝte.
> (695–96)

The Maiden asserts God's infinite liberality which annihilates degree,
that is, "more or less"—a humanly inconceivable notion in itself. But
the Maiden's comparison of the innocent with the righteous makes that
liberality appear strangely partial, diminishing, in effect, the worth of
man's moral struggle. I believe that the poet contrives this exaggeration
in order to reflect man's anxiety about that aspect of divinity which
responds to perfection by an impassive ontological affinity rather than
by a personal recognition of its painful attainment.

The author intensifies the inscrutability of divine justice by further
complicating the conceptual order of its scriptural expression. When
Christ concluded his parable of the vineyard, saying, "so the last shall
be first, and the first last" (Matt. 20:16), he was referring by "last" to
the late-repentant. Already in Christ's utterance we confront the mys-
tery of God's judgment, where one moment's sincere yearning for God
counterbalances a whole life span of spiritual effort. The Pearl Poet
deepens this moral enigma by incorporating various medieval interpre-
tations of this scriptural passage (summarized by René Wellek and D.
W. Robertson)[47] into an adaptation of his own. By "last" he means here
not only the late-repentant but also the least tested. He creates a tem-
poral paradox by matching the "euentyde" (582), the end of day, to the
dawn—not the conventional evening—of human life. Through trans-
ference, the dawn becomes the evening and the evening the dawn. We
have an illogical syllogism, which in its absurd dialectic incarnates
another inscrutable principle governing God's mercy: his view of time.
To him, the past, the present, and the future are an Eternal Now.[48] If
he measures time in this fashion, how does he measure, then, man's
spiritual effort, which takes place in time?

This conflation of temporal opposites is too vast a notion to examine
here. As moral paradox it no doubt puts man's faith to a crucial test. Its
emancipation from familiar order stimulates the human mind to cease-
less activity on an intellectual but also on an imaginative level, challeng-
ing it to discover its principle of coherence. I have already pointed to
the dynamic interplay between unity and multiplicity, in a simultaneity
of opposites, as artistic principle in the poem, derived from God's cos-

mological framework. In its present doctrinal expression, we observe its integrative force even further: Theology and art interpenetrate here. Art is more than mere artifact luxuriating in its own order; it acquires a profound metaphysical function at the service of philosophical or theological wisdom. Theology, on the other hand, is more than pure intellectual activity; it takes on an artistic order, becoming also an aesthetic experience in its vision of the world. This integration, one may well claim, is the achievement of the Christian Middle Ages.

The poet's preoccupation with the paradoxes of the Christian faith, their existential impact, and the eschatological anxiety they elicit should not be taken as evidence of a paralyzing skepticism on his part. Nor does he mean to present divine reality only in its awesome form. On the contrary, the poet reminds us of that divine aspect which has been accessible to man, enveloping him with its providence and leading him to salvation. This becomes evident in God's plan of redemption, as the Maiden shows it unfolding within human history.

She begins with the fall of "oure forme fader" (639), which condemned the rest of mankind "to dyʒe in doel" (642). She offers no explanation for the justice of this condemnation. Its mystery is heightened by the homely style of its expression, by the vast distance we discern between the simple, rustic act of "biting an apple" (640) and its awful spiritual significance—its devastating, age-long consequences as an act of rebellion against God (640 ff.). The Maiden then recalls God's own forgiving, redemptive act: his Incarnation and his Crucifixion. The Incarnation restates the hope of man's reconciliation with him in a union of natures; the Crucifixion reminds us of God's ardent love for man to the point of self-sacrifice. He does not remain a distant metaphysical principle or a majestic, detached spiritual entity. He takes on man's nature and man's suffering. Through his pain, he sanctifies man's pain. The Maiden's recounting of Christ's Passion is somewhat self-condemning, because the presence of God bleeding for man elevates the worth of man's spiritual struggle and his sorrows; in relating God's self-sacrifice for man, she reveals the divine compassion of which she in her perfection is curiously incapable.

These events in the history of redemption are essentially irreducible and mysterious. Yet man partook in their reality through God's first sacrament, the Incarnation. He continues to participate in their efficacy through the sacraments, "þe water [of] baptem" and "þe blod [that] vus boʒt fro bale of helle" (649–56), which the Maiden presents as sequel to the initial redemptive act that instituted them.

Through the Maiden's exposition of the ministry of Christ, the poet has deliberately counterbalanced the image of God the "Dryʒtyn" with the image of God as man's fellow sufferer, revealing his complementary nature: his inexorable, arbitrary justice and compassionate mercy, his awesomeness and sweet humility, his *ira* and his providential love. How is man to reconcile these opposing aspects? The image of God has softened here; yet it has become more enigmatic than ever before in the poem.

The following stanzas display the poet's skill at transition, the more so because he uses conventional scriptural material with natural ease to move the poem toward the direction he desires. As part of Christ's ministry, when "hym welke in areþede" (711), the Maiden recalls his summoning the children to him "swetely" (717):

> "Do way, let chylder vnto me tyʒt.
> To suche is heuenryche arayed."
>
> (718–19)

The children bring to mind the quality of purity, which all men—including the dreamer—must regain in order to enter the kingdom of God (722–28). The virtue of spiritual purity invokes, in turn, its symbolic embodiment in the poem: the pearl. The Maiden urges the dreamer to imitate the wise merchant of the biblical parable (Matt. 13:45–46) and give up all he possesses in order to attain "this makelleʒ perle." The pearl is identified now with "þe reme of heuenesse clere" (733–35): the kingdom of heaven itself.

Can the reader turn to conventional exegesis to comprehend this identification? Or has the poet, through the symbolic development that has taken place in the poem, cast this identification toward a specific, irrevocable direction, seeking to unveil some unique aspect in the nature of the kingdom of heaven? The answer lies in the dreamer's final confrontation.

5

The New Jerusalem

APPROACHES

When the pearl is identified with the kingdom of heaven, the object of the dreamer's quest reaches its anagogic form. The poet began with a private symbol, expanded it to an ideal universe, shaped it into an idealized self-image, and now fuses it with the sacred symbolic prototype of ideality as described by the Word itself. His private desire becomes one with man's universal ultimate nostalgia *"to find oneself always and without effort* in the Centre of the World, at the heart of reality . . . to transcend the human condition, and to recover the divine condition."[1] The quest to transcend the paradoxes of his earthly existence brings the hero, in the world of dream and wish fulfillment, *facie ad faciem* with the image of absolute reality. Here he seeks the final resolution, wherein opposites coalesce on a plane of higher unity, to be perceived in a moment of total, unmediated vision. To further establish this expansion from personal to universal quest and from private to eschatological symbol, the poet makes it appear that the anagogic realm—like the visionary landscape and the Maiden—germinates from the dreamer's object of desire, the pearl. He diffuses throughout the New Jerusalem the pearl's physical qualities and engulfs it with its substance—and, potentially, its enigma.

The pearl takes on the vast scope of the kingdom of heaven, which in turn inherits the symbolic and dramatic valences of the pearl thus far developed in the poem. The poet effects this transference not merely by identifying one with the other but also by highlighting the qualities shared by them:

> "This makelleȝ perle, þat boȝt is dere,
> Þe joueler gef fore alle hys god,
> Is lyke þe reme of heuenesse clere:

So sayde þe Fader of folde and flode;
For hit is wemleȝ, clene, and clere,
And endeleȝ rounde, and blyþe of mode,
And commune to alle þat ryȝtwys were.
Lo, euen inmyddeȝ my breste hit stode.
My Lorde þe Lombe, þat schede hys blode,
He pyȝt hit þere in token of pes.
I rede þe forsake þe world wode
And porchace þy perle maskelles."

(733–44)

"Makelleȝ," "wemleȝ, clene, and clere, / And endeleȝ rounde"—these epithets echo the description of the pearl symbol in its diverse manifestations throughout the poem: the pearl lost in the garden was "So rounde" (5) and "wythouten spot" (12); the pearl on the Maiden's breast was "wythouten wemme" (221), "clene and clere and pure" (227); the Maiden herself was called a "makeleȝ may and maskelleȝ" (780). The New Jerusalem thus gathers the various forms of the poem's central symbol and consummates them.

To accomplish this symbolic integration, the poet resorts to Christ's own metaphor, aware of its sacramental, fusive power. By skillfully uniting in it private desire and anagogic nostalgia, the poet reminds us—like Augustine and Dante—that all human quests are incarnations of the final quest for union with God and ultimately tend toward it. By weaving the divine similitude into his own symbolic fabric, he further claims that his own metaphors function like Christ's and partake of their incarnational authority in some way. That the poet was especially interested in the pearl's physical and affective qualities as incarnational vehicle most appropriate to his spiritual meaning becomes more evident by his conscious choice among several similitudes available to him. Christ, as metaphorist, compared the kingdom of heaven to several objects (Matthew 13:24–52), most of them familiar and commonplace—the seed of wheat, the seed of mustard, the leaven of bread, a fishing net, as well as the pearl of great price—showing how each similitude possessed some analogical relevance depending on the spiritual aspect to be incarnated and underscored in that kingdom. It is significant that the Pearl Poet chose from these objects the most perfect, yet most inaccessible one.

The preceding fusion of the various aspects of the pearl symbol and its identification with the kingdom of heaven bring the dreamer to the intuition of some unique relationship between the Maiden and this kingdom. He tries to fathom her true nature, voicing also the reader's mounting curiosity:

"O maskeleʒ perle in perleʒ pure,
Þat bereʒ," quod I, "þe perle of prys,
Quo formed þe þy fayre fygure?
Þat wroʒt þy wede, he watʒ ful wys.
Þy beauté com neuer of nature;
Pymalyon paynted neuer þy vys,
Ne Arystotel nawþer by hys lettrure
Of carped þe kynde þese propertéʒ."

(745–52)

The poet-dreamer does more than strike a pose of affected modesty.[2]
By observing that the Maiden's beauty does not come from familiar
nature, he hints at her remote, supernatural character; he has noticed
her unearthly complexion and demeanor, her "angel-hauyng" (753–
54). By placing her "vys" beyond the skill of Pygmalion—his kinsman,
the archetypical wishful artificer—he implicitly admits his own incapac-
ity to capture in her, through the vision of his art, a meaningful image
of human ideality. So too, in his reference to Aristotle, he acknowl-
edges the limits of philosophic thought—and hence the failure of the
dialectic exchange between him and the Maiden earlier—to rationally
clarify divine mystery and its spokesman in the poem. In short, he has
failed thus far as artist and thinker on both a symbolic and a discursive
level of perception and representation. The admission of such a failure
charges with renewed energy the work's dramatic pattern of visionary
discovery and frustration, involving us further in its progress through a
heightened sense of precariousness and even impending reversal.

To emphasize the dreamer's inability to gain any further insight,
despite his prolonged instruction, the poet has him hark back to his
earthbound criteria of judgment: "Quat kyn offys," what position in
the hierarchy, he asks, entitles her to "þe perle so maskelleʒ"? (755–
56). In her response, the Maiden mentions the mysterious being that
has formed her nature, her apocalyptic bridegroom. "Quat kyn þyng
may be þat Lambe?" (771), the dreamer presses on, and his question
raises the curtain on the whole spectrum of universal history, with the
Lamb moving in it as its central figure. The author's aim at re-creating
this universal setting as frame to the poem's private experience will
become progressively clearer.

The Maiden follows the Lamb through his various stages within sa-
cred history. She starts with Isaiah's prophetic portrait of patient self-
sacrifice and mute suffering: "So closed he hys mouth fro vch query"
(803). Then ensues the historical fulfillment of Isaiah's prophecy in the
New Testament. The Maiden selectively recounts the Lamb's ministry
on earth. He is the incarnate Christ encountered by John, coming to

his baptism "trwe as ston" (822), finally meeting death at the hands of those whose sins he took on (823–24). The Crucifixion is described with a few powerful strokes in the stark realism of the late medieval style mixed with the anguished lyricism pervading the mysticism of the Passion at the time:

> "In Jerusalem watȝ my lemman slayn
> And rent on rode wyth boyeȝ bolde.
>
> . . . .
>
> Wyth boffeteȝ watȝ hys face flayn
> Þat watȝ so fayr on to byholde."
>
> (805–10)

God is shown in the image of man's "meke" (832) fellow sufferer. The poet focuses on the events of the Baptism and the Crucifixion to establish indelibly the sources of the two central sacraments that perpetuate the Lamb's ministry, spanning and uniting within them historical time: the original event in the past and our participation in it in the present. This historical pattern finally leads to its anagogic consummation, where the Lamb stands now triumphant and terrible in the midst of God's throne, holding the book with the seven seals (833–38). In a gesture of cosmic sweep, the poet shows all creation "in helle, in erþe," cowering in awe and fear before "þat syȝt" (839–40).

By reconstructing this figural framework, the poet accomplishes several things. To begin with, we are made to witness the image of God taking on various shapes throughout the course of history. The poet aims at establishing the mysterious complementarity of God himself in order to prepare us for its most awesome manifestation at the climax of the work.

Furthermore, the poet reminds us that, in the universal economy, not only physical creation but also history is a theophany, functioning in an essentially symbolic manner, one event standing for and completing the other to its consummation and final significance at the end of time. I shall not delve into the details of figural sacred history and its operation—a subject already extensively discussed[3]—except to recall Père Chenu's comprehensive statement that, to the medieval symbolist mentality, "knowledge of God and his designs was derived from nature and from history" as his two "books" in which he taught man.[4] The poet shows here how indispensable the historical reality of the literal event is to its figural fulfillment. On that basis, he asserts also the importance of the historical reality of the symbol as *res*—its literal, concrete aspect—to the derivation of its spiritual meaning. As symbolic process, history, like creation, carries within it the dialectic tension between historical, physical fact and its ulterior spiritual meaning. This tension is expressed here, through the stages of the Lamb, in temporal opposites: the prophetic past, the historical present, and the eschatological future. All these are tending toward an ultimate coalescence in a simultaneous eternal Present on the anagogic level. This coalescence has its counterpart in the ultimate sacramental fusion of the opposing realities in the symbol. By merging the eternal with the historical, the spiritual with the physical, in the person of Christ, the Incarnation stands as the promise and the fulfillment of this dynamic reconciliation in historical and creational as well as poetic symbolism.

I am somewhat puzzled by the breezy facility with which Spearing passes over this typological pattern in *Pearl* as "explicitly completed by the poet, rather than left hidden as an allegory."[5] The fusive operation of the figural principle in sacred history is anything but explicit: it is at the core of Christian mystery. For no human intellect can conceive how the temporal and spatial polarities in history will finally collapse and fuse into an Eternal Now or Infinite Here. Furthermore, this annihilation of time and space takes place on an imaginative level as well, offering the artist the freedom to impose his own temporal and spatial order. It challenges the poetic imagination to attain to a godlike simultaneous perspective of contrary dimensions and to capture it in representational terms. In *Pearl*, as well as in the *Divine Comedy*, the poet attempts such a perspective by showing his hero breaking out of profane time and space and intruding upon absolute reality. A fraction of historical time in a man's life is engulfed in eternity; yet it suddenly expands and possesses eternity within itself—if only for a flashing moment of powerful vision.

So the poet uses this universal setting with its multiple expressions of the divine as a cosmic backdrop and total perspective against which to project the hero's personal drama. To the extent that this drama is a private affair—that is, the experience of one man in one fleeting historical moment—it becomes infinitely diminished against such a vast design, whose artificer is God. But to the extent that it is a universal drama of loss and spiritual crisis and of the irrepressible desire for a higher vision of reality, it invests its hero with great figural significance, making him stand for the men who preceded him and the men who will come after him in such a quest to the end of time. Already the poet has intimated the figural dimension of his experience by the Adamic and Christological suggestiveness of his "slepyng-slaȝte." As dreamer, he has indirectly claimed equal footing and visionary penetration with Paul, being "out of the body," his "spyryt" having sprung "in space," while his "body on balke þer bod in sweuen" (61–62).[6] And now he comes to stand on the same promontory as his sacred prototype:

As John þe apostel hit syȝ wyth syȝt,
I syȝe þat cyty of gret renoun.

(985–86)

Like Dante's "vidi, vidi," the repeated "syȝ . . . syȝt . . . syȝe" emphasizes
the poet's claim to have been granted the same revelation as John, to
have encountered *facie ad faciem* ultimate reality. But, in a sense, more
than that. He is not a mere spectator to that reality; instead, he moves
and suffers in it. He dares take the anagogic telos of the Bible and
make it the denouement of his private spiritual drama. His vision is the
eschatological vision of all mankind. It becomes obvious, then, in what
position the poet-dreamer places himself in the figural continuum of
universal history. What he forgoes in surprising invention by not con-
structing his own anagogic cosmos, as Dante does, he aims to gain in
authority.

Before discussing the poem's apocalyptic encounter, I would like to
consider for a moment the Maiden's description of the New Jerusalem
and its denizens that precedes it. Respectable critics like Kean and
Spearing have viewed this description as an artistic lapse; they see it as
little more than a redundant repetition producing a static, weakening
effect, which robs—to Kean, intentionally—the climactic event of its
full impact by anticipating it.[7] I do not think we can easily absolve the
poet of such an unhappy effect. Yet we need to understand his inten-
tions, from a thematic and dramatic standpoint, in having the Maiden
rehearse the apocalyptic world before its actual confrontation by the
hero.

First, as Kean and Spearing also observe,[8] he wishes to delight his
audience—according to the poetic practice of his time—by amplified
description. Second, he reasserts the Maiden's role as visionary guide
by letting her survey with some intimate knowledge and authority the
realm to which she is about to lead him; further on, she claims that she
herself had arranged for his vision through special divine dispensation
(966–69). Her description also acts as bait, as dramatic motivation to
the dreamer—and to the reader—to press on more urgently for the
final discovery. It excites the anticipation that, by some sudden turn,
description will become immediate reality with wondrous and curious
results, as this particular mortal presumes to intrude upon this inacces-
sible and inviolate sacred realm, succeeding perhaps in upsetting its
divine composure. Suspense and the marvelous are thus called into
play, energizing rather than enervating the otherwise familiar narra-
tive. Let us also note that, although the Maiden dwells on some
details—the Lamb's qualities (841–44) and the faces of the apocalyptic
throng engraved with the Lamb's name (869–72)—her description re-

mains rather general, without any spatial organization or concrete focus. She merely enumerates the central figures of the realm and describes its general atmosphere of ritual majesty and unshaded joy. The actual vision does not go back and repeat all that the Maiden has mentioned; it only materializes the key elements in her description and brings them into direct confrontation with the dreamer.

The Maiden's preamble is aimed, moreover, at establishing the apocalyptic realm as the preexisting, eternal framework against which the poem's climactic event will take place. She sets it as an absolute, irrevocable reality independent of the human condition and thus impervious to any human intrusion. This counterpoise between helpless man and self-sufficient, omnipotent divinity is thematically central to the work; it also constitutes its main conflict, which becomes charged with dramatic power, more so because of its stupendously uneven antithesis.

Perhaps most significantly, the poet enunciates through the Maiden the traditional, almost inviolate *significatio* of the New Jerusalem as the " 'ceté of God' . . . þe borȝ þat we to pres [to which we hasten]" (952–57). Unlike the case of the pearl and the rose, it would be superfluous to elaborate on the all too familiar significance of the New Jerusalem as the *civitas Dei*. Mircea Eliade's description of the archetypal image of the "center," to which man tends in his anagogic ascent, fits well the Christian Apocalyptic City and confirms its validity within the history of human consciousness. It is the sacred mountain or city that stands as the *axis mundi*. It represents "the zone of the sacred, the zone of absolute reality"; it exists beyond profane time and space in "a consecrated space" and in "sacred time."[9] "The final apocalyptic vision," Angus Fletcher tells us, "promises to mankind an eternal fruitfulness. It shows a triumph of love and creation. . . . [It] coincides with an access of power" to the initiate in a moment of total consciousness.[10] In the Christian "center," the initiate recovers the divine condition and thus unites with God. The New Jerusalem has been established by the Word itself in John's vision as an absolute reality full of eternal life and bliss, where, according to the Maiden, "pes . . . ay schal laste wythouten reles" (955–56).

As structure, this cosmic center represents conquest over chaos, enveloping man in an all-coherent, reassuring framework. Yet the path to it is difficult:

> The road is arduous, fraught with perils, because it is, in fact, a rite of the passage from the profane to the sacred, from the ephemeral and illusory to reality and eternity, from death to life, from man to the divinity. Attaining the center is equivalent to a consecration, an initiation.[11]

Its attainment is man's supreme dream, but the way to it almost annihilates him. The anagogic ascent, therefore, is an ambivalent and fearsome experience, as man views it from his plane of existence before he sets out for it. It is full of ecstasy as well as dread—contrary elements that the artist tries to capture and control in an enigmatic but ordered surface in his representation of it.

The enigma of the sacred or the duality of the image of God is not an invention of modern sophistication. Such complementarity is expressed, for example, in the Old Testament, in Job's address to God: "Let not thy dread make me afraid" (Job 13:21). Although God's visage softens in the New Testament, the event of the Last Judgment and John's Revelation revive our awareness of the mysterious and terrible aspect of divinity. The medieval mind was no less responsive—metaphysically and aesthetically—to the mingling of beauty and terror in the face of God. We sense this responsiveness in Pseudo-Dionysius's spellbinding description of God's "many appearances" and in his depiction of the Seraphim in all their fiery, grotesque splendor.[12] According to Saint Bonaventura, as Edgar de Bruyne paraphrases him, "en Dieu, il y a une profondeur qui nous remplit de terreur, une beauté qui nous comble d'admiration, une douceur qui soulève nos désirs."[13] The Pearl Poet not only is aware of this complementarity—brought into the poem by tradition itself—but manipulates it for his own thematic and artistic aims. The ambivalence of the *sacer* and the numinous operates in the apocalyptic world of *Pearl* as a means of initiation into the nature of ultimate reality; at the same time, it elicits much pleasure through its complex interplay of sensuous, affective, and conceptual contraries, intensified and patterned by the author into self-subsistent aesthetic order, into an intricate, bewitching rhythm of attraction and repulsion—even within the same object.

The re-creation of a prototype—such as the Pearl Poet undertakes in his representation of the New Jerusalem—inevitably asserts the ideological and artistic impulses that prompted it. There is no retelling unless the author wants to cast the prototype into a new coherence. Such an intention demands, however, the shaping force of a new poetic context.

Throughout the poem's symbolic process, we have been led to new insights as to the nature of the reality represented through the interaction the author obtains between traditionally accepted, and therefore expected, significances and the work's unique context. I have shown this interaction and its transformative impact in the poet's handling of the pearl symbol, the visionary landscape, the Maiden, and the biblical similitude of the vineyard. However hallowed and inviolate it stands in its scriptural authority as the central image of Christian eschatology, the New Jerusalem, too, once placed within the context of the poem's historical, private event, becomes subject to a similar interaction of valences, resulting in its partial reconstruction as symbolic entity. As with most of his imagery, the poet wants the reader to be aware of the Apocalyptic City's established symbolic value, so that he may perceive more keenly the poet's particular treatment of it and the intention behind it. In fact, through the Maiden's theological evaluation, the author sets up the anticipation that the sacred prototype will remain unchanged in its traditional meaning—only to betray such an anticipation by design through his own altering context. This tense dialectic between traditional expectation and contextual frustration in the work's imagistic development objectifies in palpable form its drama of spiritual perception, culminating appropriately at the poem's dramatic climax—which is, at the same time, the point of maximum analogical tension, as we shall see. The new context, then, into which the poet places the New Jerusalem as image of ideality is the poem's skillfully interwoven symbolic and dramatic development. The dreamer's confrontation with the Apocalyptic City brings this development to its summit.

The New Jerusalem culminates the crescendo of symbolic and discursive paradoxes that has built through the poem's drama of spiritual perception. In that sense, it functions in the work as the dissimilar similitude par excellence of absolute, anagogic reality about to be encountered by the hero in his spiritual quest. In employing the "dissimilar similitude" as the most efficacious metaphoric concept in the representation of anagogic reality, I do not mean to imply that the medieval symbolist mentality was guided entirely by Pseudo-Dionysian theory. Père Chenu has shown that Augustine had, in fact, exerted a greater influence on the analogical thinking of the Middle Ages through his own distinctive approach.[14] Since the Areopagite was, nonetheless, the symbolist most concerned with the representation of the apocalyptic—exploring it essentially as a theological problem but with definite aesthetic implications—and since his views were eventually adapted in this context by the Victorines, Thomas Aquinas, and even Dante,[15] I intend to use his insights as points of departure in my discussion of the Pearl Poet's eschatological symbolism.

Before applying the anagogic dissimilar similitude as metaphoric principle on the apocalyptic world of *Pearl*, I wish to summarize its operative dynamics. As symbol, it functions, according to Hugh of Saint Victor, as "a juxtaposition, that is, a coaptation of visible forms brought forth to demonstrate some invisible matter" (*symbolum collatio videlicet, id est coaptatio visibilium formarum ad demonstrationem rei invisibilis propositarum).*[16] As analogical vehicle—incapable by nature of representing divine reality yet at the same time participating in it—it carries within it the dialectic tension of God's transcendence and immanence, which is reflected in its paradoxical metaphoric function: It reveals higher truth while veiling it with an enigmatic, incongruous imagistic surface, which incarnates the poet's direct intuition of the mystery of that truth. It thus also embodies the dialectic between man's own contradictory impulses of penetrating the mystery of the divine while protecting its sanctity and preserving its remoteness:

Ὅτι μὲν γὰρ εἰκότως προβέβληνται τῶν ἀτυπώτων οἱ τύποι, καὶ τὰ σχήματα τῶν ἀσχηματίστων, οὐ μόνην αἰτίαν φαίη τις ἂν εἶναι τὴν καθ' ἡμᾶς ἀναλογίαν ἀδυνατοῦσαν ἀμέσως ἐπὶ τὰς νοητὰς ἀνατείνεσθαι θεωρίας, καὶ δεομένην οἰκείων καὶ συμφυῶν ἀναγωγιῶν, αἵ τὰς ἐφικτὰς ἡμῖν μορφώσεις προτείνουσι τῶν ἀμορφώτων καὶ ὑπερφυῶν θεαμάτων ἀλλ' ὅτι καὶ τοῦτο τοῖς μυστικοῖς λογίοις ἐστὶ πρεπωδέστατον, τὸ δι' ἀποῤῥήτων καὶ ἱερῶν αἰνιγμάτων ἀποκρύπτεσθαι, καὶ ἄβατον τοῖς πολλοῖς τιθέναι τὴν ἱερὰν καὶ κρυφίαν τῶν ὑπερκοσμίων νόων ἀλήθειαν.

[That, on the other hand, images are suitably put forth for the imageless and shapes for the shapeless is not only because, as one may say, our rational thinking is unable to extend itself directly to intellectual contemplation and [because it] needs fitting and natural upliftings which make accessible to us semblances for spectacles that are formless and supernatural; but also because it is most proper to hide the mystical oracles through ineffable and sacred enigmas and to render inaccessible to the many the sacred and secret truth of the supermundane Intelligences.][17]

The obscurity of the dissimilar similitude becomes in the hands of the poet a calculated device not only to shield his truth from the unprepared and uninitiated but also to involve his reader in an interpretive response. As I have noted earlier (chapter 1), to Augustine such obscurity results from the rich confusion of meaning built by God into every symbol, scriptural or creational. As process of discovery into the analogical relationship between two incongruous levels of being—the human and the divine, finite expression and its infinite object—symbolic obscurity becomes a source of metaphysical insight as well as aesthetic pleasure.[18]

Since the dissimilar similitude operates on two opposing but inextricable principles—its incongruity with, yet participation in, the reality it represents—it stimulates the human imagination to invent new analogical forms and relationships. In these, the imagination tries to reconcile what it is tautly and simultaneously aware of: the difference and similarity that coexist dynamically between the means and the object of its symbolic representation. The inevitable irresolution of this attempt generates immense artistic energy; its resulting frustration compels the mind into further creative activity, into further invention.

Its essential tendency toward the incongruous liberates this kind of similitude from the strictures of the familiar and the actual. It thus allows the imagination to shape its own metaphoric patterns with the maximum formative autonomy, captivating us often with its untrammeled play within the marvelous, the fantastic, and even the grotesque. In his depiction of the angelic order of the Seraphim, based on Isaiah's vision (6:3–13), Pseudo-Dionysius displays the grotesque as an inseparable part of the anagogic similitude as visible form.[19] Through this element, he unveils before us—while veiling it—the terrible and awesome aspect of sacred reality. At the same time, the self-luxuriating flamboyance of his descriptions—the sumptuous brilliant colors and the transfixing fiery shapes—reflects his utter fascination with the apocalyptic and its formal freedom.

It was this creative exuberance inherent in the anagogic dissimilar similitude that impelled Pseudo-Dionysius—and later the author of *The Cloud of Unknowing* and Walter Hilton, both contemporaries of the Pearl Poet—to warn us against the beguilements of its "veil." Such renunciation, of course, belies itself, for, in the process of denying his image, the theologian paints it more intensely. His deprecation of it as ultimately insubstantial and irrelevant only betrays his awareness of how much its corporeal qualities help shape its ulterior spiritual significance in the human sensibility. Even for Pseudo-Dionysius, the proponent of the *via negativa,* there is no similitude that is totally negative or self-annihilating, despite its analogical incongruity. For it succeeds in its revelatory function only to the extent that it states, not negates, its own reality. Its absurdity is paradoxically its meaning, its enigma the revelation. So, despite these misgivings and public denials, the medieval poet did not hesitate to use the dissimilar similitude, even in its most debased and scandalous form, to startle the mind into some apprehension of the nature of the ineffable.[20] Its inexhaustible ontological and formal dialectic—the vital counterpoise within it of contrary essences and multiple patterns—allowed him to express his deepest eschatological anxieties while controlling them in his own created order as visionary and artist.

As we have already seen, the impulse to control infinite, inscrutable reality compels the poet to project his desire upon it to the maximum within the realm of the dream and to exercise the full autonomy of his art in giving it shape. And by its very nature as visionary event and fecund form the anagogic dissimilar similitude serves this very purpose—or, rather, is created by it. The emancipation from familiar actuality, which is afforded to the human imagination in its vision of the apocalyptic, elicits in the artist an inner exultation, an inebriating sense of demiurgic independence. For, in the eyes of the medieval poet, the making of a poem becomes in essence the making of a world.[21] This is also how Northrop Frye views anagogic literature, except that he sees it as finally "existing in its own universe, no longer a commentary on life and reality, but containing life and reality in a system of verbal relationships [i.e., its own creative order]."[22] Such a comment, however, would strike the medieval poet as metaphysically and aesthetically solipsistic, since all human art, though it partakes in the divine creative act, is a construction of time and space and thus inevitably limits, if not betrays, its infinite object. In the representation of anagogic reality, then, all art can do is function as a "commentary" on that reality—for representation here becomes totally interpretation—and on man's ability to conceive and express it. While the apocalyptic frees the imaginative mind from the restrictions cast upon it by the actual world, allowing it the power of cosmogonic creativity, it also brings it *facie ad faciem* with its own devastating limitations. For such autonomy eventually imprisons itself in its own created cosmos, imposing its own rhythm and structure, leading finally to the ironic realization of the absurdity, irrelevance, and essential failure of its constructions in relation to ultimate reality.

In the dream world of *Pearl*, the poet projects his desire and casts his own form on ultimate reality through the pearl, the object of desire of the "I" in the poem, making it function as germinating seed and shaping force of that reality. As we have seen, by a clever stroke he has elevated his private symbol, through the authority of the Word, to the universal sacred prototype of ideality: the kingdom of heaven. A look at the New Jerusalem shows it, indeed, as an expansion of the pearl, at least in its corporeal qualities. In such an identification, the poet challenges the reader's imagination to achieve an instantaneous awareness of contrary, irreconcilable dimensions—between pearl and kingdom of heaven, between finite symbol and its infinite object—one existing simultaneously in the other as a spatial "conceit" in mutual microcosmic condensation or macrocosmic expansion. The poem's central symbol is made to contain the universe in which it exists. In its juxtaposition of vastly distant analogical entities, a paradox of this kind evokes an authentic sense of mystery and awe; the daring of its invention, on the other hand, communicates the visionary artist's sense of liberation and creative exuberance. More than any other period, the medieval age, Edgar de Bruyne reminds us, delighted in dwelling on the tantalizing notion of the mutual, simultaneous containment of the immense infinite and the infinitely small, not only on the speculative but also on the aesthetic plane.[23]

Yet, while the Pearl Poet luxuriates in the imaginative freedom of his anagogic construction, he is keenly aware of its limitations as conception and representation. More than that, he manipulates these limitations into becoming instruments of insight. Since human art tries to reproduce the immutable principles of beauty that form God's masterpiece, the created universe, it represents one of man's supreme efforts to actualize the ideal in this world. The poet, therefore, uses the creative process itself—with its accomplishments and frustrations—as supreme symbolic action incarnating man's ceaseless endeavor toward a clearer vision of absolute reality. In other words, he makes the creative process the vehicle of his symbolic irony. The anagogic image gains in symbolic irrelevance—and hence in metaphysical penetration into the reality it represents—to the extent that it succeeds as artistic order. In that sense, poetry functions as a cognitive force leading to philosophical wisdom. Philosophical wisdom and the struggle for its attainment, on the other hand, take on greater validity, greater resonance and depth, by involving the total man also as aesthetic experience.

THE APOCALYPTIC CITY

Although he borrows his anagogic construction from sacred tradition, the Pearl Poet subjects it to his own thematic and artistic aims through a unique process of selection and intensification. His success in the depiction of the Apocalyptic City is twofold: He presents a vehicle that incarnates a profound metaphysical enigma through its ontological disparity with its ineffable tenor. At the same time, he captures this ontological dialectic in aesthetic form, the vehicle displaying a complex coherence of its own as product of the poetic imagination. I wish to observe more closely how the poet, as medieval artist, ties the creative process and some of its controlling values to his symbolic intention, making the one serve the other.

As in the visionary landscape, the author casts a definite artistic order on his representation of the apocalyptic realm, although, significantly, with greater autonomy. The entire city is patterned as a beautiful mosaic of precious stones and metals, riveted to each other with their seams and grout, so to speak, clearly visible, their color and luminescence accented by the poet's selective but concentrated description. In depicting the city, the poet employs the materials of the art of his time: the stones gleam as polished glass or burnished gold; the walls of jasper glint "as glayre" (1026), that is, like egg white used as fixative to gold leaf in medieval illumination.[24] He thus invites us to judge his anagogic image as a work of art built according to the aesthetic principles of his time.

Looked at from the standpoint of medieval aesthetics, the New Jerusalem as a construction of beauty meets at least the criteria of symmetry, clarity of form, brilliance of surface, and immutability. Augustine, who together with his God-inebriated lyricism brought into medieval aesthetics a definite geometric spirit, viewed symmetry as the embodiment of the key cosmological and aesthetic principle of "integrity" and "due proportion" of form. At one point, he expresses an almost obsessive distaste for the random inequality of size and distance between objects arranged in an architectonic order, such as doors and windows in a building.[25] In describing the New Jerusalem, the Pearl Poet emphasizes the perfect symmetry of its dimensions: its length, breadth, and height are equal; its gates are situated symmetrically, three in each of the four sides (1025–35).

Thomas Aquinas complements Augustine's aesthetic criteria of integrity and due proportion with *claritas,* that is, clarity and rationality of form as well as brilliance of surface.[26] I should interject here, however, that in medieval aesthetics eccentricity of form and the element of the fantastic and the irrational were also considered as sources of beauty. As Edgar de Bruyne states this notion, referring to Hugh of Saint Victor and his views on the subject,

> Les unes [formes] nous plaisent parce qu'elles nous sont familières, ainsi la lumière, d'autres parce qu'elles sont rares. Il y en a qui nous frappent à cause de leur harmonie rationnelle et équilibrée, d'autres à cause de la logique de leur incohérence ou de l'estétique de leur bizarrerie: "aliquando quia pulchrae, aliquando, ut interim ita loquar, quia quodammodo convenienter ineptae." [Sometimes forms please us because they are beautiful and sometimes, if I may say so, because they are fitly absurd.][27]

The monstrous itself, despite its horror, fills us with aesthetic emotions, whether we merely conjure it up in our imagination (Alexander of Hales) or depict it in works of art and literature.[28] The Apocalyptic City measures up to the first notion of *claritas* in its fine delineation of jointure and the coherence of its visual organization, as we shall see. At the same time, we also discover that the eccentric and irrational begins to play an increasingly important role as aesthetic value and symbolic instrument.

In regard to the second notion of *claritas*, we see the city enwrapped in a resplendent effulgence of brilliant light and rich color whose intensity never diminishes:

> Byʒonde þe brok fro me warde keued [the city],
> Þat schyrrer þen sunne wyth schafteʒ schon.
>   (981–82)

Much has been written on the predominance of light and bright color in the lavish surfaces of medieval art. It involves one of the central impulses in the emergence of·Gothic architecture. The architects and artists of the Gothic period were propelled toward bringing brilliance into their structures and onto their artifacts by the Pseudo-Dionysian view of light as a similitude of God, in a universal order structured on a hierarchy of participation in the divine light by each level of being.[29] Abbot Suger, the proponent of this movement and builder of its first known edifice, the abbey of Saint Denis, put to full incarnational use— though with unmistakable Neoplatonic reservations—precious stones and metals, marble and stained glass, hoping that the human mind might rise through the experience of their physical luminosity to the true light which is Christ:

> Mens hebes ad verum per materialia surgit,
> Et demersa prius hac visa luce resurgit.
>   (*De admin.* XXVII, 189)[30]

To Suger and his collaborators, these sumptuous and translucent artifacts were as "veils at once shrouding and revealing the ineffable."[31] Saint Bernard of Clairvaux belied his acrid protestations against Suger's abandon to such opulence by admitting that, in Canticles 1 and 10, borders of gold and studs of silver served as the mirror and enigma through which the human mind could perceive what it could not look upon face to face: divine wisdom.[32] So too, like Suger and like the author of the Canticles, the Pearl Poet attempts in his poem to lead the mind through the visual splendor of his precious symbol to a keener apprehension of its invisible object.

We finally come to the Pearl Poet's handling of immutability as a symbolic and aesthetic value. Although medieval thinkers esteemed greatly the dynamic coexistence of multiplicity and unity as supreme universal formative principle, they responded with equal urgency to an almost contradictory impulse: the desire for permanence, both as ultimate mode of being and as criterion of perfect beauty. Permanence of being and the indestructibility of the order of things—these aroused the welcome feelings of safety, coherence, and tranquillity, especially in an age of deepening melancholy at the transience of earthly beauty and the time-bound fragility of the work of man, a sentiment that eventually led to the obsessive, horrified preoccupation with mortality and death. Immutability of form, on the other hand, was for the medieval thinker—beginning with Augustine[33]—the mark of ideal beauty. Alexander of Hales proclaims that "non est pulchritudo in re transeunti secundum seipsum accepta" (nothing of a transient nature can be beautiful).[34] Saint Bonaventura sees the artist constantly striving to achieve in his work, besides beauty and utility, permanence: "Omnis enim artifex intendit producere opus pulchrum, utile, et stabile."[35] After all, human art attempts to re-create and model itself after the ideal immutable laws of God's art, the cosmos. In this sense at least, the permanence of art becomes for the medieval poet[36] a kind of defense against decaying, destructive change. In its inherent aim to actualize the ideal in this world, art captures beauty—which in this life is fluid and ephemeral—and fixes it into an ideal permanent form. Its effort, however, is an extension of man's search for permanence on the metaphysical level as well. What, indeed, in the Middle Ages adds immense urgency to the artistic ideal of immutability, taking it beyond the plane of dispassionate aesthetic contemplation to that also of existential anxiety, is its close tie, if not fusion, with man's deepest eschatological concerns. In no other pursuit, therefore, does the artistic creative process—with its successes and failures—embody as symbolic action man's aspiration for the ideal with such poignancy, and even compelling pathos, than in the pursuit of permanence. This becomes evident in the ideal world of *Pearl.*

In *Pearl,* the New Jerusalem is presented, like its biblical prototype, as the anagogic fulfillment of man's desire for permanence, in both a metaphysical and an aesthetic sense. This desire was first expressed in the "erber." We heard it in the dreamer's desperate appeal—in defiance even of cosmic law—to preserve his buried pearl from decay (34–35). We found it in the poet's comforting rhetoric of beauty: the lush verbal tapestry of his description and his intent imposition of a fixed architectonic order on the garden of mutability through the floral mosaic of the "huyle." His wish for permanence began to materialize in the world of the dream and of uninhibited desire, when the earthly landscape, subject to change and decay, was transformed to an ideal realm of precious, enduring substance. Similarly, the Maiden as the dreamer's self-projection into potential ideality was rescued by the vision and shaping force of his art from change and dissolution into plastic perfection. Through its powerful interplay between thematically announced symbolic meaning and the contradictions of sensuous and affective experience, this transformation initiated in the reader's mind the dialectic that reflects one of man's most gripping eschatological preoccupations: What stands best for eternity and perfection—the renewal of the transitory or the deathlike stasis of the permanent? It remains to be seen whether the New Jerusalem as image of ultimate reality resolves or perpetuates this dialectic. That depends on the way the poet, as a medieval artist, employs his controlling aesthetic values—symmetry, clarity or eccentricity of form, brilliance of surface, as well as immutability—to articulate this symbolic dialectic while creating, of course, a self-subsistent, self-celebrating work of art.

Patricia Kean gives voice to the prevailing view among critics today when she observes that, although the description of the New Jerusalem functions well as "an effective set piece . . . , it does not, in fact, seem to engage the poet's concentrated attention; and he seems to depend on the reader's reaction to the general effect, and to recognition of a familiar context, rather than his usual technical skill."[37] I have already discussed the presence of a unique context in the work. As to the poet's description, we discover that, on the contrary, he takes great pains to make his New Jerusalem a more arresting image than its biblical prototype by a concentrated yet subtle manipulation of its visual surface. He gives it a concrete topography, for example, which is absent in John's version. The apostle's visionary position can hardly be defined spatially, for all he says is "I saw . . . I saw . . ." According to the Maiden's strict instructions, the dreamer moves opposite her in a parallel direction along the barrier of the stream (973–76). They pass through woods "by launce3 so lufly leued [by boughs so beautifully covered by leaves]" (978). Because of this definition of locality and the walk through foliage—possibly obscuring the vision—the poet achieves a sense of surprise when at a certain turn the dreamer unexpectedly comes upon the city as a single, powerful impression:

> Tyl on a hyl þat I asspyed
> And blusched on þe burghe, as I forth dreued,
> By3onde þe brok fro me warde keued,
> Þat schyrrer þen sunne wyth schafte3 schon.
> (979–82)

Spatial relationship is used here, however, for more than narrative surprise. Although it appears rationally conceived in a physical sense, it operates primarily as metaphysical and moral relationship.[38] It is also determined, as in mythopoeic thought, "not by objective measurements, but [by] an emotional recognition of values," referring "to localities which have an emotional colour; they may be familiar or alien, hostile or friendly" to the intruder.[39] The stream barrier in *Pearl* functions with just such metaphysical and affective value, demarcating the protagonists' disparate spheres of existence. So does their parallel but never-meeting movement along the stream's opposite banks. Spatial relationship—like the entire visionary landscape that contains it—must be viewed simultaneously as an imagistic projection of the dreamer's intuitive sense of his relationship to the entity he is encountering and as the poet's conscious symbolic construction defining spiritual distance as objective reality. Space, then, in *Pearl*'s apocalyptic topography is employed as both psychological and metaphysical metaphor. However, contrary to the generally accepted view of medieval plastic and literary space as relatively uninterested in the object's sensuous appearance— that is, as tending toward abstraction in order to facilitate the union between the physical and spiritual spheres[40]—the Pearl Poet uses space to accentuate, rather, sensuous appearance as a crucial means to spiritual significance. He sharpens, therefore, the physical outlines of his topography in order to translate into concrete kinesthetic and experienceable terms the dreamer's spiritual tension, with desire and fulfillment arrayed impassably opposite each other.

Each object or physical block in the Apocalyptic City is delineated with intense precision. Its corporeal attributes are powerfully stated, signaling to us their centrality as vehicles to higher meaning. Visual perception becomes metaphysical penetration in one act of apprehension. The city's brilliance, despite its composite impact, is not a vague effluence; instead, it is concentrated on and emanates from the city's dense surface, which shines as gold burnished like gleaming glass (989–90), a material frequently used in medieval art. The poet describes the foundations as "gemmeȝ an-vnder pyȝt" and "of riche tenoun" (991–93), huge blocks of precious stones "admirably joined" to each other. Each layer or "tablement," however, is strongly defined from the other (994). It is as if the "rych rokkeȝ" met initially in the visionary landscape (68)—standing as archetypal images of power and permanence in contrast to the precariousness of the human condition and suggesting a mode of absolute being[41]—have taken on in their precision a more immovable and intent stance as forces countering the intruding dreamer.

The Pearl Poet goes beyond the mere listing of the biblical narrative to dwell on the material texture of each stone, thus intensifying its corporeal qualities. The chalcedony is "wythouten wemme" with a pearllike pallor to it (1003–4); the surface of the emerald is "so grene" (1005); and the beryl is clear and white (1011). The poet's eye delights in tracing the double hue of the topaz (1012) and the exquisite blend of purple and indigo in the amethyst (1016), which he calls "þe gentyleste in vch plyt" (the most excellent in each plight or peril), recalling the magical, exotic lore of the lapidaries (1015). Our gaze shifts to the walls of jasper that glint like gleaming glass (1017–18), then penetrates the walls to the streets shining like lustrous glass and to the houses—not found in the biblical version—which are adorned with precious stones of every kind (1025–28). Finally, the poet describes the twelve gates covered with sumptuous metal plate, each gate crowned with or composed of "a margyrye, / A parfyt perle þat neuer fateʒ" (1034–38).[42]

"Pat neuer fateʒ"—this is the human aspiration that the New Jerusalem, in all its scriptural authority, embodies in *Pearl* as the image of immutable perfection. Let us recall the historical impulses that gave this aspiration an added urgency in the late Middle Ages. The transfixion of the poem's milieu on the concrete image of death demanded an equally palpable and convincing image of eternity as comforting counterpoise. Although the Pearl Poet does not fully share this feeling, he does display a keen sensual preoccupation with mortality, which inevitably leads to an equally material conception of immortality. Added to this material orientation are certain characteristic tendencies of the late medieval style. One is its obsessive "visuality" rigidifying thought into image. Another is its infatuation with artistic surface and with flamboyant effect. In dealing with the experience of mortality, such extravagance becomes part of the desperate rhetoric of beauty attempting to anesthetize the sensibility toward the gruesome reality of death and to capture eternity in a convincing and permanent form. As a result, the New Jerusalem as an image of anagogic transcendentality here becomes subject to the same representational betrayal as the visionary landscape, but with more profound implications since it is a universal symbol of ideality and not a private construction.

Contrary to the spiritual reality it represents, the New Jerusalem is enveloped in an almost orgiastic, though marvelous, materiality: its brilliant colors, its precious sumptuousness, and its dense metal plates. The poet intensifies this materiality, as we saw, by concentrating with lavishing care on the surface of his image. The reader is too distracted by the rhetoric on the surface of the image to penetrate its density to its ulterior spiritual significance. His senses become suffocated not by a rich overripeness, as in the earthly garden, but by a glutting opulence that has a similar numbing effect on the intellect and its free play. The

transcendental is weighed down by matter. Hence, the hallowed ana-
gogic image, as a product of the poetic imagination, cannot escape the
limits of its own conception and the conditions of time and space. The
more tenaciously it asserts its emancipation from this world's physical-
ity, the more irrevocably earthbound it becomes by the physical inten-
sity of its statement. In trying to transcend the values of this world as a
symbol of spirituality, the New Jerusalem becomes caught in them
ironically by the very act of transcending.

If the density and flamboyant splendor of its imagistic surface despi-
ritualizes the anagogic world of *Pearl,* blunting any contemplative pene-
tration, its spatial arrangement elicits an equally complementary effect.
Its geometrically explicit symmetry makes for beauty; it also communi-
cates a comforting sense of stability and rationality. Yet the sheer force
of this symmetry—the city's square shape with its heavily defined mea-
surements, the unalterable outline and cubical bulk of its physical
blocks—creates an overpowering impression of static monumentality:

> Þe cyté stod abof ful sware,
> As longe as brode as hyȝe ful fayre;
> . . . .
> Þenne helde vch sware of þis manayre
> Twelue forlonge space, er euer hit fon,
> Of heȝt, of brede, of lenþe to cayre.
> (1023–31)

Furthermore, during the city's description and until the coming of the
procession, there is no movement whatever within its thickly framed
Romanesque structure. The effect is, indeed, one of deathlike stasis,
exacerbating the dialectic as to what constitutes an appropriate simili-
tude for eternity—unless eternity, the entity symbolized here, is meant
to participate in some mysterious fashion in the reality of its symbol. We
cannot assume that this effect is accidental or that it results solely from
the biblical version. This ambivalence is the conscious product of the
poet's strategy of material intensification, structural rigidification, and
retardation of movement. It complicates and enriches the function of
the New Jerusalem as a dissimilar similitude of eternity. Also, it is part of
the poet's gradual process of symbolic alienation, incarnating an increas-
ing sense of estrangement between the dreamer and divine reality.

To appreciate more fully the Pearl Poet's intention in this instance, it
is helpful to note how Dante—whose anagogic symbolism tends toward
the ultimate reconciliation and mystic union between God and man—
overcomes stasis within his equally well-defined and structured heav-
enly universe. He vitalizes its architectonic frames through a process of

perpetual transformation and inner movement. In the sphere of Jupiter (*Paradiso* XVIII–XX), for example, the figure M is made of souls, which, like a flock of birds rising from the riverbank, change shape in their constant motion. Then the M is miraculously transformed before us into an eagle, with thousands of souls gathering in it and then spurting from it like the sparks of a burning log. Both of these configurations contain familiar images of vigorous life. Though the eagle is seen as a vast heraldic mosaic of rubies and precious jewels, it throbs with life through the full-throated sound that comes from its beak like "the murmur of a stream that fell limpid from rock to rock" (*un mormorar di fiumel che scende chiaro giù di pietra in pietra*) (XX, 19–20). Finally, the Rose, Dante's anagogic superstructure, begins as a very active image, a river of light on whose banks the angelic hosts move to and fro like sparks (XXX, 61 ff.). Then the river is changed into the vast, thousand-tiered Romanesque edifice, clearly defined in its geometric hierarchy. But the souls of the blessed continue its interior vital movement by descending to it and then ascending like intoxicated honeybees (XXXI, 1–12).

Though he depicts a universal frame rigid and immutable in its cosmological and moral design, Dante achieves a balance between hierarchical structure and inner vitality—both essential analogical qualities to eternal order as well as eternal life. In attempting to fully capture permanence, the Pearl Poet, on the other hand, applies the condition of space too stringently, allowing it to tyrannize over transcendent reality. His effort is thus betrayed by the intensity of his means—again, as part of his symbolic strategy. Immutability as ideal metaphysical value is undercut by immutability as aesthetic, representational value, that is, by the very means of its self-assertion. Such symbolic irony translates itself instantaneously into dramatic irony. For the reader sees the dreamer, in his attempt to liberate himself from the paradoxes of earthly existence, encountering now an ideal, anagogic reality whose own enigma is caught in the incongruity between its spiritual nature, on the one hand, and its material appearance and spatial confinement, on the other.

We should remember, nevertheless, that the New Jerusalem in *Pearl* does not function as a dissimilar similitude of divine reality only on the basis of its ontological difference, as material construction, from its object of representation, the spiritual city of God. After all, when we talk of medieval poetic symbolism we refer not merely to a process of ontological participation but, rather, to its aesthetic expression.[43] In other words, we refer to the sacramental process cast into aesthetic order. Consequently, the New Jerusalem as anagogic symbol gains in irrelevance—and therefore insightful irony—to the extent that it succeeds also as autonomous artistic form. To fulfill its own order, art submits its object to its own formal principles: it stylizes it, refracts it under its own vision, and finally dehumanizes it, removing it from its actual biological context. This process of dehumanization inherent in the creative process is used by the Pearl Poet to implement his strategy of progressive symbolic alienation. The images are further removed from familiar experience, taking on a less representational and more arbitrary form. Since we can no longer interpret their identity, we lose contact with their analogical operation and symbolic relevance. The reader's mental search for a new metaphoric coherence between image and idea translates into the dreamer's increasing visionary frustration as well as his gradual isolation from the reality he tries to comprehend and unite with. Artistic autonomy thus carries out a key symbolic function with serious thematic implications for the poem. Let us observe how this symbolic distancing is effected through the city's artistic patterning.

The poet visually intensifies each detail in the apocalyptic landscape through sharp delineation and local enrichment, rendering it a discrete aesthetic moment with an emphasis of its own. As we saw, he fixes the twelve foundation stones in a mosaiclike pattern as precisely defined geometric shapes. Though organized into a formal structure, each block is heavily framed from the other in a stunting of any possible interaction. The poet, furthermore, enriches the texture of each stone by lavishly describing the play of its various hues. Then follow in a clean-cut design the walls of refulgent jasper and the streets paved with gold. The gates stand isolated from one another, each adorned with opulent metal plates, culminating in a visually high point, its crowning pearl. However beautiful as plastic conception, the apocalyptic landscape is a paratactic arrangement of separate objects, taking on a highly refracted and surrealistic character. Paradoxically, the heavy schematization, while evoking a powerful sense of order, patterns the image so intensely as to fragment it, creating at the same time an effect of isolation and discontinuity. This complementary effect possesses great symbolic potency. It recalls the self-enclosed perfection of the poem's central symbol, "clanly clos in golde so clere" (2) and set "sengeley in synglere" (8). In that connection, then, it hints that the New Jerusalem, as an anagogic expansion of the pearl, might be governed by the same principle of ingathering isolation as self-sufficient reality and ideal schema. How can the restless, fluid figure of the dreamer fit into this configuration, unless it becomes one of these frozen, isolated images in it?

Such fragmenting schematization results in a physically and emotionally arid landscape. Already the anagogic realm has been purified to precious substance and brilliant light. It is a world of immutable being where no generative process can unfold within its perfect geometric precision. Its never-fading effulgence mirrors the splendor of God; it sheds *claritas* on the apocalyptic image as a work of art. But it also acts as objective correlative to the realm's emotional atmosphere: its unshaded, never-varying joy, to be encountered more fully in the society of the blessed. This purification of essences, sensuous and affective, symbolizes the attainment of unity, the return of the Many to the One, impelled by the anagogic (upward) proclivity of all levels of being in the medieval cosmos. Such unity affects us, to be sure, as supreme coherence, yet also as a form of impoverishment—a denuding of the life principle and of vital feeling to a state of sterile, static, strangely dispassionate permanence, a loss of nuance that renders this blissful world paradoxically oppressive and desolate. This complex effect makes the New Jerusalem as similitude of anagogic reality—of palpitating life and eternity—truly "dissimilar" and contradictory. And yet, having in mind the incarnational principle that a similitude participates in the reality it represents, we develop the disconcerting suspicion that anagogic reality has an awesome aspect to it that annihilates the life principle, as we understand it at least, changing it to a form of its own strange perfection.

Suspicion soon turns into dreadful certainty as the poet completes the perversion of all natural order begun earlier in the poem. After alchemizing the Apocalyptic City into pure precious stone and metal, the poet takes from it the sun and the moon, illuminating it only with the light of the Lamb:

> Of sunne ne mone had þay no nede;
> Þe self God watȝ her lombe-lyȝt,
> Þe Lombe her lantyrne, wythouten drede;
> Þurȝ hym blysned þe borȝ al bryȝt.
>
> (1045–48)

Because of its illumination, A. C. Spearing has reacted to it with highly evocative terms: it is a world of harsh, glittering light, a technicolor vista, "a kind of science-fiction landscape."[44] I rather share Spearing's strong response but quarrel with his flighty, anachronistic description of it. Furthermore, his impressionistic reaction stops well short of a serious analysis of the symbolic function and artistic merit of this unique vista. The absence of the sun and the moon is to be expected in a realm beyond our world of change and corruption, yet its unearthly iridescence elicits an ambivalent, if not frightening, effect. Moreover, while the absence of any temporal cycle marked by these natural elements suggests timelessness, it resembles time stopped at a deathlike standstill rather than ongoing eternity, an impression reinforced by the monotony of the unchanging light. The lack of any cycle incarnates immutability and incorruption, but it cancels rebirth and regeneration and the whole life process with which these ephemeral images have been associated since the beginning of human consciousness. Pure, "Wythouten fylþe oþer galle" (1060), the river flows out of the throne of God with the illogicality of surrealistic iconographic space, a stream of solid, unvarying light. While it courses through the streets, one cannot sense any motion in it by focusing on any particular point; it is fixed like a gold-leaf thread in an icon. Human art, in its quest for perfection and permanence, brings the life process here to stillness, contradicting in our perception the traditionally established symbolic value of the image as "the river of the water of life" (Rev. 22:1). Rather, it asserts the image's complementary character as being also the river of death, which annihilates the crossing initiate. The poet finally brings us to the trees by the riverbanks bearing the twelve fruits of life. It is perhaps by design that he omits here John's comforting statement that "the leaves of the trees were for the healing of the nations" (Rev. 22:2). Their shimmering brilliance ("ful schym") (1077) reminds us of the metallic trees seen earlier in the visionary region. Cast on an arid landscape, they intensify the unfamiliarity of this realm, not by being infertile but by their abnormal, sustained fruition. Once more, there is no cycle of renewal. The statement that

> Twelue syþe3 on 3er þay beren ful frym,
> And renowle3 nwe in vche a mone
> (1079–80)

is absurd, having already been nullified by the absence of time and its measurer, the moon. In addition, their hybrid character—they are both fruits and bright, metallic artifacts—reintroduces the element of the grotesque, which will finally complete the dissolution of all familiar order, thus culminating the process of symbolic estrangement and, consequently, the hero's alienation at the climax of the work.

To grasp more fully the Pearl Poet's view of divine reality and man's relationship to it, we must turn once again for contrast to Dante's representation of the anagogic realm, since it reflects a different conception of them. I shall not elaborate on Dante's incarnational symbolic method. That he was aware of the metaphysical and aesthetic dynamics of the dissimilar similitude becomes apparent at least from the symbol of the griffin in the *Purgatorio* on to the more incongruous and enigmatic images of the *Paradiso.* His acquaintance with Pseudo-Dionysian symbolist thought has been extensively discussed by some of his critics.[45]

Dante, as metaphorist of divine reality, relies on familiar experience to act as the reader's criterion of judgment concerning the analogical relevance of each similitude. He understands and exploits thematically and artistically the tension that can develop between human vehicle and divine tenor. In the initial stages of the *Paradiso,* Dante represents the supernatural world by selectively heightened natural scenes into which he injects elements of the fantastic and the artificial without, however, allowing them to predominate. As we saw earlier in his configuration of the Eagle, the souls are shown as rubies glittering with a gemlike flame. Still, they never freeze into total artifact. They are "happy in their sweet fruition" (XIX, 1–6); they are vitalized with natural life by being compared to a flock of birds rising from a riverbank and to sparks spurting from a burning log. As he ascends closer to the divine center, Dante increases the incongruity of his images and renders them more difficult to interpretation, so as to evoke a sense of the awesome mystery about to be confronted. Yet he controls their alienating effect by avoiding a total transformation to an order of unfamiliar forms which might elicit fear or revulsion in the reader. Because of his eschatological optimism, which is evident in the poem's conciliatory, unitive ending, Dante does not abandon the earth; instead, he redeems it as a similitude of heaven, thus making heaven more accessible and intelligible to man. Even at its most remote, he continues to relate heaven to familiar, comforting experience. In the Empyrean, which is beyond time and space, the river of light, though strange and sublime, remains close to the human sensibility with its celestial honeybees (XXIX). Paradise is Eden rediscovered, a pastoral idealization of our world—lofty, yet a distillation of the most delectable moments found in the human and earthly landscape. In the *Commedia,* anagogic reality fulfills rather than negates earthly reality.

Accordingly, in Dante's heaven, the moon and the sun are spiritually elevated; they are made part of its physical and moral superstructure. The sun, as symbol of God, warms with its touch the *rosa sempiterna* into blossoming (XXX, 124–26). Through this active image, we experience a sense of perpetual renewal in the anagogic cosmos as well as the pilgrim's own spiritual fruition. In the heaven of the Pearl Poet, meanwhile, our world is totally deleted, its sun and moon literally eclipsed by the unearthly light of the Divine Presence. Although this cancellation is justified conceptually in an image incarnating immutable being, its threatening unfamiliarity repels and alienates the human sensibility at least on an affective and sensory level. By thus estranging us from the vehicle, the poet has cut us off from participating even analogically in the experience of its tenor. Consequently, our sense of distance from the metaphorized reality—in this case, heaven and its perfection—becomes more palpable and final. For we relate to perfection only as the fulfillment of what we have experienced imperfectly.

The Pearl Poet does not convey to us the complementarity of the anagogic world only through our own perceptual stress, where sensory, affective, and conceptual values are held in perpetual tension with one another. The hero of the work, too—though on a more intuitive level of perception—reacts to the landscape with mixed feelings of rapture and dread:

> An-vnder mone so great merwayle
> No fleschly hert ne myȝt endeure,
> As quen I blusched vpon þat bayle,
> So ferly þerof watȝ þe fasure.
> ....
> Þat felde I nawþer reste ne trauayle,
> So watȝ I rauyste wyth glymme pure.
> (1081–88)

He becomes tautly aware of the impending self-annihilation that threatens him as an intruder:

> Hade bodyly burne abiden þat bone,
> Þaȝ alle clerkeȝ hym hade in cure,
> His lyf were loste an-vnder mone.
> (1090–92)

Being a skilled dramatist, the poet knows how to relieve the tension of such concentrated moments—while at the same time heightening it through imagistic contrast and a play of false optimism. He achieves this paradoxical effect by describing the dreamer's stupefaction upon encountering the Apocalyptic City not in elevated terms but in a rustic image whose exaggerated expressiveness verges on comedy:

> I stod as stylle as dased quayle
> For ferly of þat frelich fygure.
> (1085–86)

The recollection of this image grounds us at first in common, protective reality, allaying for the moment our sense of estrangement and suspenseful anxiety in this forbidding realm. The sudden presence of this remarkably earthbound scene promises with its welcome familiarity some comprehensible point of reference in this strange, remote order of being to which the dreamer may be able to relate his personal crisis and thus resolve it. Yet simultaneously, by mere juxtaposition, the image sharpens the contrast between the Maiden's sphere of existence and the dreamer's; its misplacement and irrelevance in the apocalyptic context only magnifies the distance between their worlds. The image thus intensifies the work's dramatic suspense by increasing our apprehension as to the dreamer's ability to reconcile himself with ultimate reality and its governing absolutes.

We recall, moreover, that earlier in the poem the dreamer had stood still as a heraldic hawk intently watching the newly appeared Maiden "lest ho me eschaped" (187). Eventually, he was depicted as a braying doe cornered into subjection by divine law (345–48) but still maintaining in our eyes some nobility through its resistance, however futile—or, rather, because futile. Now the aristocratic predatory bird has itself become the prey, dazzled and immobilized into captivity in the stupid, graceless stance of a defenseless quail. The image thus completes the pattern of animal images aimed at the gradual diminution of the hero's stature. The resulting comic devastation of his human dignity reveals his pathetic, almost ludicrous helplessness before the divine; yet it heightens his humanity and therefore his appeal and relevance to us as protagonist. Above all, it energizes the work's dramatic conflict—between God and man—by accentuating its absurdity.

After establishing the *donnée* of Christian eschatology as the setting for the ensuing dramatic event, and after expressing his reaction to this setting to remind us of his presence in it—although still as a spectator—the poet mobilizes the anagogic realm into action, so that he may confront it and act in it directly, making it part of his private experience. Drama, which so far has been caught and transfixed into symbol, is finally released into action. This unfastening of pent-up stress, of concentrated antinomy and conflict, from frozen image to action gives that motion a startling power, adding to its surprise and dramatic impact. And yet, deriving from an essentially imagistic milieu, dramatic action maintains here a strongly iconographic and schematized character, symbolic rather than realistic. In other words, it is controlled by ritual order—a key organizing principle in the poem as well as its anagogic world.

Despite my indebtedness to past definitions, I do not view ritual strictly from Frye's archetypal standpoint, that is, as a self-perpetuating pattern of desire in opposition to reality, present in all literature.[46] Neither do I view it in what seems to me an anachronistic, extrinsic fashion, that is, ritual as a compulsive defense mechanism against the emotional anxiety elicited by the literary object.[47] Instead, I view ritual as any recurrent pattern, any coherent and balanced construction, established by emphatic reduplication, that helps us to order our experience within both an ideological and an aesthetic framework. As Angus Fletcher rightly observes, ritual allows for "a degree of certainity in a world of flux." By "certainty," however, we should mean not only the defensive alleviation of anxiety—as Fletcher does—but also the willful achievement of self-celebrating order, existing for its own sake and significance as created form. Fletcher speaks of "a higher effect" in ritual—besides its function as compulsive defense mechanism—that can lead to "a positive moment of exuberance and delight."[48] Although he points to certain aesthetic qualities in ritual, especially within a literary context, still, his evaluation of it is primarily a psychological one. To the medieval thinker, however, the aesthetic-literary experience is more than a psychological state—whether it be anxiety or exuberance. Thomas Aquinas, whose influence on medieval aesthetic theory remains undisputed, claims that aesthetic pleasure, while it involves all levels of perception and response, derives fundamentally from a disinterested contemplation of beautiful forms and their harmonious relationship. Such contemplation is intellectually cognitive in nature rather than emotionally arousing or sensually gratifying.[49] Consequently, although I shall be dealing with the emotive and sensory values of ritual as a vital part of its human meaning in the poem, my approach to it will be essentially formal, studying it both as autonomous aesthetic order and as an element carrying out an important symbolic and dramatic function. For it too springs from the poet-dreamer's desire to control inscrutable reality—earthly and anagogic—within a framework of his own making, imposing on it coherence and permanence.

In its regularity and precision of structure and rhythm—architectonic and kinetic—as well as in its visual splendor, ritual order is an expression of the ideals of symmetry, clarity of form, and brilliance of surface. In its reduplication of the same pattern or pulse, it suggests to our perception an open-ended, uninterrupted movement toward the infinite and invariable. Each interval in the uniform pattern is a symbolic reassertion of the One into which the Many ultimately merge in total, unalterable unity. In that sense, ritual order reflects an order of immutable being. In sum, as a product of the artistic imagination and the creative process, ritual order tries to actualize certain human aspirations for the ideal, at once metaphysical and aesthetic. In this attempt, then, ritual order too becomes an instrument of the poet's symbolic strategy, leading us to crucial "ironic" insights concerning the nature of divine reality and man's capacity to comprehend and express it. Ritual order acts, furthermore, as a key dramatic force in the hero's quest for reconciliation with God's absolutes, yet also for self-realization. Finally, it becomes the artist's means of organizing and guiding our responses as the work unfolds.

We experience ritual pattern in *Pearl* as visual or verbal form, that is, in imagistic or syntactical terms. The two work together, one reinforcing the other—a collaboration that we shall witness often. Ritual as syntax is created by the repetition of certain verbal structures which we have encountered from the beginning of the poem and which continue into the section of the New Jerusalem. Since I am studying the Celestial City primarily as symbolic image rather than linguistic construction, I will concentrate on the visual rather than the verbal expression of ritual order in the poem.

We found ritual order already imposed by the poet-dreamer as a principle of coherence and control over the contradictions of earthly existence—such as the symbiosis of life and death—in the garden of mutability, the "erber." It was visually expressed in the patterning of the floral mosaic on the "huyle," while verbally sustained by the syntactical rhythm of the catalogue of the various flowers placed there (41–44). As a manifestation of the poet-dreamer's wish for permanence, ritual order begins to materialize more fully—because uninhibited by actual reality—in the world of dream and wish-fulfillment: the visionary landscape. It becomes strongly evident in the careful arrangement of its objects in an unalterable architectonic scheme unfolding before us in a definite descriptive sequence. The poet's *effictio* of the Maiden, too, obeys a ritual pattern; each detail in her appearance follows a particular descriptive order and is then fitted into a strict, sharply drawn configuration.

Ritual order as architectonic form, nevertheless, finds its most powerful expression in the visual organization of the Apocalyptic City. The poet guides our eye systematically from the general to the specific: from a broad view of the city shining "schyrrer þen sunne" (982) to its individual sections. In a pattern moving from bottom to top, he describes the twelve foundation stones, next the walls, and finally the twelve gates, each topped by a pearl. Then this stepwise visual movement changes direction—from the exterior to the interior. We enter the city, trace its streets and houses (absent in the less definite topography of the biblical version), until we come to the river of light emanating from the throne of God. Our view finally shifts to the twelve trees on the banks of the river bearing the twelve fruits of life. Strengthening the structural pattern is the progressive description of the foundation stones, which follows an unswerving, predictable numerical and spatial sequence. It is further reinforced by the list's rhythmic syntax and the repetitive pulse of the recurring number twelve—twelve foundations, twelve gates, twelve trees—throbbing also in each stanza with its twelve lines. This architectonic ritual structure incarnates in its monumentality and rigid delineation an overarching framework of absolute values governing the anagogic world. The Maiden's divine imperatives take on palpable form as powerful, permanent images whose geometric logic suggests a hierarchical order in which they exist as indisputable, immutable theses. At the same time, the uninterrupted regularity and diagrammatic fixity of the apocalyptic landscape convey a sense of eternal destiny and unalterable design.

In such a schematized cosmology, all activity, too, is controlled by a ritual framework. Ritual movement activates the system of absolute values in which it takes place and which have been rigidified into visual form. It translates them from symbolic image into symbolic action.

The poem itself as a spiritual quest has obeyed what Fletcher calls in allegory a "ritualistic necessity" as opposed to mimetic, realistic probability.[50] Its hero moves in a single direction: toward repossessing the pearl and attaining to the "center" in order to penetrate the mystery of ultimate reality. The alternation between discovery and frustration, between human desire and divine resistance, the back-and-forth movement of the ideological conflict in the debate, the dialectic of attraction and revulsion permeating the work—all these establish a definite rhythm that builds up to the poem's climax in the final encounter. In other words, the work's plot and dramatic action unfold as ritual pattern. Similarly, sacred history as rehearsed earlier by the Maiden—that is, the timeless narrative and universal plot that encompasses the poem's human temporal event—moves in an inexorable ritual order from the prophetic to its eschatological phase. The poem's syntax, meanwhile, reinforces its ritual action much as it does its ritual architecture. The extended repetition of the same stanzaic structure, rigidly divided into independent verbal blocks but forged into an unbroken sequence by the linking words; the methodical listings and enumerations of objects; the set recurrence of the rhyme and the alliteration—all create a linguistic movement, balanced and symmetrical in pace, schematized but relentlessly progressing within a preordained framework, that echoes and sustains the narrative action. Such verbal movement as patterned sound produces, furthermore, an incantatory effect, which gives the poem an elusive liturgical quality, conditioning our responses for the forthcoming climactic ritual event in the New Jerusalem.

That all anagogic action is subject to an all-encompassing ritual order becomes evident with the appearance of the Maiden in the visionary landscape. Her description by the poet presages his manner of description of the apocalyptic landscape itself: from systematically scrutinized immobility to measured, structured gesture (177–238). Her hieratic movement foreshadows the central event of the apocalyptic realm, its "mes" (892), where

> Þe Almyʒty watʒ her mynster mete,
> Þe Lombe þe sakerfyse þer to refet.
> (1063–64)

Anagogic reality manifests itself as action in a cosmic liturgy, an eternal sacramental ceremony.

THE PROCESSION

The procession of the Lamb with his apocalyptic entourage is the triumphal point of this cosmic liturgy, and it comes to the dreamer with wondrous unexpectedness. Appearing suddenly in motion in a world thus far transfixed in immobility, the procession has a startling effect, visually and dramatically:

> Ryʒt as þe maynful mone con rys
> Er þenne þe day-glem dryue al doun,
> So sodanly on a wonder wyse
> I watʒ war of a prosessyoun.
> Þis noble cité of ryche enpryse
> Watʒ sodanly ful wythouten sommoun. . . .
> (1093–98)

Critics have promptly responded to the simile's poetic power, the way it captures the haunting, mysterious emergence of the moon at such an hour.[51] But none have commented on its studied irrelevance. This is the kind of simile that Phillip Damon, in his study of Homer's analogical practice, defines as that type "whose most immediately accessible effect lies in an explicit antithesis"; through contradiction rather than likeness, it brings to our consciousness the opposite of what it ostensibly describes.[52] Dante continues this practice when he depicts the souls in Cocytus:

> E come a gracidar si sta la rana
>   col muso fuor dell'acqua, quando sogna
>   di spigolar sovente la villana. . . .

[And as the frog sits with its muzzle out of the water to croak
when the peasant-girl dreams often of her gleaning. . . .]
                    (*Inferno* XXXII, 31–33)

Such a comparison intensifies through contrast the horror and desola-
tion of hell by bringing to mind the good earth with its peaceful,
delectable moments that the damned have lost for eternity. Similarly,
the Pearl Poet, after dismissing the moon from the apocalyptic realm,
makes us feel its absence more poignantly by suddenly introducing it in
an incongruous simile. He thus heightens our sense of the impending
dissolution of all familiar order in anagogic reality. At the same time,
the lyrical beauty of the image evokes an inexpressible sense of home-
sickness for our world. The dreamer's wistful forgetfulness in recalling
it in such an irrelevant context adds a stabbing pathos to his attempt to
relate himself to this strange realm and to find in it meaning and
consolation.

Both as visual form and as movement, the apocalyptic procession
obeys a ritual structure. The thousands of virgins appear in "þe same
gyse" (1099). They move with a uniform pace and sway: "þay glod in
fere [they glided together]" (1105). Even the Lamb, despite his icono-
graphically central position and unique features (1111, 1142), does not
upset the regularity of the movement. All of them proceed in one
direction, toward the apex of the "center," the throne of God. Mean-
while, the aldermen kneel together as if before the passing Host
(1119–20). The poet magnifies the awesome beauty of the spectacle by
expanding it to cosmic dimensions. "Legyounes of aungeles" sum-
moned together glorify the Lamb. Their song resounds through the
limits of the universe, from heaven "þurȝ þe vrþe to helle" (1124–26).
The poet attains a sense of immensity by the synesthetic manner in
which sound measures space with its echo. He expresses the comple-
mentarity of the sacred in musical, contrapuntal form, once again cap-
turing metaphysical polysemousness in aesthetic order. There is first
the dreadful sound,

> Lyk flodeȝ fele laden runnen on resse,
> And as þunder þroweȝ in torreȝ blo.
>   (874–75)

Above this rumbling organ tone can be heard "a gentyl carpe . . . as
harporeȝ harpen in her harpe" (881–83), a more delicate tessitura of
sound. To establish the musical metaphor, the poet refers specifically
to "þe modeȝ" (884), the system of musical scales in the medieval pe-
riod. As they sing, the angelic multitudes cast incense before the throne

of God in one ritual motion (1121–24). Thus, architecture as well as action in the apocalyptic realm are subject to a definite diagrammatic schematization.

Still, ritual order, especially in the representation of the ineffable, elicits a complex effect. On the one hand, it strikes us as a form of triumph for the poetic imagination, for it imposes structure, coherence, and stability—in both a metaphysical and an aesthetic sense—on an unknown reality that tends to shift under the varying perception of the onlooker. As Fletcher shows, though mostly in terms of relieving man's psychological anxiety, it neutralizes and harnesses ambivalence or the threat of the dissolution of the order of things.[53] In that sense, it reflects the hero's wish to become part of a stable, permanent schema and to find repose in it. Paradoxically, though, this very ritual order becomes the source of ambivalence and anxiety. When we view the procession in the New Jerusalem, its perfect orderliness of design and movement suggests a perfect order of being, existing and acting outside the limits of human time and space, that is, in the realm of the eternal and the infinite. Yet, in essence, ritual order as symbolic form and action is shaped by human time and space; therefore, within any representation of the eternal and the infinite, it can only stand as its contradiction, that is, as a symbolic conceit. For, in it, spiritual abstract values rigidify into sharply delineated material forms; motion tends toward strict schematization, which, paradoxically, verges on immobility. At least sensuously and affectively this stasis negates the presence of vital life and, hence, its eternity. The implications of this paradox for the individual human personality are profound.

These implications become clearer and more striking in *Pearl* if we turn once again to Dante for comparison. The kingdom of heaven in the *Commedia*, too, is governed by an overarching framework of absolute values and a ritual hierarchy. It does not efface, however, the individual self but fulfills it. Though enveloped in a common beatitude and its luminosity, Dante's blessed are extensions of their earthly identity, manifesting themselves in their full historical intensity and uniqueness. Dante preserves the diversity of their character and gesture as much as their separate destinies. The soul is perfected not as an otherworldly general type or abstraction but as a distinct, recognizable personality, a center of consciousness that is never lost or enfeebled in the anagogic realm but is enriched and expanded. Relying on the doctrine of the resurrection of the body and its reunion with the soul in a final reintegration of the self at the Last Judgment, Dante reaffirms in his blessed the sacred unity and indestructible continuity of the human personality.[54] As if to emphasize this continuity, Dante shows in the Rose a great throng of children still frolicking as children—not as transformed adults—"their childish voices" shedding a bright, light air on heaven, saving it from monotonous sacerdotal solemnity (*Paradiso* XXXII, 46–48).

The blessed in the heaven of *Pearl,* on the other hand, reflect a different conception of the ultimate fate of the individual personality: death here leads to a different kind of transfiguration. As spectacle of a transhumanized, ideal society, the apocalyptic procession elicits a mixed response in the reader. The white effulgence of the thousands of virgins as well as the sense of vast symmetry in their reduplicative appearance and regularity of movement invest the divine pageant with an awesome splendor. Yet all this beauty is counterbalanced by a disturbing collectivity: the faces engraved with the name of the Lamb, their unchanging expression, and finally their constriction into one absolute configuration. Emotion here—like its objective correlative, the light of the landscape—maintains an unvarying brilliance. It is conflated to perpetual, ritualized joy, unshaded by the variety of joyful expression found in Dante's blessed, for example. However justified theologically, the absence of degree of intensity purifies and impoverishes this sublime society emotionally, making it seem unresponsive—even incapable of responding—to the dreamer's private human sorrow. Such collective, unmitigated joy becomes crystalline in its impersonality; it lacks the nuance that would make it the expression of a particular personality and temperament, as in Piccarda's faint melancholy wistfulness. Because we do not witness change in the personality—even for a moment—we cannot witness the process of its fulfillment and therefore feel fulfillment as somehow suspended.

Ritual hierarchy in the anagogic world of *Pearl* constricts the individual within an absolute tectonic and ideological superstructure. It strips him of his selfhood; it purifies his yearning for self-realization as a distinct personality into the desire for self-absorption within one ideal form, one model of perfection. Thus, the individual is transformed into a hieratic, iconographic stereotype. He becomes an absolute value that rigidifies into a permanent image, an emblematic entity to be fixed in a ritual configuration, a cosmic mosaic, for eternity. In its strict segregation of parts and heavy schematization, the apocalyptic pageant creates the impression of such a mosaic. As instrument of the poet's symbolic strategy, art in its idealizing, and thus "dehumanizing," process rescued the garden of mutability from time and decay by changing it into a landscape of plastic perfection and permanent beauty. Now it enwraps, transmutes, and orders the human personality itself.

Although the individual might seek repose in a world of flux by becoming part of this eternal configuration, he also rebels against it because it threatens the loss of his selfhood—an apprehension that

accompanies the anagogic ascent, making it an experience of both ec-
stasy and dread. Hence, ritual order is simultaneously comforting and
horrifying. As meaningful form, it allays our eschatological anxiety; as
depersonalizing scheme, it exacerbates and magnifies it. How ironic
that man's own construction for controlling ultimate reality should at
the same time be the symbol of his fear against his own ordering, his
own rigidification by that reality! In the encounter between dreamer
and anagogic framework two poles of values are poised against each
other: man's search for individual fulfillment versus God's demand for
total subjugation and self-negation. Through this ideological counter-
poise and the emotional conflict resulting from it, ritual order emerges
in the work as a powerful dramatic force.

In his process of divine depersonalization, the poet goes beyond the
reduction of the individual to a ritual stereotype. Just as he dissolved all
familiar order in the apocalyptic landscape, he now cancels all recogniz-
able relationship in the life of his elect. In the world of the *Commedia*,
even if there has been no personal bond between the blessed while on
earth, the love that binds them in heaven expresses itself in the familiar
terms of human kinship, as if imitating its sacred analogue: the rela-
tionship between the first two persons of the Holy Trinity as Father
and Son. Dante addresses Virgil as "dolce padre"; Virgil shields and
embraces Dante as his "figlio." Cacciaguida behaves still as the patriar-
chal, protective ancestor. The canto (*Paradiso* XV) brims with familiar
names and localities. The old warrior falls back upon his old Florentine
dialect, a "voce più dolce, / Ma non questa moderna favella" (32–33), as
if yearning to recapture rather than wipe away the memory of his
earthly ties. He addresses Dante affectionately as his "fronda" (branch)
whose "radice" (root) he was (XV, 88–89). It is significant that Dante
reestablishes their relationship through an image of fertility and un-
eradicable growth, asserting the life principle and the abounding love
of Paradise in powerful, concrete terms. So Dante's heaven does not
erase the human bond but fulfills it. True to his intention, Dante makes
heaven appear more accessible to man as the consummation of what
man has experienced imperfectly in this life rather than as its deletion
or total transformation, however transcendent.

Spearing has perceptively observed that the Pearl Poet ties the pearl to
several relationships, keeping them vague for a while, so that the pearl
comes to embody all earthly relationship, which may be lost or fully
transformed by her death. Spearing points to the absurdity of the
dreamer's effort to revive the bond that existed between them on earth
by recalling Christ's comment to the baiting Sadducees that in the resur-
rection people will not be related to each other in any earthly way (Matt.
22:23–30). Human individuality is the result of a network of many

relationships, which, according to Christ's foregoing statement, dissolve in the other world and are replaced by a strange and ineffable new relationship.[55] It is therefore appropriate—we may conclude from Spearing's comments—that the Maiden spurns her previous filial connection with the dreamer as irrelevant and even unrecognizable in her new mode of existence. However scripturally tenable it might be, the absence of any recognizable human relationship deprives the apocalyptic world of *Pearl* of the capacity for feeling. By having transcended feeling, it seems to have transcended also individual selfhood. The dreamer as Everyman cannot relate his private sorrow—an extension of his identity—to an ideality where there is no identity and where sorrow is transcended and forgotten. Consequently, our sense of his alienation from divine reality increases with ominous dramatic forebodings.

The Maiden, nevertheless, calls herself the "bride" of the Lamb, using the terms of human kinship, which she has denied, to describe her relationship to God. In fact, she resorts to the dreamer's courtly, languishing terms—which she had dismissed as equally absurd—to describe the Lamb as her wooer: he is the "lemman swete" who makes her his mate (756–64). Her apocalyptic marriage, however, transforms these terms to a new function in which the poet can use them now as veils revealing the nature of anagogic existence. We note that the poet omits the biblical description of the Celestial City "coming down out of heaven from God, *prepared as a bride adorned for her husband*" (Rev. 21:2; my italics). Having died a child, plucked as "newe fryt" (894), and presented as a figure of plastic perfection unresponsive to the dreamer's wooing, the Maiden has become, like the pearl, an image lacking biological fulfillment. There is no ravishment or fecundity in her bridehood but only a chaste purification (presaged imagistically by the purification of her landscape), a spiritual desexualization suggesting sterility and the absence of any generative capacity. She is above the mutable world of becoming, which leads to decay—but only after satisfying ripeness. Here she is frozen into perpetual unripeness and suspended fulfillment, elements that negate the marital term "bride" in its analogical function by denuding it of its passion and life process. Aridity, seen earlier in the apocalyptic landscape, finds a more gripping expression now in the transfigured human personality. Is the soul's bridehood, then, on the anagogic level a state of frigid perfection? This question, too, becomes part of the poem's eschatological dialectic, stimulated further by the author's calculated choice of the virginal, perfectly ingathered pearl as symbol of eternity over the mutable but life-emanating rose.

Another element that complicates—yet enriches immensely—the soul's apocalyptic bridehood is its odd mixture of love and death. The Maiden's love language toward the Lamb refers constantly to his suffering and death. In recalling his mating, her language brims with the fragrance and tender lyricism of erotic passion, while, in describing his death, she dwells over the details of his torture with a curiously tenacious physicality, as if reliving and savoring it again in its full intensity:

> He calde me to hys bonerté:
> "Cum hyder to me, my lemman swete,
> For mote ne spot is non in þe."
> He gef me myʒt and als bewté;
>
> . . . .
>
> My Lombe, my Lorde, my dere juelle,
> My ioy, my blys, my lemman fre,
>
> . . . .
>
> In Jerusalem watʒ my lemman slayn
> And rent on rode wyth boyeʒ bolde.
>
> . . . .
>
> Wyth boffeteʒ watʒ hys face flayn
> Þat watʒ so fayr on to byholde.
> (762–810)

Erich Auerbach has surveyed the development of the "gloria passionis," the mingling of passionate love and suffering, in the mysticism of the Passion in late medieval spirituality. In his ardor for God—expressed often in the language of amorous longing—the believer yearns to become one with him by sharing in his suffering. Thus, pain becomes the means to an ecstatic, self-obliterating union with the crucified Christ.[56] But just as intense suffering passes into ecstasy, so ecstasy passes disturbingly into death. Death becomes a form of ravishment, the ultimate consummation in such mystic ardor. Auerbach does not dwell on the fascinating, self-luxuriating grotesqueness of the experience, the passionately erotic but macabre language of Jacopone da Todi's *Cantico dell'amor superardente* or the bizarre, almost repugnant imagery of Saint Bonaventura's mystical exhortation: "O handmaiden, to Jesus wounded . . . do not merely look at the marks of the nails in his hands . . . but enter wholly by the gate of his side [his wound] to the very heart of Jesus."[57] In her recollection of her vision of the bleeding Christ and her ecstatic desire to share in his suffering, Juliana of Norwich, a contemporary of the Pearl Poet, articulates forcefully the tantalizing mixture of rapture and revulsion in the unitive experience: "This revelation," she remembers well, "was . . . horrifying and dreadful, sweet and lovely."[58] The Maiden's mystical love language recalls just this kind of experience in all its affective and sensuous complexity, making it part of her apocalyptic bridehood. Inevitably, we are drawn

by our eschatological anxiety to a more awful question: If such comple-
mentarity pervades the soul's anagogic relationship to God, how far
does it touch the divine image itself? To determine that, we must look
carefully at the figure moving at the center of the procession: the
Lamb, God in his apocalyptic form.

Dante's representation of the godhead stands in significant contrast
to that of the Pearl Poet. In the three concentric circles, Dante creates
an analogical image which by its very ineptitude incarnates "negatively"
the paradox of the Holy Trinity. According to symbolic tradition, the
circles represent perfection by their self-sufficient shape; in Dante's
case, they also suggest the existence of the Three in One by their
overlapping, yet distinct, three colors. As geometric forms limited by
space, however, the three circles are totally irrelevant to the infinitude
of God. Left to gaze at this configuration alone as a symbol of divine
mystery, the visionary hero would have been diagrammatically ex-
cluded from its self-enclosed perfection and its alienating incongruity—
alienating on an abstract, intellectual level of perception rather than as
an unfamiliar, repelling form. But Dante's vision culminates in the
reconciliation between human and divine nature. Hence, in the midst
of the puzzling shape is seen "nostra effige" (*Paradiso* XXXIII, 131),
restating the achievement and the promise of the Incarnation. Al-
though the poet's "alta fantasia" cannot sustain the flash of illumination
so that he can fathom the meaning of that effigy standing thus in the
center of divine mystery, his "disio e'l velle" (desire and will) are ful-
filled in a moment of intense union followed by the profound serenity
of the last few words (*Paradiso* XXXIII, 142–45). Through his potential
identification with the familiar figure in the center of the configura-
tion, the visionary hero has entered the symbol on some ineffable level
of perception. He has become part of the spiritual diagram.

The image of God in *Pearl,* on the other hand, is shaped by different
thematic aims and a different symbolic strategy. The Lamb's meek and
humble mien and his torn side usher before us the Franciscan Christ of
the Gothic tympana, pointing to his wounds and reaching out to men
as one of them for their sympathy. The Lamb's mute suffering un-
leashes great pathos, so much so that critics have tended to overlook his
unusual features and the temper of his final action toward the human
dreamer. Focusing on his wound and his blithe mood, Kean does not
see the Lamb as being "described in apocalyptic terms"; to her, the
more terrifying elements of the figure in John's Revelation are missing
in *Pearl.*[59] Spearing, however, discerns the ambivalence in the Lamb's
description: "squalor in majesty, pain in triumph." He notices that the
Pearl Poet brings out "the almost nightmare quality of St. John's appre-
hension of the nature of God," a description that "suggests for the

moment the god of a totemistic cult stranger and crueller than Christianity as we usually think of it." But only for the moment—Spearing thinks—because the Lamb's "loke3 symple" (1134) and bleeding wound soften and humanize him ultimately, to the point that the dreamer himself pities the Lamb for his injury.[60] His sensitive reaction notwithstanding, Spearing does not pursue the symbolic significance of the apocalyptic form of God in this case, nor does he relate it to the poem's drama, a relationship that is ostensibly his main subject of interest.[61]

Despite his humility and appealing pathos, the Lamb is the summation and apotheosis of the grotesque element in the poem, which we witnessed emerging for the first time in the visionary landscape, eventually enwrapping the human personality in its transfigured state. The Pearl Poet does not construct a blatant monstrosity by any means. He allows, rather, an intricate suggestiveness to operate freely enough in the reader's imagination, the Lamb's image shifting between the humble and the almost barbarically majestic, the meek and the terrifying. In medieval art—in certain late thirteenth-century depictions of the Apocalypse in English illumination, for example[62]—this transfixing, arresting ambiguity is annulled precisely because definite form restricts the free play of the imagination. The sheep with seven horns centrally located in the celestial orb in these depictions has little of the suggestive power of John's or the Pearl Poet's description.

The Lamb behaves in a human manner:

> Þe Lombe byfore con proudly passe
> . . . .
> Best wat3 he, blyþest, and moste to pryse,
> . . . .
> His loke3 symple, hymself so gent.
> . . . .
> So wern his glente3 gloryous glade.
> (1110–44)

At the same time, he appears as a scintillating, precious effigy, significantly vested with the imagistic qualities of the poem's central symbol:

> As praysed perle3 his wese3 wasse
> . . . .
> . . . þat gay juelle.
> (1112–24)

Finally, he has the shape of an animal:

Þe Lombe byfore con proudly passe
Wyth horneȝ seuen of red golde cler.
(1110–11)

In other words, the Lamb is a hybrid creature, the sum of the unnat-
ural crossing of natures—the human, the artificial, and the animal. His
animality is further perverted by the unnatural number of his horns
and their bright, artificial red-gold color. The image of the seven horns
is a doctrinally explicit symbol of the seven sacraments. Yet the poet
exploits the antithesis between it as clear intellectual construction and
its irrational impact as abnormal, even unpleasant, visual form in order
to emphasize perceptually the awesome complementarity of the image
of God. Altogether, the laws of proportion and relationship are
wrenched out of their familiar shape in the Lamb's aspect.

It is this haunting distortion that results in the grotesque, threatening
by its visual absurdity not only the dissolution of external, protective
reality but also the derangement of the mind by destroying its laws of
coherence. Seen as vision, such absurdity takes on the aura of a bad
dream. One is reminded of Dürer's observation that, to represent the
world of the dream and the nightmare, the painter need only mix all
kinds of creatures and incongruous natures. When this grotesque fu-
sion appears on the visage of the godhead itself, the dissolution of
external order and the self seems even more final and cataclysmic, not
because it threatens oblivion but because we confront the possibility of
finding ourselves in another mode of existence molded by abysmal and
demonic forces beyond our control. In that threat, anagogic reality in
its apocalyptic form alienates us with its ominous quality, while simulta-
neously it rivets us with a nightmarelike irresistibility in its mingling of
beauty and horror. In this sense, then, the Lamb becomes the apex of
the poet's symbolic strategy, incarnating man's eschatological dread yet
beguiling wonder and attraction.

The Lamb moves in majesty, dressed in white, effulgent garments,
yet on his side he has a wound that is open and perpetually bleeding.
But the Lamb is unperturbed by it; his mood remains meek and joyful:

Paȝ he were hurt and wounde hade,
In his sembelaunt watȝ neuer sene,
So wern his glenteȝ gloryous glade.
(1142–44)

The effect is complex. We face the image of triumph over pain, which,
after all, is at the center of the Christian promise of victory over suffer-
ing. Nevertheless, it is a ritual triumph; the wound becomes an isolated

emblem, a separate, discrete aspect that does not affect the divine composure. To the extent that such imperturbability takes on a hieratic and emblematic form, it is elevated above familiar experience and thus loses its touch with or relevance to human reality. It is a triumph that man cannot share in or identify with because of its strange nature.

Furthermore, such imperturbability soon takes on a quality of unnatural insensitivity, which adds to the alienating grotesqueness of the figure. I do not wish to "sensationalize" the point by belaboring it. However, the effect here is similar—in a different context, of course— to that experienced in Bosch's *Millennium* with its piked and torn figures reclining on a hill. The indifference of the tormented to their tortures puzzles and disturbs the onlooker profoundly. Dante creates the same nightmarish effect by the hypnotic, almost languorous reaction of the thieves to the horrible embracements of the snakes in hell (*Inferno* XXV). The human sensibility is jarred by the juxtaposition between the bleeding wound and the unruffled joy and odd impassivity of the Lamb. The unnatural crossing of incongruous sensations and emotions makes the grotesque an even more palpable experience here. This juxtaposition, now within the image of the godhead, revives a central motif in the poem: the disturbing transference between ravishment and self-devastation, between ecstasy and death, suggesting an indefinable kinship between them in the anagogic experience.

Again, we cannot overlook the sense of liberation felt here by the poetic imagination in its ability to portray the *sacer* and to control its "demonic" aspects by capturing them in concrete form and casting them into aesthetic order. It is in this sense that I regard the New Jerusalem and the apocalyptic procession with the figure of the Lamb in its center as a powerful construction. It results in what I will term "the Romanesque tension." Here we have creative exuberance, a kind of delirious fantasy, contained within a heavy architectonic frame. The interaction between explosive inner content and strongly defined outer form energizes the anagogic symbol to the utmost as ideogram and as iconographic shape.

By rendering the Lamb's triumph over pain into hieratic form, the poet attains a distinctly complementary effect in it: He elevates it sacramentally while he depersonalizes it by subsuming it in a cosmic ritual superstructure. The Lamb's transcendent imperturbability forebodes a similar lack of response to the dreamer's own pain or its personal recognition. In our eyes, then, the dreamer is distanced even further from the divine reality in which he seeks consolation by uniting with it.

It strikes the reader almost as a rebuke against God that the human dreamer should be suddenly touched by the Lamb's injury, forgetting his own for the moment:

> Alas, þoȝt I, who did þat spyt?
> Ani breste for bale aȝt haf forbrent
> Er he þerto hade had delyt.
>
> (1138–40)

I cannot agree with Patricia Kean's comparison of the dreamer's reaction with the "brief, impersonal comment" of the dreamer in Chaucer's *Book of the Duchess* (lines 1308, 1310) as another means of "playing down of the supreme moment of vision," since there is no personal triumph involved here for the visionary hero.[63] On the contrary, the startled question, the breast burning with pity, and the touching directness of the language add to the poignancy of the dreamer's reaction, increasing rather than diminishing the emotional force of the approaching climactic event. His tender, protective address to the "lyttel quene" in the procession (1147), who had used him so imperially, intensifies the dramatic irony of the moment, as we sense the irrelevance of his human compassion in a transcendent world that does not reciprocate. Before turning her gaze "all'etterna fontana," Beatrice smiles back at Dante from the Rose (*Paradiso* XXXI, 91–93), as if to reaffirm their personal bond and her continuing solicitude in his spiritual quest. But in the anagogic world of *Pearl*, no one notices the dreamer. The apocalyptic throng passes him by, unperturbed by his agonized presence, totally absorbed in their divine perfection.

As dramatist, the poet uses this increasing sense of isolation to exacerbate the dreamer's urgency to hold on to the ideal realm passing before him, bringing it to its desperate, climactic expression. The "lufdaungere" felt initially in the "erber grene," the desire to recover his daughter, expands now to the "luf-longyng" of regaining Paradise and penetrating the mystery of absolute reality. This anagogic nostalgia, raised here to its maximum, makes him forget the confines of his mode of existence, despite the Maiden's warnings. Ecstasy overcomes dread for the moment; he defies self-annihilation or is willing to abandon himself to it as the ultimate ravishment and fulfillment:

> Delyt me drof in yȝe and ere,
> My maneȝ mynde to maddyng malte;
> Quen I seȝ my frely, I wolde be þere,
> Byȝonde þe water þaȝ ho were walte.
> I þoȝt þat noþyng myȝt me dere
> To fech me bur and take me halte,
> And to start in þe strem schulde non me stere,
> To swymme þe remnaunt, þaȝ I þer swalte.
>
> (1153–60)

Like Dante, the Pearl Poet handles dramatic climax with the utmost economy; compression here makes for intensity. After many cantos or stanzas of accumulated tension, we expect a full release, either when Dante encounters Satan and the triune godhead or when the Pearl dreamer is confronted by the Lamb as he is about to plunge into the stream. Instead, these climaxes are concentrated into brief, pinpointed moments of immense energy—and it is all over. The dramatic tension explodes in the reader's imagination in a delayed pattern of response, as he arrives at successive stages of increasing awareness as to the full significance of the event. Thus, the poem's dramatic power remains to the end instead of being dissipated at the point of climax.

The hero attempts to break through the barrier of sacred time and space but is held back within his mortal limits. While the stream maintains the character of the river of the romance—beckoning yet perilous with its "meruelous mereʒ" (1166)—as symbolic image, it acts as an impassable boundary in a definite spiritual topography. Explosively yearning, yet irrevocably constrained by this barrier, the dreamer is reduced to the image of the frenzied, cornered animal used earlier by the Maiden—as if with premonitory intent—to describe man in his impotent rebellion against God's inexorable decrees and in his presumption to penetrate divine mystery:

> For þoʒ þou daunce as any do,
> Braundysch and bray þy braþeʒ breme,
> When þou no fyrre may, to ne fro,
> Þou moste abyde þat he schal deme.
>
> (345–48)

The image re-creates itself:

> . . . I so flonc
> Ouer meruelous mereʒ, so mad arayde.
> Of raas þaʒ I were rasch and ronk,
> Ʒet rapely þerinne I watʒ restayed.
>
> (1165–68)

The poet leaves it to the reader to imagine the glance or gesture that must have transfixed the dreamer. By indirect suggestiveness, the meek Lamb suddenly takes on a terrible aspect, baring his *ira Dei:* "Of þat munt I watʒ bitalt [shaken] . . . / Out of þat caste I watʒ bycalt [summoned]" (1161–62). The words bring to mind the awful "Dryʒtyn," who restrains him now as he expelled once his "ʒorefader" from Eden, to be encountered again at the Last Day of Judgment.

The vision rises to its highest point of tension—and then it snaps off. As he rushes toward the stream, the dreamer is suddenly awakened. His head is still lying on the mound in the "erber," where he had lost his pearl, where, numbed with grief, he had fallen asleep (1169–73).

The dreamer fails in his unitive attempt. He is excluded from the self-sufficient transcendent diagram in which he yearned to become a permanent image. The symbol rejects him. The kingdom of heaven withdraws into an icon, a frozen image of ideal ritualistic stasis. Like its germinal source, the pearl,[64] it ingathers and encloses so "clanly clos in golde" the mystery the dreamer—and we with him—seeks to possess. Its apocalyptic form stuns human penetration. The New Jerusalem thus brings to a climax the poet's symbolic and dramatic strategy. As dissimilar similitude, it incarnates in its enigmatic surface and its con-flicting sensuous, affective, and conceptual values the awesome comple-mentarity of divine reality. In its juxtaposition of ravishing beauty and frigid inaccessibility, we are made to experience the ecstasy and dread of the anagogic ascent, a duality that pervades the life of belief not only on an intellectual level but on an existential one as well, teasing the imagination with its hidden truths and enrapturing man with its eternal promise.

The poet achieves the incarnation of divine mystery through a pat-ern of mounting symbolic irony in which the creative process itself plays a central role. The essential antithesis of this symbolic irony is caught very concretely in this paradox: The ideal world, which is meant to transcend time and space, is represented here by its very contradic-tion—an image, an artifact of time and space. The apocalyptic realm in *Pearl* is, then, an imagistic conceit not of eternity but of its enigma. It is at this point of total symbolic irrelevance that the dreamer and we are cut off inevitably from the vision of the ideal, to be thrust back upon our reality—but with a new consciousness.

6

Conclusion

It is often overlooked that, unlike Dante, the Pearl dreamer fails in his unitive effort. Some critics have acknowledged this failure, but mainly in order to patronize the dreamer—though he stands for every man, including the critics—as spiritually dull and insensitive, since his theological ratiocination can neither bring him to an explicit understanding of God's decrees nor argue away his human grief.[1] Others, lulled by the dreamer's words of abject obeisance, see the poem's ending as one of full illumination and happy acceptance.[2]

To be sure, the dreamer resigns himself to his failure in compellingly earnest and self-effacing terms. He seems even grateful that his Pearl continues to exist and that he will rejoin her one day. Yet we cannot fail to note that, despite his statement of utter submission, "Now al be to þat Prynceȝ paye" (1176), he is overcome with "gret affray [dismay]" (1174); upon fully realizing his expulsion from "þat fayre regioun," he swoons with grief (1174–80). He recovers in a chastened and sober mood, but a feeling of heartless injustice and humiliation continues to rankle in him. His parting words to the Maiden are filled with a forced exultation toward her blessed state, choked by a note of bitter forlornness. We hear verbal echoes of his earlier complaint against his exclusion from her realm (245–48). His farewell to her sounds more like a rebuke, thinly veiled in self-pitying language:

> Þat þou so stykeȝ in garlande gay,
> So wel is me in þys doel-doungoun. . . .
> (1186–87)

When he expresses his resignation to God's will, reproaching himself for his presumption, his choice of words betrays unmistakably his resentment at having been tamed into acceptance. They are words of resistance, "hade I ay bente" (1189), and of dismaying defeat: "Lorde, mad hit arn þat agayn þe stryuen" (1199). One recalls in contrast to this seething utterance the fulfilled serenity of Piccarda's words: "E'n la sua volontade è nostra pace" (*Paradiso* III, 85). Is this, then, the language of an enlightened, reconciled man? How much insight and consolation has he derived from his visionary experience?[3] The dark despair of his mourning early in the poem comes back to mind now, and we ask: Would he have begun recounting his visionary experience in that disconsolate, prostrated mood if, indeed, he had been fully taught and comforted by it? The answer is uncertain. But even if the hero remained untouched by the experience, that would not have prevented him from becoming the instrument of our instruction at the hands of the poet, the all-controlling intelligence in the work. For we have noted from the beginning how the poet has often detached us from the hero, raising us to a higher level of awareness, to a superior perspective, very close to his own.

Much of the poet's perspective becomes clearer by the way he handles his protagonist, namely, as Everyman striving to transcend the anguished paradoxes of his earthly existence and attempting to grasp the meaning of ultimate reality. The dreamer's human helplessness before the divine, his emotional instability, and the comic quality of his pathos seem devastating to his stature as man. Deflated, impotent, and thus bereft of his human dignity, he has been viewed by several critics essentially as a comic anti-hero. Guided by the prevailing pessimism of the age, they have promptly posited their view of him as the "image of man" current in late medieval art and literature and, more especially, in the works of the Pearl Poet.[4]

Despite the ludicrous absurdity that often characterizes the thoughts and actions of the Pearl dreamer, I do not agree with the notion that the Pearl Poet has meant to make him entirely the object of our superior judgment or amusement, as many have contended. I believe, rather, that this human diminution hides or, better, "reveals by veiling" the poet's own reproach to God for man's helplessness—not the reproach of a disillusioned skeptic but that of one who is trying desperately to understand God and to unite with him. For he is a God of many faces and of many demands: "A God, a Lorde, a frende ful fyin" (1204). How is man to reconcile these loving yet awesome aspects in the divine image? I believe that in pitting human weakness in all its comic pathos against divine omnipotence this medieval poet is trying to justify not only God's ways to man but also man's ways to God. A certain view of man emerges, therefore, out of the poem's event, which I think is truer of the Pearl Poet, though perhaps atypical of his age.

It is in this connection that I regard the dreamer's rejection from the New Jerusalem as a reenactment and a restatement of the Fall. It brings back to mind something central to man's puzzling existence: it was in quest of the absolute that he fell; it is by this quest alone that he can ever be redeemed. When the poet shows man capable of encompassing and suffering such a vast paradox, he elevates rather than diminishes man almost in a tragic sense. The poet drives this sense home through some pathetic irony, when the dreamer tries to reassure himself and us that "To pay þe Prince oþer sete saȝte / Hit is ful eþe to þe god Krystyin" (1201–2). The poem as drama has just demonstrated the contrary and with great poignancy.

The dreamer fails in his quest to penetrate divine mystery as a forestep to his union with God. Looking back at the event, he now reflects ruefully:

> To þat Prynceȝ paye hade I ay bente,
> And ȝerned no more þen watȝ me gyuen,
> And halden me þer in trwe entent,
> As þe perle me prayed þat watȝ so þryuen,
> As helde, drawen to Goddeȝ present,
> To mo of his mysterys I hade ben dryuen.
>
> (1189–94)

In this lament, the poet states explicitly the poem's central event; I have therefore related all other elements to it. It is, after all, this quest that leads to the poem's climactic action: the final desperate attempt to cross over the human barrier to absolute reality. The abortiveness of this attempt climaxing a process of symbolic alienation in the work reflects, no doubt, the poet's radical sense of man's spiritual alienation and the inaccessibility of divine reality to him. Its mystery appears now even more complicated and intensified by another act of vision and representation. That does not mean, however, that no insight has been gained. For the poem's event is like an initiation in which we mature not by understanding but by mere encounter. Furthermore, the poet offers to the dreamer and to us powerful sources of consolation, while in this life.

Having been shown before the apocalyptic vision God's plan of man's salvation, we are reminded of Christ's promise of redemption and immortality. Through his symbolic dramatization of the paradoxes of the Christian faith—their existential impact and the eschatological anxiety they elicit—the poet does not mean to weaken that promise. Instead, he demands that we view it with some spiritual maturity—not as facile and explicit but as fraught with excruciating mystery and anguish. The author, whose voice begins to emerge more clearly now as the poem's "I," offers us specifically two main sources of consolation: the sacrament of Communion and the almost sacramental sharing of his art.

At the end of the poem, we confront, still, an inscrutable and many-faceted divinity: "A God, a Lorde, a frende ful fyin" (1204). Having failed to understand him, we are exhorted to assimilate him in an essentially symbolic manner,

> . . . in þe forme of bred and wyn
> Þe preste vus scheweȝ vch a daye.
> (1209–10)

The sacrament of Communion has a definite dramatic and symbolic function in the poem's denouement. As sacrament, it carries on the achievement of its sacred prototype, the Incarnation: the reconcilement and final fusion of two opposite natures, the material and the spiritual, the human and the divine. This is what each symbol aspires to inherently in its warring terms. This is the union that the dreamer desires as the resolution to his spiritual drama. Besides such ontological reconciliation, the sacrament brings into fusion the temporal opposites of sacred history by the past event it commemorates, by its revivification of that event in the present, and by foreshadowing its anagogic fulfillment in the future. Thus, history and nature as two different sources of analogical symbolism and of theophany are blended into one. The poet invites us, through the sacrament, to participate in this vast integration of disparate realities, although we cannot fathom with our limited perception its mysterious operation.

As a source of consolation, the sacrament gives us also the comfort of discovering God once again in his creatures, in the things close to us. The poet has brought us back to a vehicle that is familiar and reassuring. It has, at least, human validity, for the bread and the wine are the fundamental sources of man's sustenance and mirth. God, therefore, is brought closer to us here than in the fantastic, incongruous symbolic juxtaposition of the New Jerusalem, where the metaphoric terms were so utterly distant from each other. Just as the estrangement between symbol and idea in the apocalyptic realm incarnated for us man's distance from divine reality and his turbulent relationship to it, so the more familiar analogical tie between the bread and the wine and God's spiritual feeding of man incarnates the hope of their final reconciliation. Symbolic resolution spells dramatic resolution in the poem's ending. But it remains, significantly, partial.

The Pearl Poet offers us also the poem itself as a source of consolation and regeneration—an idea introduced by the comforting "sange" in the "erber." As a product of the symbolic imagination, attempting to represent the ideal and the eternal, *Pearl* is essentially a failure. But as a human work of art it imitates and re-creates within itself the laws of coherence and beauty in God's work of art, the world—an all-encompassing notion which is part of the common medieval inheritance and which I have reiterated throughout this study. A cathedral, a motet, or a poem is an analogical reproduction of God's universal order, structured on the same cosmological and aesthetic principles. In this connection, the human artist stands as an analogue to *Deus artifex,* God the arch-artist.[5] He becomes in a sense God's collaborator by carrying on the divine creative act, producing new patterns and relationships in an unending process of regeneration of form, and therefore meaning. In such a supreme collaboration, the human artist finds consolation and assurance—even a sense of conquest—in the midst of potential chaos.

If the world is a theophany, so is the poem by participation. For in it the poet has rebuilt symbolically the whole divine *ordo,* erecting it before us for our contemplation and assimilation as ordering principle, as model, for our inner reconciliation and integration. As we share in the poem's experience through our active spiritual and aesthetic response, we share also in its reconstruction of God's universal order and thus of the self. In this function, then, art itself becomes a sacrament.

Finally, in giving tangible form to spiritual truth and in bringing together contrary realities, the poem, like the comforting "sange" in the garden, has carried on the integrative work of the "kynde of Kryst," rendered into artistic form. The poet manifests this most memorably in the way he binds his work with the first and last lines:

> Perle, plesaunte to prynces pay
> (1)

> Ande precious perle₃ vnto his pay.
> (1212)

The verbal form is the same, unifying the poem through repetition of its initial motif. But the meaning has shifted, energizing the ending through contrast, planted in the very center of its aesthetic opposite— another expression of the pervasive formative principle of unity in diversity and diversity in unity. The poet has moved from the pleasure of the worldly prince to that of the Heavenly Prince as criterion of excellence. Or, rather, he has reconciled the two pleasures in mutual participation and fulfillment: divine pleasure takes on the warm familiarity of earthly pleasure, and earthly pleasure is redeemed and elevated to its ideal form, which is in God. Through this sacramental reconciliation between opposite poles of experience standing at each end of the work—a reconciliation caught in aesthetic order as verbal play—the poet reminds us with a sense of finality of his guiding metaphysical and poetic principle: the incarnate Word. Here, revealed truth and its artistic form have become one.

Notes

Chapter 1

1. All quotations from *Pearl* in my text are from E. V. Gordon, ed., *Pearl* (Oxford, 1953); hereafter cited as Gordon, *Pearl*.

2. Walter S. Ong, S.J., "Wit and Mystery: A Revaluation in Medieval Latin Hymnody," *Speculum*, 22 (1947), 310–41. See Johan Huizinga, *The Waning of the Middle Ages*, trans. F. Hopman (Garden City, N.Y., 1954), in his discussion of late medieval pessimism; and A. Bartlett Giamatti, *The Earthly Paradise and the Renaissance Epic* (Princeton, N.J., 1966), pp. 80–81.

3. See J. A. Burrow, *Ricardian Poetry: Chaucer, Gower, Langland, and the Gawain Poet* (New Haven, 1971), p. x; D. W. Robertson, Jr., *A Preface to Chaucer: Studies in Medieval Perspectives* (Princeton, N.J., 1963), p. 223; and A. C. Spearing, *The Gawain Poet: A Critical Study* (Cambridge, 1970), p. 149.

4. Northrop Frye, *Anatomy of Criticism* (Princeton, N.J., 1957), pp. 105 ff.

5. I am borrowing this term from Mircea Eliade, *Images and Symbols: Studies in Religious Symbolism*, trans. P. Mairet (New York, 1961), p. 55.

6. A. R. Heiserman, "The Plot of *Pearl*," *PMLA*, 80 (1965), 164–71.

7. Rudolph Otto, *The Idea of the Holy*, trans. J. W. Harvey (New York, 1958; rpt. 1971), passim; Eliade, *Images and Symbols*, pp. 27–56, and *The Myth of the Eternal Return; or, Cosmos and History*, trans. W. R. Trask (New York, 1954; rpt. Princeton, N.J., 1971), pp. 6–21; Frye, *Anatomy of Criticism*, pp. 131–60; and Angus Fletcher, *Allegory: The Theory of a Symbolic Mode* (Ithaca, N.Y., 1964), pp. 220–36.

8. *De mystica theologia*, cap. I, 2, in *PG*, III, col. 1000, hereafter cited as *Myst. theol.; De coelesti hierarchia*, cap. I, 2, in *PG*, III, col. 121, hereafter cited as *Coel. hier.;* ibid., cap. II, cols. 136–45; *Myst. theol.*, cap. I, cols. 997–1001; also *Coel. hier.*, cap. II, col. 140. Cf. Cacciaguida's hiding and revealing smile in Dante's *Paradiso* XVII, 36.

9. τὸ ἀκρατὲς . . . τοῦ συντόνου καὶ ἀνεπιστρόφου, καὶ πρὸς μηδενὸς ἐκκόπτεσθαι δυναμένου . . . τῆς θείας καλλονῆς ἔρωτα." *Coel. hier.*, cap. II, col 144; my translation.

10. *St. Augustine's "Confessions,"* vol. II, trans. W. Watts, (London, 1912; rpt. 1960), bk. XIII, esp. chap. xxx, pp. 458–59; *On Christian Doctrine*, trans. D. W. Robertson, Jr. (Indianapolis and New York, 1958), I, i and iv, pp. 7–10; *The Trinity*, trans. S. McKenna (Washington, D.C., 1963), XV, xxi, pp. 234–36, and *On Christian Doctrine*, II, xvi, pp. 50–51; *The Trinity*, III, pp. 27–29, and *On Christian Doctrine*, II, xvi, p. 51.

11. Rom. 1:20; *On Christian Doctrine*, I, iv, p. 10. Pseudo-Dionysius repeats this notion in *De divinis nominibus*, cap. IV, 4, in *PG*, III, col. 700.

12. M. D. Chenu, *Nature, Man, and Society in the Twelfth Century*, trans. and ed. J. Taylor and L. Little (Chicago and London, 1968), p. 125, has observed that Hugh of Saint Victor, though fundamentally an Augustinian, was highly responsive to Pseudo-Dionysian symbolist thought; see also Glunz, *Die Literarästhetik des europäischen Mittelalters* (Bochum-Langendreer, 1937), p. 167; de Bruyne, *Etudes d'esthétique médiévale* (Bruges, 1946), II, 203–50.

13. Hugonis de St. Victorae, *Commentariorum in hierarchiam coelestem S. Dionysii Areopagitae*, lib. II, cap. i, in *PL*, CLXXV, col. 949; *Eruditionis didascalicae*, lib. VII, cap. iv, in *PL*, CLXXVI, col. 814. Père Chenu considers this work as wrongly printed with the above name; instead, he calls it *De tribus diebis* (*Nature, Man, and Society*, p. 115, n. 39).

14. Hugonis de St. Victorae, *Eruditionis didascalicae*, caps. xii–xiii, cols. 820–21; Hugh of Saint Victor, *Soliloquy on the Earnest Money of the Soul*, trans. K. Herbert (Milwaukee, 1956), pp. 29–31.

15. Saint Thomas Aquinas, *Summa Theologica*, I, q. 84, a. 7 (hereafter cited as *ST*), in *Basic Writings of St. Thomas Aquinas*, trans. and ed. A. C. Pegis (New York, 1945), I, 808–10.

16. *ST*, I, q. 12, a. 12, in ibid., pp. 109–10.

17. *ST*, I, q. 1, a. 9, in ibid., pp. 14–16. See also Ong, "Wit and Mystery."

18. Marcia Colish, *The Mirror of Language: A Study in the Medieval Theory of Knowledge* (New Haven and London, 1968), p. 222.

19. Saint Bonaventura, *The Mind's Road to God*, trans G. Boas (Indianapolis and New York, 1953), pp. 7–21.

20. For a discussion of this sentiment and of Franciscan spirituality in general, see Erich Auerbach, *Literary Language and Its Public in Late Latin Antiquity and in the Middle Ages*, trans. R. Manheim (New York, 1965), pp. 76–81; Ong, "Wit and Mystery"; and F. J. E. Raby, "The Franciscan Poets," *A History of Christian-Latin Poetry from the Beginnings to the Close of the Middle Ages*, 2nd ed. (Oxford, 1953), pp. 415–52.

21. *On Christian Doctrine*,III, xxv, pp. 99–101. See also Alanus de Insulis's discussion of the lion as representing variously Christ, Antichrist, the Devil, the tribe of Juda, just men as well as thieves and plunderers, in *Liber in distinctionibus dictionum theologicalium*, s. v. "leo," *PL*, CCX, cols. 834–35.

22. Alanus, *Distinctiones dictionum*, s. v. "ignis," *PL*, CCX, col. 815.

23. Alanus, *Elucidatio in Cant. cant.*, *PL*, CCX, cols. 54, 62, 79, 98, 100.

24. Augustine, *On Christian Doctrine*, III, xxv–xxvii, pp. 99–102.

25. Ibid., II, vi, p. 38. I would quarrel with D. W. Robertson's contention that Augustine saw in the figure of the Church in the Canticle of Canticles only "an abstract pattern of philosophical significance" (*On Christian Doctrine*, p. xv). When Augustine speaks of the "pleasure of discovery" afforded him by this similitude, he appears quite aware of the stimulating incongruity between the terms of the analogy.

26. Boccaccio, *Life of Dante*, cited in Fletcher, *Allegory*, p. 234, n. 22. See also Charles G. Osgood, trans., *Boccaccio on Poetry* (New York, 1956), p. 62.

27. Chenu, *Nature, Man, and Society*, p. 137. For further discussion on medieval symbolic polyvalence, see D. W. Robertson, Jr., and Bernard F. Huppé, *"Piers Plowman" and Scriptural Tradition* (Princeton, N. J., 1951), pp. 56 ff.; and Morton W. Bloomfield, "Symbolism in Medieval Literature," *Modern Philology*, 56 (1958), 73–81.

28. Gerhart B. Ladner, *Ad Imaginem Dei: The Image of Man in Medieval Art* (Latrobe, Pa., 1965), p. 1.

29. See Colish, *The Mirror of Language*, pp. 69–73, for Augustine's view of man's own analogical relationship to God; pp. 220–21, for Thomas Aquinas's view.

30. Ladner, *Ad Imaginem Dei*, pp. 59–60, 63.

31. Augustine, *On Christian Doctrine*, II, xvi, p. 51.

32. Charles S. Singleton, "Dante's Allegory," *Speculum*, 25 (1950), 78–83; idem, "The Other Journey," *Kenyon Review*, 14 (1952), 189–206; idem, *Dante Studies I. Commedia: Elements of Structure* (Cambridge, Mass., 1954), pp. 58–59, 61–83; idem, "The Irreducible Dove," *Comparative Literature*, 9 (1957), 129–35.

33. Richard H. Green, "Dante's 'Allegory of Poets' and the Medieval Theory of Poetic Fiction," *Comparative Literature*, 9 (1957), 118–28; Phillip Damon, *Modes of Analogy in Ancient and Medieval Verse* (Berkeley and Los Angeles, 1961), pp. 329–34; and Robert Hollander, *Allegory in Dante's "Commedia"* (Princeton, N.J., 1969), pp. 3–56. Judson B. Allen, *The Friar as Critic: Literary Attitudes in the Later Middle Ages* (Nashville, Tenn., 1971), passim, deals with the problem of the fictive literal element and its spiritual meaning in late medieval English criticism, arriving at a conclusion similar to those of the foregoing critics on Dante.

While acknowledging the fictionality of the parables and much of the figurative language in the Bible, Augustine chides the reader who would dare call them "lies," emphasizing their spiritual truth (*Liber contra mendacium*, x, 24, in *PL*, XL, col. 533, cited in Chenu, *Nature, Man, and Society*, p. 141, n. 78).

34. Howard R. Patch, *The Other World According to Descriptions in Medieval Literature* (Cambridge, Mass., 1950), esp. pp. 80–229.

35. For example, Patricia M. Kean, *The Pearl: An Interpretation* (London, 1967), passim; Ian Bishop, *Pearl in Its Setting* (New York, 1968), passim; O. D. Macrae-Gibson, "*Pearl:* The Link-Words and the Thematic Structure," *Neophilologus*, 52 (1968), 54–64.

36. Honorius of Autun, *Liber XII quaest. ii*, in *PL*, CLXXII, col. 1179, describes creation as a great zither, made by the supreme artisan God, combining a variety of sounds in one cosmic harmony. Spirit and matter in all their multiplicity of expression and form, though antithetical to each other, are consonantly joined into one universal order. Similarly, Alanus de Insulis, *De planctu naturae*, in *PL*, CCX, col. 453, speaks of the dynamic interplay between unity and diversity throughout the universal order in aesthetic terms: "Ad unitatem pluralitas, ad identitatem diversitas, ad consonantiam dissonantia, ad concordiam discordia."

Chapter 2

1. For example, Heiserman, "The Plot of *Pearl*"; Spearing, *The Gawain Poet*, pp. 135–37.

2. W. H. Schofield, "Symbolism, Allegory, and Autobiography in *The Pearl*," *PMLA*, 24 (1909), 585–675, reminds us that "a learned man of the fourteenth century was so used to interpretations of the pearl that the word could hardly be mentioned without a great many rising to his memory instantly" (p. 639).

3. Ibid.; P. J. Heather, "Precious Stones in the Middle English Verse of the Fourteenth Century," *Folklore*, 42 (1931), 217–64, 345–404. The Latin poem *De Gemmis* by the Abbot Marbodus (d. 1124), *PL*, CLXXI, col. 1725, served as basis to most medieval lapidaries. One of them was the influential Anglo-Saxon version of the *Lapidaire* in L. Pannier, ed., *Les lapidaires français* (Paris, 1882), referred to by Chaucer in *The House of Fame*, lines 1350 ff. Others are cited in P. Studer and J. Evans, *Anglo-Saxon Lapidaries* (Paris, 1924).

4. In *Purity*, ed. R. J. Menner (New Haven, 1920), lines 1124 ff., the poet displays his knowledge of gems, repeating Pliny's directions for restoring their luster. Cf. Pliny, *Natural History*, bk. X, chap. 56.

5. A power dramatized by Lunete's magic ring making Yvain invisible to his enemies in Chrétien de Troyes's *Yvain*.

6. Heather, "Precious Stones," p. 232.

7. See *Floris and Blanchfleur* (lines 618–24), in Donald B. Sands, ed., *Middle English Romances*, (New York, 1966), p. 297.

8. *Legenda Aurea*, ed. T. Graesse, 3rd ed. (Bratislava, 1890), p. 400.

9. W. W. Skeat, ed., *Complete Works of Geoffrey Chaucer*, Supplement (Oxford, 1894), pp. 1–145.

10. Schofield, "Symbolism, Allegory," pp. 593–94.

11. See ibid.; and Sister Margaret Williams, R.S.C.J., "Oriental Backgrounds and the Pearl-Poet," *Tamkang Review*, 1, no. 1 (April 1970), 93–107.

12. For a survey of various exegetical interpretations of the pearl, see Charles G. Osgood, Jr., ed., *"The Pearl," a Middle English Poem* (Boston, 1906), pp. 82–83; and René Wellek, *"The Pearl:* An Interpretation of the Middle English Poem," *Studies in English by Members of the English Seminar of Charles University*, 4 (1933), 5–33, in Robert J. Blanch, ed., *"Sir Gawain" and "Pearl": Critical Essays* (Bloomington, Ind., 1966), pp. 3–36.

13. Kean, *The Pearl*, p. 150; see also Schofield, "Symbolism, Allegory," p. 633.

14. Kean, *The Pearl*, pp. 155–56.

15. *PL*, XCII, col. 69.

16. See references to Albertus's *De Laudibus B. Mariae Virginis* in Jefferson Fletcher, "The Allegory of the *Pearl," Journal of English and Germanic Philosophy*, 20 (1921), 1–21.

17. Aldhelm, *De Virginitate*, cited in Gordon, *Pearl*, p. xxvii. See also C. A. Luttrell, "The Medieval Tradition of the Pearl Virginity," *Medium Aevum*, 31, no. 3 (1962), 194–200.

18. *Purity*, ed. R. J. Menner; *Sir Gawain and the Green Knight*, ed. J. R. R. Tolkien and E. V. Gordon (Oxford, 1925; rpt. 1966).

19. From Caxton's translation of Voragine's *Legenda Aurea*, in Osgood, *The Pearl*, pp. xxxi ff.

20. *Compendium theolog. veritatis*, 2, 4, in Kean, *The Pearl*, p. 142.

21. Rabanus Maurus, *Allegoriae in sacram scripturam, PL*, CXII, col. 996.

22. Schofield, "Symbolism, Allegory," p. 598; and Gordon, *Pearl*, p. xxxiv.

23. Walter Hilton, *The Ladder of Perfection*, trans. L. Sherley-Price (Harmondsworth, Middlesex, 1957), bk. II, chap. 39, p. 219.

24. Sister Mary V. Hillmann, "Some Debatable Words in *Pearl* and Its Theme," *Modern Language Notes*, 60 (1945), 241–48; John Conley, *"Pearl* and a Lost Tradition," *Journal of English and Germanic Philology*, 54 (1955), 232–47.

25. Gordon, *Pearl*, p. xxvii.

26. In Sands, *Middle English Verse Romances*, p. 195.

27. Joan Evans, *English Art, 1307–1461* (Oxford, 1949), V, 1–8, 139–72.

28. A good example of this kind of criticism is Patricia Kean's learned and comprehensive book, *The Pearl: An Interpretation*. Although the author promises at the outset not to allow any search for a "common medieval tradition" to obscure the poem's artistic uniqueness—which she has experienced "most forcibly" in her reading (pp. ix–x)—her book soon turns into a compendium of precisely such background material, betraying her original intentions for a close and more personal analysis. She brings out of medieval tradition a formidable array of symbolical and rhetorical analogues, which she fails, in my view, to integrate into one thesis or artistic aim.

29. Cf. Chaucer's description of Criseyde: "Hire sydes longe, flesshly, smoothe, and white." *Troilus and Criseyde*, III, 1248, in *The Works of Geoffrey Chaucer*, ed. F. N. Robinson, 2nd ed. (Cambridge, Mass., 1957), p. 434.

30. Schofield, "Symbolism, Allegory," p. 588.

31. Heiserman, "The Plot of *Pearl*."

32. Kean, *The Pearl*, p. 27; Gordon, *Pearl*, p. 47, n. on 19–22. W. A. Davenport, "Desolation, Not Consolation: *Pearl* 19–22," *English Studies*, 55 (1974), 421–23, denies the "sange" any consolatory value in this context.

33. See also Spearing, *The Gawain Poet*, pp. 140–41.

34. The seed's incarnational function here undercuts Wendell S. Johnson's thesis that the poem's aim is to contrast heaven and earth by a neat, exclusive dichotomy between the eternal, precious images of heaven and the transient and far less worthy images of the earth. Despite his discussion of the poem's "sacramental" images, Johnson maintains this dichotomy throughout. "The Imagery and Diction of *The Pearl:* Toward an Interpretation," *Journal of English Literary History*, 20 (1953), 161–80.

35. Kean, *The Pearl*, pp. 61–52. Gordon, *Pearl*, supports this view through his translation of the lines.

36. Edward Vasta, *"Pearl:* Immortal Flowers and the Pearl's Decay," *Journal of English and Germanic Philology*, 66 (1967), 519–31, in John Conley, ed., *The Middle English "Pearl": Critical Essays* (Notre Dame, Ind., 1970), pp. 185–202. Vasta cites five editions and five translations that translate *fede* into "faded," "withered," "decayed," in order to define the prevailing opinion—with which he disagrees.

37. Huizinga, *The Waning of the Middle Ages*, esp. "The Vision of Death," pp. 138–51; T. S. R. Boase, *Death in the Middle Ages: Mortality, Judgment, and Remembrance* (New York and London, 1972), passim.

38. Huizinga, *The Waning of the Middle Ages*, p. 141.

39. Boase, *Death in the Middle Ages*, p. 19.

40. Patch, *The Other World*, esp. pp. 134–229.

41. For instance: Gordon, *Pearl*, p. 47, n. on 39; Kean, *The Pearl*, p. 48; Spearing, *The Gawain Poet*, p. 140, n. 2; Bishop, *Pearl in Its Setting*, pp. 85–88; and William J. Knightley, Jr., *"Pearl:* The 'hy seysoun'," *Modern Language Notes*, 76 (1961), 97–102.

42. C. A. Luttrell, *"Pearl:* Symbolism in a Garden Setting," *Neophilologus*, 49 (1965), 160–76, in Blanch, *Critical Essays*, pp. 60–86.

43. Most of these plants did not grow in August, and some never in England. See R. M. V. Elliot, *"Pearl* and the Medieval Garden: Originality or Convention?" *Les langues modernes*, 45 (1951), 85–98; Luttrell, *"Pearl:* Symbolism in a Garden Setting"; Bishop, *Pearl in Its Setting*, p. 85; and Marie P. Hamilton, "The Meaning of the Middle English *Pearl*," *PMLA*, 70 (1955), 805–24, in Blanch, *Critical Essays*, pp. 37–59. For a general survey of garden symbolism in medieval literature, see D. W. Robertson, Jr., "The Doctrine of Charity in Medieval Literary Gardens: A Topical Approach through Symbolism and Allegory," *Speculum*, 26 (1951), 24–49.

44. Luttrell, *"Pearl:* Symbolism in a Garden Setting."

45. For example, Hamilton, "Meaning of the Middle English *Pearl*"; and Elliot, *"Pearl* and the Medieval Garden."

46. Sister Mary Madeleva, *Pearl: A Study in Spiritual Dryness* (New York, 1925), p. 144; Louis Blenkner, O.S.B., "The Theological Structure of *Pearl*," *Traditio*, 24 (1968), 43–75; and Spearing, *The Gawain Poet*, pp. 111–15, although he denies the dreamer any significant mystical penetration.

47. Julian of Norwich, *Revelations of Divine Love*, trans. C. Wolters (Baltimore, 1966), pp. 65–66, 71–72.

48. Eliade, *Images and Symbols*, pp. 50–51.

49. On the poem's medieval audience, see, for example, Dorothy Everett, *Essays on Middle English Literature*, ed. P.M. Kean (Oxford, 1964), p. 69; and John Gardner, trans., *The Complete Works of the Gawain-Poet: In a Modern English Version with a Critical Introduction* (Chicago and London, 1965), p. 15.

50. The problem of interpretation as it relates to an ideal medieval audience and to the intrusion of our own critical sensibility is at the center of the debate in Dorothy Bethurum, *Critical Approaches to Medieval Literature* (New York, 1960), passim.

51. "Allas! *I* leste hyr on erbere" (9); "Ofte haf *I* wayted, wyschande þat wele" (14); "To þat spot þat *I* in speche expoun / *I* entred in þat erber grene / In Auguste . . . " (37–39); " 'O perle', quod *I* . . ." (241).

52. Among the early critics supporting an autobiographical interpretation of the poem were Ten Brink, *Early English Literature* (London, 1883); Sir Israel Gollancz, ed. and trans., *"Pearl," an English Poem of the Fourteenth Century* (London, 1891 and 1921); Osgood, *The Pearl;* and G.G. Coulton, "In Defense of *Pearl*," *Modern Language Review*, 2 (1906–7), 39–43. Later, Mother Angela Carson, "Aspects of Elegy in the Middle English *Pearl*," *Studies in Philology*, 62 (1965), 17–27, proposed the interesting notion that the dead person was not the poet's child but his newly baptized beloved who had just come from a foreign land. The allegorical-symbolical approach was initiated by W. H. Schofield, "The Nature and Fabric of *The Pearl*," *PMLA*, 19 (1904), 154–215, and restated in his "Symbolism, Allegory," where the pearl is a symbol of pure maidenhood. This approach was followed by others in divergent directions: R. M. Garrett, *The Pearl: An Interpretation* (Seattle, 1918), views the pearl as a symbol of the Eucharist. Fletcher, "The Allegory of the *Pearl*," sees the pearl as symbolizing the Blessed Virgin. Madeleva, *Pearl*, considers the dead child a personification of the poet's own soul, suffering initially "spiritual blues" until it attains full mystic illumination and joy. Madeleva's view has been readapted more recently by Sister M. V. Hillmann, trans. and ed., *The Pearl: Mediaeval Text with a Literal Translation and Interpretation* (Convent Station, N.J., 1961), and by Blenkner, "Theological Structure of *Pearl*." D. W. Robertson, Jr., "The Pearl as a Symbol," *Modern Language Notes*, 55 (1950), 155–61, studies the pearl as a symbol of innocence according to the fourfold allegorical method. To Hamilton, "Meaning of the Middle English *Pearl*," the pearl stands for the regenerate rediscovered soul, for eternal life, and for heavenly bliss.

53. Gordon, *Pearl*, pp. xi–xix.

54. For example: Kean, *The Pearl*, pp. 114 ff.; Heiserman, "The Plot of *Pearl*"; and Spearing, *The Gawain Poet*, pp. 134–35.

55. Charles Moorman, "The Role of the Narrator in *Pearl*," *Modern Philology*, 53 (1955), 73–81, in Conley, *Critical Essays*, 103–21.

56. Heiserman, "The Plot of *Pearl*."

57. Damon, *Modes of Analogy*, p. 317. Leo Spitzer, "Note on the Poetic and Empirical *I* in Medieval Authors," *Traditio*, 4 (1946), 414–22, responds to the complexity of the "I" in medieval visionary allegory to the point that he considers it seminal to the development of the modern fictional "I."

Chapter 3

1. For English translations, see *The Ante-Nicene Fathers*, ed. Rev. A. Roberts and J. Donaldson (Buffalo, N.Y., 1885), II, 3–55; and Montague R. James, *The Apocryphal New Testament* (Oxford, 1924), pp. 525–55. For a more comprehensive description of otherworld visions and journeys to Paradise, see Patch, *The Other World*, esp. pp. 80–174.

2. Synesius, *De insomniis, PG*, LXVI, cols. 1281–1320.

3. Macrobius, *Commentary on the Dream of Scipio*. trans. W. H. Stahl (New York, 1952), pp. 87–92.

4. Saint Augustine, *De genesi ad litteram*, ed. J. Zycha, in *Corpus Scriptorum Ecclesiasticorum Latinorum*, XXVIII, 1 (Leipzig, 1893), p. 388.

5. Richard Saint Victor, *De eruditione hominis interioris*, lib. II, cap. ii, in *PL*, CXCVI, cols. 1299–1300; Bernard of Clairvaux, *Sermones in Cantica canticorum*, sermo LII, 3, in *PL*, CLXXXIII, col. 1031; Walter Hilton, *The Scale of Perfection*, ed. E. Underhill (London, 1923), pp. 424–25.

6. René Wellek and Austin Warren, *Theory of Literature* (New York, 1956), p. 81.

7. I am using here Pseudo-Dionysius's terminology on the ineffable: *alogian pantele*. *Myst. theol.*, cap. III, in *PG*, III, col. 1033.

8. Charles Muscatine, "Locus of Action in Medieval Narrative," *Romance Philology*, 17, no. 1 (August 1963), 115–22, relates this literary practice to medieval iconography.

9. For instance, Osgood, *The Pearl*, p. xv; Schofield, "Nature and Fabric of *The Pearl*" and "Symbolism, Allegory"; Gordon, *Pearl*, p. xxxii; Herbert Pilch, "The Middle English *Pearl*: Its Relationship to the *Roman de la Rose*," *Neuphilologische Mitteilungen*, 65 (1964), 427–46, in Conley, *Critical Essays*, pp. 163–84.

10. Kean, *The Pearl*, pp. 98–113.

11. Heiserman, "The Plot of *Pearl*."

12. Frye, *Anatomy of Criticism*, p. 111.

13. Ibid., p. 119.

14. Ibid., pp. 141–50.

15. I am still concerned primarily with the literary, rather than the mythic or anthropological, aspect of the dream vision.

16. Patch, *The Other World*, pp. 83–320; Kean, *The Pearl*, pp. 89–113.

17. Everett, *Essays on Middle English Literature*, p. 91.

18. Kean, *The Pearl*, p. 97.

19. Mircea Eliade, *Patterns in Comparative Religion*, trans. R. Sheed (New York, 1958; rpt. 1974), p. 216; see also idem, *The Sacred and the Profane: The Nature of Religion*, trans. W. R. Trask (New York, 1959), pp. 155–56.

20. Ian Bishop's apt term in *Pearl in Its Setting*, p. 89.

21. Gordon, *Pearl*, p. 49, interprets "in space" to mean "after a time," a common ME idiom (see also *OED*). Nevertheless, the phrase has also definite spatial connotations, since ME "space" meant an interval of either time or space. We cannot ignore, furthermore, the kinetic words "sprang" and "gon" or the narrator's explicit separation of body and spirit in the dreamer. The phrase appears to be another instance of the Pearl Poet's skillful word play, juxtaposing different dimensions of reality.

22. See Wolfgang Kayser, *Das Groteske: seine Gestaltung in Malerei und Dichtung* (Oldenburg and Hamburg, 1957), for a perceptive though somewhat sketchy discussion of the grotesque in art and literature. Most of his examples are derived from the Renaissance and later.

23. Arnold Hauser, *The Social History of Art*, (New York, 1951), I, 189.

24. For a thorough discussion of the use of these materials in medieval art, see Daniel V. Thompson, *The Materials and Technique of Medieval Painting* (New York, 1956); Margaret Rickert, *Painting in Britain: The Middle Ages*, 2nd ed. (Baltimore, 1956); and Evans, *English Art*.

25. Fletcher, *Allegory*, p. 105, describes the visual effect of such an arrangement as a "surrealistic ordering of parts."

26. Frederick Goldin, ed., *German and Italian Lyrics of the Middle Ages* (Garden City, N.Y., 1973), pp. 48–49 (lines 1–8); my translation.

27. C. S. Lewis, *The Allegory of Love* (New York, 1936; rpt. 1958), pp. 105–9.

28. Alanus de Insulis, *Anticlaudianus*, *PL*, CCX, col. 513.

29. Robertson, *Preface to Chaucer*, pp. 211–28. Elizabeth Salter, "The Alliterative Revival," *Modern Philology*, 64 (1966–67), 146–50, compares the style of *Pearl* to the art and architecture of the time.

30. Huizinga, *The Waning of the Middle Ages*, pp. 151–53, 277, 285.

31. Whereas in the Old English line the third stressed word always contains the key alliterative sound, in *Pearl* it need not be so always. Also, the lines in *Pearl* are accentually more regular than in Old English verse.

32. Because of its "circular" narrative form—the return to the "erber"—emphasized by the repetition of the first line's words in the end, Everett (*Essays on Middle English Literature*, pp. 87–88) and Bishop (*Pearl in Its Setting*, pp. 29–30) view the poem as a verbal reconstruction of the pearl, the poem's central symbol. I am pointing here to the work's interior texture as additional evidence of this reconstruction.

33. Bishop, *Pearl in Its Setting*, pp. 27–39; Kean, *The Pearl*, passim.

34. Kean, *The Pearl*, pp. 8–11.

35. Ernst R. Curtius's definition in *European Literature and the Latin Middle Ages*, trans. W. R. Trask (New York, 1953; rpt. 1963), p. 492.

36. Hugonis de St. Victorae, *Eruditionis didascalicae*, lib. VII, in *PL*, CLXXVI. (See Introduction, chapter 1, herein.)

37. Coolidge O. Chapman, "The Musical Training of the *Pearl* Poet," *PMLA*, 46 (1931), 177–81; Sandy Cohen, "The Dynamics and Allegory of Music in the Concatenations of *Pearl*, a Poem in Two Movements," *Language Quarterly*, 14, nos. 3–4 (1975–76), 47–52.

38. Gordon, *Pearl*, pp. xxxvi–xxxix; Everett, *Essays on Middle English Literature*, p. 89; Macrae-Gibson, "*Pearl:* The Link-Words and the Thematic Structure."

39. Ong, "Wit and Mystery."

40. Carleton Brown, ed., *English Lyrics of the Thirteenth Century* (Oxford, 1932), p. 1.

41. Yvor Winters, *In Defense of Reason* (Denver, 1947), pp. 61–64, 72. The poet becomes, in other words, "like Whitman trying to express a loose America by making loose poetry" (p. 62).

42. *ST*, I, q. 39, a. 8, and q. 44, a. 4, in Pegis, *Basic Writings*, I, 376–81, 429–31. The other two qualities are wholeness or perfection ("integritas sive perfectio") and proportion or harmony among parts ("debita proportio sive consonantia").

43. *The Works of Geoffrey Chaucer*, ed. Robinson, p. 290.

44. Kenneth Sisam, ed., *Fourteenth Century Verse and Prose* (Oxford, 1955), pp. 58–59. By "matter" I assume he means thematic aim.

45. Constance Hieatt, "*Pearl* and the Dream-Vision Tradition," *Studia Neophilologica*, 37 (1964), 139–45.

46. Lewis, *The Allegory of Love*, pp. 251–52.

47. Robert M. Jordan's characterization of medieval poetic form in *Chaucer and the Shape of Creation* (Cambridge, Mass., 1967). "Indeed, the overt manipulation of fixed structural elements seems to impart a distinctly *in*organic quality to Chaucerian narrative. . . . An analogy exists between Chaucer's art and that of the Gothic builders. . . . The typical Chaucerian narrative is literally 'built' of inert, self-contained parts, collocated in accordance with the additive, reduplicative principles which characterize the Gothic edifice" (pp. ix, xi).

48. Macrae-Gibson, "*Pearl:* The Link-Words and the Thematic Structure."

49. Gordon, *Pearl*, pp. xxxix, 63–64, notes that most of these meanings were used infrequently at the time, although he warns that what appears to us strained "may well have seemed to contemporaries a form of verbal wit."

50. See Spearing's excellent evaluation of the Pearl Poet's plain, realistic style in all four poems in the MS. Cotton Nero A. x, *Purity, Patience, Pearl*, and *Sir Gawain and the Green Knight* (*The Gawain Poet*, passim).

51. Moorman, "The Role of the Narrator in *Pearl*"; Heiserman, "The Plot of *Pearl*."

52. The earthly Paradise was considered as a real though ordinarily unapproachable

place in the medieval cosmos. Maps often showed its location. See Patch, *The Other World*, passim; and Giamatti, *The Earthly Paradise and the Renaissance Epic*, pp. 4–9, 14–15, 48–122.

53. Eliade, *Images and Symbols*, pp. 151–57; Frye, *Anatomy of Criticism*, pp. 145, 152.

54. *Homil. in Joh.*, XXV, 2, cited in Eliade, *Images and Symbols*, p. 154.

55. Eliade, *Images and Symbols*, p. 155.

56. Patch, *The Other World*, pp. 3, 120, 231, 237, 241, 244 ff., 247–49, 255, 276, 278, 281, 321–23.

57. Gordon, *Pearl*, p. 52, n. on lines 139–40.

58. David O. Fowler, "On the Meaning of *Pearl*, 139–40," *Modern Language Quarterly*, 21 (1960), 27–29. He refers to the *OED* (*device*, 6) and to a comparable passage in *The Wars of Alexander* (ed. Skeat, EETS, e.s., vol. 47 [1886]).

Chapter 4

1. Paul Piehler, *The Visionary Landscape* (Montreal, 1971), passim.

2. See also my article, "*The Shepherd of Hermas* and the Development of Medieval Visionary Allegory," *Viator*, 8 (1977), 33–46, on Rhoda as the first historical beloved ever to appear in visionary allegory.

3. See Curtius, *European Literature*, pp. 83–85, on the topos of affected modesty and self-disparagement in late antique and medieval literature.

4. Carson, "Aspects of Elegy in the Middle English *Pearl*," has identified the Maiden as the dreamer's newly baptized, foreign-born beloved. On the other hand, further sustaining the prevailing opinion, Norman Davis, "A Note on *Pearl*," *Review of English Studies*, 17 (1966), 403–5, after a study of medieval English letters, has shown that the following parting statement of the dreamer was a common formula of greeting from parent to child: "And syþen to God I hit bytaȝe / In Kristeȝ dere blessyng and myn" (1207–8).

5. This is the consensus of most modern critics.

6. Morton W. Bloomfield, "A Grammatical Approach to Personification Allegory," *Modern Philology*, 60, no. 3 (February 1963), 161–71.

7. Robert W. Frank, Jr., "The Art of Reading Medieval Personification Allegory," *Journal of English Literary History*, 20 (1953), 237–50.

8. Schofield, "Symbolism, Allegory," pp. 654–59, has pointed to the Maiden's connection with Machaut's courtly-allegorical beloved in *Dit de la Marguerite* and with Loyalty, the preciously bedecked figure in the *Assemblé de Dames*, a poem contemporary with *Pearl*.

9. Schofield, "Nature and Fabric of *The Pearl*," pp. 183–84.

10. Gordon, *Pearl*, pp. xxxiv, 56, n. on line 228.

11. See, for example, Fletcher, "The Allegory of the *Pearl*"; Kean, *The Pearl*, pp. 150–68; Bishop, *Pearl in Its Setting*, pp. 101–21.

12. Bishop, too, notices this omission (*Pearl in Its Setting*, p. 113).

13. Gordon, *Pearl*, p. 55, n. on lines 215–16.

14. Edwin Honig, *Dark Conceit: The Making of Allegory* (Evanston, Ill., 1959), pp. 131–32, 202, n. 1, refers to this notion, though in a different context.

15. For example, Johnson, "The Imagery and Diction of *The Pearl*"; Louis Blenkner, O.S.B., "The Pattern of Traditional Images in *Pearl*," *Studies in Philology*, 68 (1971), 26–49; Edwin D. Cuffe, S.J., "An Interpretation of *Patience, Cleanness*, and *The Pearl* from the Viewpoint of Imagery" (Ph.D. diss., University of North Carolina, 1951), pp. 145–233.

16. Kean, *The Pearl*, esp. pp. 53–85, 167–72.

17. My summary derives to some degree from the extensive surveys made by Kean (ibid.) and Barbara Seward, *The Symbolic Rose* (New York, 1960), pp. 1–52.

18. Allen, *The Friar as Critic*, pp. 110–16. For additional biblical analogues to this metaphor of mortality as well as exegetical comments on it by Augustine, Jerome, Bede, Alcuin, and Rabanus Maurus, see Robertson, "The Doctrine of Charity in Medieval Gardens." The flower or rose as a symbol of the fading glory of the flesh and of human love is seen repeatedly in medieval art (Robertson, *Preface to Chaucer*, pp. 190–91).

19. Allen, *The Friar as Critic*, pp. 115–16.

20. C. 1370. Robert D. Stevick, ed., *One Hundred Middle English Lyrics* (Indianapolis and New York, 1964), p. 69, no. 43, lines 29–44.

21. Seward, *The Symbolic Rose*, pp. 2–17.

22. *"The Vision of William Concerning Piers the Plowman" in Three Parallel Texts together with "Richard the Redeless" by William Langland,* ed. W. W. Skeat (London, 1886; rpt. 1965), I, 274–75. This passage is omitted from texts B and C.

23. *PL*, CLXXXIV, col. 1020.

24. *The Poems of William Dunbar*, ed. W. M. Mackenzie (Edinburgh, 1932), p. 162.

25. Richard L. Greene, ed., *The Early English Carols* (Oxford, 1935), no. 173, pp. 130–31.

26. Raymond Oliver, *Poems Without Names: The English Lyric, 1200–1500* (Berkeley, Calif., 1970), pp. 82–83.

27. For a more extensive discussion of Thomistic and Franciscan spirituality and poetic on the Continent and in England, see Ong, "Wit and Mystery"; and Raby, *A History of Christian-Latin Poetry*, pp. 376–457.

28. The connection between the rose and martyrdom is evident in the lives of the martyrs Saint Cecilia and Saint Dorothy in *The Golden Legend*, ed. F. S. Ellis (London, 1900), VI, 247–53.

29. Seward, *The Symbolic Rose*, p. 22. See also Rabanus Maurus, *PL*, CIX, cols. 930, 1041, 1115, speaking of the rose of martyrdom in connection with divine love and patience.

30. "Look, and see the rose of the bloody passion, how it reddens as a sign of the most ardent love. For love and the passion are contending, one to burn hotter, the other to become more red. But, in a marvellous way, the passion is reddened by the heat of love, for, unless He had loved He would not have suffered. And in the passion, in the redness of the passion, He showed the greatest ardour and an incomparable love." (Saint Bonaventura, *Decem opuscula*, pp. 454, 463–64, quoted in Kean, *The Pearl*, pp. 170–71.)

31. Spearing, *The Gawain Poet*, pp. 102–3, 152–53; and "Symbolic and Dramatic Development in *Pearl*," *Modern Philology*, 60 (1962), 1–12, in Blanch, *Critical Essays*, pp. 98–119.

32. I am highly indebted to Walter Ong's analysis of Thomas's comments on metaphor in theology and poetry ("Wit and Mystery").

33. Ibid., p. 336.

34. Spearing, *The Gawain Poet*, p. 152.

35. Heiserman, "The Plot of *Pearl*," makes a similar point.

36. Everett, *Essays on Middle English Literature*, p. 95.

37. Dorothy Everett and Naomi D. Hurnard, "Legal Phraseology in a Passage in *Pearl*," *Medium Aevum*, 16 (1947), 9–15; and Kean, *The Pearl*, pp. 185–86.

38. Spearing, *The Gawain Poet*, p. 156.

39. Concerning Pseudo-Dionysius's view of analogy and its aesthetic implications, see Introduction (chapter 1 herein). See also negative comments on the analogical representation of God and his angels in *The Cloud of Unknowing*, trans. C. Wolters (Baltimore, 1961; rpt. 1967), pp. 121, 136–38.

40. Gordon, *Pearl*, pp. xx–xxi, defines "cortaysye" in the poem as "the spirit of divine grace in Christian love and charity," as a quality of courteous generosity that binds the inhabitants of heaven. W. O. Evans, " 'Cortaysye' in Middle English," *Medieval Studies*, 29 (1967), 143–57, regards courtesy as heaven's ordering principle, as God's liberality, which rewards not according to merit but by its own dictates, and as Mary's concern for mankind. He insists on a thorough distinction from its earthly counterpart. But if the earthly court has been used as an extended and apt metaphor for God's court, I think it impossible that its courtly and even amorous associations can be deleted by mere statement.

41. E.g., Spearing, "Symbolic and Dramatic Development in *Pearl*," p. 99. Although in *The Gawain Poet*, pp. 152–59, Spearing admits that the Maiden's discourse leaves many mysteries unsolved for the dreamer, he insists, as in the earlier work, that "the parable of the vineyard is given a full and explicit exegesis by the poet" (p. 102).

42. Auerbach, *Literary Language and Its Public*, pp. 51–52.

43. Spearing, *The Gawain Poet*, pp. 152–53.

44. Various critics consider this view of divine rewards to be the general consensus of the Church Fathers, which the poet apparently follows in orthodox fashion. See Fletcher, "The Allegory of the *Pearl*; Wellek, "*The Pearl*"; Hamilton, "Meaning of the Middle English *Pearl*"; and D. W. Robertson, Jr., "The 'Heresy' of *The Pearl*," *Modern Language Notes*, 65 (1950), 152–55.

45. Cf. Hamilton's linguistic analysis in "Meaning of the Middle English *Pearl*." James Sledd, "Three Textual Notes on Fourteenth Century Poetry," *Modern Language Notes*, 55 (1940), 379–82, points to a similar distinction in the word "rewarde."

46. See extensive discussion by the critics mentioned in nn. 44–45, above. See also Bishop, *Pearl in Its Setting*, passim; and Kean, *The Pearl*, passim.

47. Wellek, "*The Pearl*"; Robertson, " 'Heresy' of *The Pearl*."

48. Augustine, *Confessions*, bk. XI, chaps. xi–xxvii, pp. 230–75.

Chapter 5

1. Eliade, *Images and Symbols*, p. 55.

2. Curtius, *European Literature*, pp. 83–85.

3. For example, in Erich Auerbach, *Mimesis: The Representation of Reality in Western Literature*, trans. W. Trask (New York, 1953), pp. 151–77; idem, "Figura," in *Scenes from the Drama of European Literature: Six Essays*, trans. R. Manheim (New York, 1959), pp. 11–49; idem, "Typological Symbolism in Medieval Literature," in R. J. Clements, ed., *American Critical Essays on the "Divine Comedy"* (New York, 1967), pp. 104–13; Charles S. Singleton, *An Essay on the "Vita Nuova"* (Cambridge, Mass., 1949), passim; idem, *Dante Studies I. Commedia*, passim; Johan Chydenius, *The Typological Problem in Dante*, in *Societas Scientiorum Fennica Commentationes Humanarum Litterarum* (Helsingfors, 1958), XXV, 1–159; Jean Daniélou, *Sacramentum Futuri: Etudes sur les origines de la typologie biblique* (Paris, 1950), passim; Hollander, *Allegory in Dante's "Commedia,"* esp. pp. 3–135.

4. Chenu, *Nature, Man, and Society*, p. 117.

5. Spearing, *The Gawain Poet*, pp. 163–64.

6. See above, chapter 3, n. 21 for interpretation of passage.

7. Kean, *The Pearl*, p. 215; Spearing, *The Gawain Poet*, pp. 165–66.

8. Kean, *The Pearl*, p. 215; Spearing, *The Gawain Poet*, pp. 165–66.

9. Eliade, *Images and Symbols*, pp. 41–59; *The Myth of the Eternal Return*, pp. 12, 17, 21.

10. Fletcher, *Allegory*, pp. 354–55.

11. Eliade, *The Myth of the Eternal Return*, p. 18.

12. Dionysius, *De divinis nominibus*, cap. ix, in *PG*, III, cols. 909–36; *Coel. hier.*, cap. xiii, in *PG*, III, cols. 300–20.

13. Edgar de Bruyne, *L'esthétique du moyen âge* (Louvain, 1947), p. 157; see also idem, *Etudes*, III, 197.

14. Chenu, *Nature, Man, and Society*, pp. 99–145.

15. Ibid., pp. 99–145; Etienne Gilson, *The Christian Philosophy of St. Thomas Aquinas*, trans. L. K. Shook (New York, 1956), pp. 137–43; H. Flanders Dunbar, *Symbolism in Medieval Thought and Its Consummation in the "Divine Comedy"* (New Haven, 1929), pp. 155 ff.; Joseph A. Mazzeo, "Dante's Conception of Poetic Expression," *Romanic Review*, 47 (1956), 241–58; and idem, *Structure and Thought in the "Paradiso"* (Ithaca, N.Y., 1958), pp. 25–49.

16. Chenu, *Nature, Man, and Society*, p. 103.

17. *Coel. hier.*, *PG*, III, col. 140; my translation.

18. Augustine, *On Christian Doctrine*, II, vi, pp. 37–38 and IV, viii, pp. 132–33.

19. *Coel. hier.*, cap. xiii, in *PG*, III, cols. 300–20.

20. For Pseudo-Dionysius's view of the dissimilar similitude as a means of initiation to divine mystery, see *Myst. theol.*, cap. I, in *PG*, III, cols. 997–1001; *Coel. hier.*, cap. I, in *PG*, III, col. 124 and cap. II, cols. 137–41. For further discussion, see Chenu, *Nature, Man, and Society*, pp. 123–31; Mazzeo, "Dante's Conception of Poetic Expression," esp. pp. 253–55. For the revelatory value of the similitude's debased form, see *Coel. hier.*, cap. II, cols. 136–45. For further discussion on this point, see Chenu, *Nature, Man, and Society*, pp. 132–33.

21. Curtius, *European Literature*, p. 444; Bruyne, *Etudes*, III, 220–21.

22. Frye, *Anatomy of Criticism*, p. 122.

23. Bruyne, *L'esthétique du moyen âge*, p. 157. See also Georges Poulet, "The Metamorphoses of the Circle," in J. Freccero, ed., *Dante: A Collection of Critical Essays* (Englewood Cliffs, N.J., 1965), pp. 151–69, for the handling of this notion by Dante, Cusanus, and other medieval poets and thinkers.

24. Salter, "The Alliterative Revival," p. 149.

25. On Augustine's view of beauty, see Bruyne, *L'esthétique du moyen âge*, esp. pp. 29–31; K. Svoboda, *L'esthétique de Saint Augustine et ses sources* (Brno, 1933), passim; Robertson, *Preface to Chaucer*, pp. 114–24; and Jordan, *Chaucer and the Shape of Creation*, pp. 23–26. On architectural form, see *De ordine* 2.11.34 and *De vera religione* 30.54–55, cited in Robertson, *Preface to Chaucer*, pp. 120–21. For further discussion on this point, see Svoboda, *L'esthétique de Saint Augustine*, pp. 25, 170.

26. On Thomas's view of beauty, see Bruyne, *L'esthétique du moyen âge*, pp. 34–35, 84–86, 131, 139, and *Etudes*, III, 278–346; and Leonard Callahan, *A Theory of Esthetic According to the Principles of St. Thomas Aquinas* (Washington, D.C., 1927), pp. 24–76. On Thomas's notion of *claritas*, see *ST*, I, q. 5, a. 5–6, in Pegis, vol. I, pp. 47–49; *ST*, I, q. 39, a. 8, in Pegis, vol. I, p. 378; *ST*, II–II, q. 145, a. 2, in *Summa Theologiae*, Blackfriars ed. (London and New York, 1964), vol. 43, pp. 72–76; Bruyne, *L'esthétique du moyen âge*, pp. 70–86, and *Etudes*, III, 307–10; Calahan, *Theory of Esthetic*, pp. 62–67.

27. Bruyne, *L'esthétique du moyen âge*, p. 105.

28. Ibid., pp. 132–33, and *Etudes*, III, 114.

29. Otto von Simson, *The Gothic Cathedral*, 2nd ed. (New York, 1962), pp. 101–41, has discussed in greater detail the connection between Pseudo-Dionysian light metaphysics and symbolism and Gothic architecture. Bruyne, *Etudes*, III, 16–29, has surveyed light, brilliant color, and luminous surface as divine similitudes in medieval symbolism and aesthetics.

30. Simson, *The Gothic Cathedral*, p. 115, n. 73.

31. Ibid., p. 121.

32. Bernard of Clairvaux, *Sermones in Cantica canticorum, PL,* CLXXXIII, col. 986.

33. Saint Augustine, *De musica, PL,* XXXII, 29, col. 1179. For general comments on the aesthetic ideal of immutability, see Bruyne, *Etudes,* III, 48–49.

34. Bruyne, *L'esthétique du moyen âge,* pp. 130–31, and *Etudes,* III, 112–13.

35. Bruyne, *L'esthétique du moyen âge,* pp. 175–76, and *Etudes,* III, 208–09.

36. I am not referring here, of course, to every troubadour or ditty maker of the time who wrote merely for the light diversion of his audience.

37. Kean, *The Pearl,* p. 215.

38. See also Muscatine, "Locus of Action in Medieval Narrative"; and Hieatt, "*Pearl* and the Dream-Vision Tradition."

39. Henri Frankfort et al., *Before Philosophy* (Baltimore, 1954), p. 30.

40. Simson, *The Gothic Cathedral,* p. xviii.

41. Eliade, *Patterns in Comparative Religion,* p. 216; see also idem, *The Sacred and the Profane,* pp. 155–56.

42. Cf. Rev. 21:21: "And the twelve gates were twelve pearls; every several gate was of one pearl."

43. ". . . le symbolisme qui n'est autre chose que l'expression esthétique de la participation ontologique." Bruyne, *L'esthétique du moyen âge,* p. 93.

44. Spearing, *The Gawain Poet,* pp. 97, 143.

45. See Dunbar, *Symbolism in Medieval Thought,* pp. 155 ff.; and Mazzeo, "Dante's Conception of Poetic Expression."

46. Frye, *Anatomy of Criticism,* p. 105.

47. Fletcher, *Allegory,* pp. 343–49.

48. Ibid., pp. 344–48.

49. Bruyne, *L'esthétique du moyen âge,* pp. 144–53, and *Etudes,* III, 287–97. Some thinkers, like William of Auvergne and Thomas Gallus, contested this intellectual approach to the aesthetic experience in favor of a more hedonistic and emotional one.

50. Fletcher, *Allegory,* p. 150.

51. For example, Burrow, *Ricardian Poetry,* p.' 134, and Spearing, *The Gawain Poet,* pp. 104, 166.

52. Damon, *Modes of Analogy,* p. 262.

53. Fletcher, *Allegory,* pp. 243–45.

54. See also Erich Auerbach, *Dante: Poet of the Secular World,* trans. R. Manheim (Chicago, 1961; rpt. 1974), pp. 69–179; and idem, "Farinata and Cavalcante," in *Mimesis,* pp. 151–77.

55. Spearing, *The Gawain Poet,* pp. 147–48.

56. Auerbach, *Literary Language and Its Public,* pp. 67–81. See also Raby, *A History of Christian-Latin Poetry,* pp. 417 ff.

57. Auerbach, *Literary Language and Its Public,* pp. 77 and 80.

58. Julian of Norwich, *Revelations of Divine Love,* pp. 71–72.

59. Kean, *The Pearl,* pp. 220–21. See also Marie P. Hamilton, "Notes on *Pearl,*" *Journal of English and Germanic Philology,* 57 (1958), 177–91.

60. Spearing, *The Gawain Poet,* pp. 166–67.

61. Ibid., p. 137: "it is through the synthesis of symbol with this human drama that the poet conveys his meaning."

62. Listed and described in Rickert, *Painting in Britain,* pp. 110–14.

63. Kean, *The Pearl,* pp. 210–11.

64. I am thinking here of Saint Ephrem's self-ingathered pearl, speaking of herself: "The daughter of the sea am I, the illimitable sea! And from that sea whence I came up it is that there is a mighty treasury of mysteries in my bosom! Search thou out the sea, but search not out the Lord of the sea! I have seen the divers who came down after me, when

astonied, so that from the midst of the sea they returned to the dry ground; for a few moments they sustained it not. Who would linger and be searching on into the depths of the Godhead?" J. B. Morris, trans., *Select Works of S. Ephrem the Syrian* (Oxford, 1847), pp. 87, 98.

Chapter 6

1. For example, Kean, *The Pearl*, pp. 213, 227–42; Spearing, *The Gawain Poet*, pp. 167–70.

2. The majority of critics share this opinion. Some are: Bishop, *Pearl in Its Setting*, pp. 92–98; Blenkner, "Theological Structure of *Pearl*"; Conley, "*Pearl* and a Lost Tradition"; Hamilton, "Meaning of the Middle English *Pearl*"; Heiserman, "The Plot of *Pearl*"; Madeleva, *Pearl*, passim; Moorman, "The Role of the Narrator in *Pearl*." For a more sensible and balanced evaluation of rebellion and insight in the dreamer and the reader, see Larry M. Sklute, "Expectation and Fulfillment in *Pearl*," *Philological Quarterly*, 52 (1973), 663–79.

3. Kean, *The Pearl*, p. 213, notes suggestively the poet's omission from the Maiden's description of the Apocalyptic City of John's celebrated words of comfort: "And God shall wipe away all tears from their eyes; and death shall be no more; nor mourning, nor crying, nor sorrow shall be any more; for the former things are passed away" (Rev. 21:4).

4. Robertson, *Preface to Chaucer*, pp. 221–24, 279, 282–85; Burrow, *Ricardian Poetry*, pp. ix–x, 41–45, 93–129; Spearing, *The Gawain Poet*, passim.

5. The fascinating and vast notion of human art being a reproduction of the divine *ordo* and man the artist acting as an analogue to *Deus artifex* has been extensively treated by several eminent medievalists: Bruyne, *Etudes*, I, 63–69, 93, 248, 326–34; II, 75–77, 81–87, 91–92, 103–7, 114–15, 121, 126, 129, 208, 266–69, 276, 298, 304, 360–61, 377–86, 390–95; III, 112–19, 128–29, 207–17, 272–79, 304–5, 317–18. Idem, *L'esthétique du moyen âge*, pp. 45–46, 64–65, 127–34, 168–78, 228–43, 250–51. Curtius, *European Literature*, pp. 501–9 and 544–46. Chenu, *Nature, Man, and Society*, pp. 7–9. Singleton, *Dante Studies I. Commedia*, pp. 58–59. Simson, *The Gothic Cathedral*, passim. Simson's views on the subject are summarized and related to literary structure by Jordan in *Chaucer and the Shape of Creation*, pp. 10–60.

Selected Bibliography

PEARL EDITIONS AND TRANSLATIONS IN CHRONOLOGICAL ORDER

Morris, Richard, ed. *Early English Alliterative Poems in the West-Midland Dialect of the Four-teenth Century.* Early English Text Society, O.S., no. 1. London, 1864; rev. 1869, 1885, 1896, 1901. Contains *Pearl, Cleanness,* and *Patience.*

Gollancz, Sir Israel, ed. and trans. *"Pearl,"* An English Poem of the Fourteenth Century. London, 1891; 2nd ed. 1897.

Osgood, Charles G., Jr., ed. *"The Pearl,"* a Middle English Poem. Boston, 1906.

Coulton, G. G., trans. *Pearl.* London, 1906; 2nd ed. 1907; rpt. 1921.

Jewett, Sophie, ed. and trans. *"The Pearl,"* a Middle English Poem: A Modern Version in the Metre of the Original. New York, 1908.

Gollancz, Sir Israel, ed. and trans. *"Pearl,"* an English Poem of the Fourteenth Century: Edited with Modern Rendering Together with Boccaccio's "Olympia." London, 1921.

———, ed. *"Pearl," "Cleanness," "Patience," and "Sir Gawain,"* reproduced in facsimile from the unique MS. Cotton Nero A. x in the British Museum. Early English Text Society, no. 162. London, 1923; rpt. 1931.

Gordon, Eric V., ed. *Pearl.* Oxford, 1953.

Hillman, Sister Mary V., trans. and ed. *The Pearl: Mediaeval Text with a Literal Translation and Interpretation.* Convent Station, N.J., 1961.

Cawley, A. C., ed. *"Pearl" and "Sir Gawain and the Green Knight."* London, 1962.

Gardner, John, trans. *The Complete Works of the Gawain-Poet: In a Modern English Version with a Critical Introduction.* Chicago and London, 1965.

Williams, Margaret. R.S.C.J., trans. *The Pearl-Poet: His Complete Works.* New York, 1967.

Borroff, Marie, trans. *Pearl: A New Verse Translation.* New York, 1977.

Andrew, Malcolm, and Ronald Waldron, eds. *The Poems of the Pearl Manuscript: Pearl, Cleanness, Patience, Sir Gawain and the Green Knight.* Berkeley and Los Angeles, 1979.

CRITICAL STUDIES OF *PEARL*

Ackerman, Robert W. "The Pearl-Maiden and the Penny." *Romance Philology,* 18 (1964), 615–23. In Conley, *Critical Essays,* pp. 149–62.

Bishop, Ian. *Pearl in Its Setting.* New York, 1968.

Blanch, Robert J. "Color Symbolism and Mystical Contemplation in *Pearl." Nottingham Medieval Studies,* 17 (1973), 58–77.

————. "Precious Metal and Gem Symbolism in *Pearl*." In Blanch, *Critical Essays*, pp. 37–59.

————, ed. *"Sir Gawain" and "Pearl": Critical Essays*. Bloomington, Ind., 1966.

Blenkner, Louis, O.S.B. "The Pattern of Traditional Images in *Pearl*." *Studies in Philology*, 68 (1971), 26–49.

————. "The Theological Structure of *Pearl*." *Traditio*, 24 (1968), 43–75. In Conley, *Critical Essays*, pp. 220–71.

Brewer, Derek S. "The Gawain-Poet: A General Appreciation of Four Poems." *Essays in Criticism*, 17 (1967), 130–42.

Carson, Mother Angela. "Aspects of Elegy in the Middle English *Pearl*." *Studies in Philology*, 62 (1965), 17–27.

Chapman, Coolidge O. "The Musical Training of the *Pearl* Poet." *PMLA*, 46 (1931), 177–81.

Cohen, Sandy. "The Dynamics and Allegory of Music in the Concatenations of *Pearl*, a Poem in Two Movements." *Language Quarterly*, 14, nos. 3–4 (1975–76), 47–52.

Conley, John, ed. *The Middle English "Pearl": Critical Essays*. Notre Dame, Ind., 1970.

————. "*Pearl* and a Lost Tradition." *Journal of English and Germanic Philology*, 54 (1955), 232–47. In Conley, *Critical Essays*, pp. 50–72.

Coulton, G. G. "In Defense of *Pearl*." *Modern Language Review*, 2 (1906–7), 39–43.

Cuffe, Edwin D., S.J. "An Interpretation of *Patience, Cleanness*, and *The Pearl* from the Viewpoint of Imagery." Ph.D. dissertation, University of North Carolina, 1951.

Davenport, W. A. "Desolation, Not Consolation: *Pearl* 19–22." *English Studies*, 55 (1974), 421–23.

Davis, Norman. "A Note on *Pearl*." *Review of English Studies*, 17 (1966), 403–5. In Conley, *Critical Essays*, pp. 325–34.

Dunlap, Louise. "Vegetation Puns in *Pearl*." *Mediaevalia*, 3 (1977), 173–88.

Elliot, R. M. V. "*Pearl* and the Medieval Garden: Originality or Convention?" *Les langues modernes*, 45 (1951), 85–98.

Evans, W. O. " 'Cortaysye' in Middle English." *Medieval Studies*, 29 (1967), 143–57.

Everett, Dorothy, and Naomi D. Hurnard. "Legal Phraseology in a Passage in *Pearl*." *Medium Aevum*, 16 (1947), 9–15.

Farnham, Anthony E. "The Principles of Allegory and Symbolism Illustrated in the Middle English Poem *Pearl*." Ph.D. dissertation, Harvard University, 1964.

Finlayson, John. "*Pearl*: Landscape and Vision." *Studies in Philology*. 71 (1974), 314–43.

Fletcher, Jefferson B. "The Allegory of the *Pearl*." *Journal of English and Germanic Philology*, 20 (1921), 1–21.

Fowler, David O. "On the Meaning of *Pearl*, 139–40." *Modern Language Quarterly*, 21 (1960), 27–29.

Garrett, R. M. *The Pearl: An Interpretation*. Seattle, 1918.

Gatta, John, Jr. "Transformation, Symbolism, and the Liturgy of the Mass in *Pearl*." *Modern Philology*, 71 (1973–74), 243–56.

Greene, Walter K. "*The Pearl*—a New Interpretation." *PMLA*, 40 (1925), 814–27.

Hamilton, Marie P. "The Meaning of the Middle English *Pearl*." *PMLA*, 70 (1955), 805–24. In Blanch, *Critical Essays*, pp. 37–59.

————. "Notes on *Pearl*." *Journal of English and Germanic Philology*, 57 (1958), 177–91.

Heiserman, A. R. "The Plot of *Pearl*." *PMLA*, 80 (1965), 164–71.

Hieatt, Constance. "*Pearl* and the Dream-Vision Tradition." *Studia Neophilologica*, 37 (1964), 139–45.

Hillmann, Sister Mary V. "Some Debatable Words in *Pearl* and Its Themes." *Modern Language Notes*, 60 (1945), 241–48. In Conley, *Critical Essays*, pp. 9–17.

Hoffman, Stanton de Voren. "*The Pearl*: Notes for an Interpretation." *Modern Philology*, 58 (1960), 73–80. In Conley, *Critical Essays*, pp. 86–102.

Johnson, Wendell S. "The Imagery and Diction of *The Pearl:* Toward an Interpretation."
    Journal of English Literary History, 20 (1953), 161–80. In Conley, *Critical Essays,* pp.
    27–49.
Kean, Patricia M. *The Pearl: An Interpretation.* London, 1967.
Kellogg, Alfred, L. "*Pearl* and the Augustinian Doctrine of Creation." *Traditio,* 12 (1956),
    406–7. In Conley, *Critical Essays,* pp. 335–37.
Knightley, William J., Jr. "*Pearl:* The 'hy seysoun.'" *Modern Language Notes,* 76 (1961),
    97–102.
Luttrell, C. A. "The Medieval Tradition of the Pearl Virginity." *Medium Aevum,* 31, no. 3,
    (1962), 194–200.
———. "*Pearl:* Symbolism in a Garden Setting." *Neophilologus,* 49 (1965), 160–76. In
    Blanch, *Critical Essays,* pp. 60–85.
Macrae-Gibson, O. D. "*Pearl:* The Link-Words and the Thematic Structure." *Neophilologus,* 52 (1968), 54–64. In Conley, *Critical Essays,* pp. 203–19.
Madeleva, Sister Mary. *Pearl: A Study in Spiritual Dryness.* New York, 1925.
McAndrew, Bruno. "*The Pearl,* a Catholic *Paradise Lost.*" *American Benedictine Review,* 8
    (1957–58), 243–51.
Moorman, Charles. "The Role of the Narrator in *Pearl.*" *Modern Philology,* 53 (1955), 73–
    81. In Conley, *Critical Essays,* pp. 103–21.
Niemann, Thomas C. "*Pearl* and the Christian Other World." *Genre,* 7 (1974), 213–32.
Pilch, Herbert. "The Middle English *Pearl:* Its Relationship to the *Roman de la Rose.*"
    Neuphilologische Mitteilungen, 65 (1964), 427–46. In Conley, *Critical Essays,* pp. 163–84.
Richardson, F. E. "*The Pearl:* A Poem and Its Audience." *Neophilologus,* 46 (1962), 308–
    16.
Robertson, D. W., Jr. "The 'Heresy' of *The Pearl.*" *Modern Language Notes,* 65 (1950),
    152–55. In Conley, *Criticial Essays,* pp. 291–96.
———. "The Pearl as a Symbol." *Modern Language Notes,* 65 (1950), 155–61.
Rupp, Henry R. "Word-Play in *Pearl,* 277–278." *Modern Language Notes,* 70 (1955), 558–
    59.
Schofield, W. H. "The Nature and Fabric of *The Pearl.*" *PMLA,* 19 (1904), 154–215.
———. "Symbolism, Allegory, and Autobiography in *The Pearl.*" *PMLA,* 24 (1909), 585–
    675.
Sklute, Larry M. "Expectation and Fulfillment in *Pearl*" *Philological Quarterly,* 52 (1973),
    663–79.
Sledd, James. "Three Textual Notes on Fourteenth Century Poetry." *Modern Language
    Notes,* 55 (1940), 379–82.
Spearing, A. C. *The Gawain Poet: A Critical Study.* Cambridge, 1970.
———. "Symbolic and Dramatic Development in *Pearl.*" *Modern Philology,* 60 (1962), 1–
    12. In Blanch, *Critical Essays,* pp. 98–119.
Stern, Milton R. "An Approach to the *Pearl.*" *Journal of English and Germanic Philology,* 54
    (1955), 684–92. In Conley, *Critical Essays,* pp. 73–85.
Tristram, Richard. "Some Consolatory Strategies in *Pearl.*" *Journal of English and Germanic
    Philology,* 54 (1955), 332–47. In Conley, *Critical Essays,* pp. 272–96.
Vasta, Edward. "*Pearl:* Immortal Flowers and the Pearl's Decay." *Journal of English and
    Germanic Philology,* 66 (1967), 519–31. In Conley, *Critical Essays,* pp. 185–202.
Watts, V. E. "*Pearl* as a Consolatio." *Medium Aevum,* 32 (1963), 34–36.
Wellek, René. "*The Pearl:* An Interpretation of the Middle English Poem." *Studies in
    English by Members of the English Seminar of Charles University,* 4 (1933), 5–33. In
    Blanch, *Critical Essays,* pp. 3–36.
Williams, Sister Margaret, R.S.C.J. "Oriental Backgrounds and the Pearl-Poet." *Tamkang
    Review,* 1, no. 1 (April 1970), 93–107.

Index of Authors Cited